D1615707

Be Your Own Motor Cycle Mechanic

HONDA

Be Your Own Motor Cycle Mechanic

John Thorpe

With a Foreword by Charles Deane

Orbis · London

Acknowledgments
Champion 64; C. Gorman/Orbis 58A, 74; Harlequin Studio/Orbis 18, 25, 35; James Neill 17; Motorcycle Mechanics Magazine 8, 146; Orbis 20, 21, 27–9, 31, 33, 39, 40, 42, 43, 45, 46, 48, 49, 53B, 54, 55, 57, 58B, 58C, 59, 60, 61, 62A–H, 85–7, 89, 91B, 101, 130, 133, 164B; F. & M. Papetti 41, 50, 51, 52, 53A, 67, 68, 69A, 71, 72, 75, 76, 78, 83, 88A, 90, 92, 94, 97, 98, 99B, 100, 102–9, 111, 113, 114, 115, 118, 119, 120, 124, 125, 127, 129, 131, 132, 134–40, 142–5, 147–52, 154, 155, 157, 158, 159, 161, 163, 164A, 165, 169, 171–86; J. Spencer Smith/Orbis 12; J. Thorpe/Orbis 91A, 99A, 116, 121, 122.

First published in Great Britain by
Orbis Publishing Ltd, London, 1980
Reprinted 1985

Printed in Czechoslovakia

ISBN 0 85613 035 4

50132/2

Contents

Foreword

What is a motor cyclist? Or should it be, who is a motor cyclist? They, or we, arrive in many different shapes and sizes, clad in a multifarious selection of clothing from wellies and anorak to race boots and leathers. Our aim is to bestride a two-wheeler of miniscule proportions as an economy conscious commuter or a superbike as a proverbial 'king of the road'. In many instances, the only thing we have in common is two wheels on tarmac, that is until it comes to a mechanical breakdown.

When that 50cc moped or 1,000cc megawhatsit splutters to a halt, we're on our own, unless you happen to be a member of the RAC or AA or belt-and-braces member of both. Finding the fault on one or six cylinders can be just as difficult in each case when you haven't a clue where to start looking for the trouble.

Exposed electrics on a Honda 'Gold Wing' – its fuel tank is under the seat

John Thorpe, as a motor cycle journalist, has to put it very mildly, 'done it all'. Staff road test rider for the original 'green 'un' *Motor Cycling*, moped test rider for *Cycling*, editor of *Motorcycling Monthly* . . . , there are not many two wheelers that the author of this book hasn't at one time or another opened the throttle of in search of a, later to be reported, new experience.

The fundamentals of looking after a motor cycle, setting up a workshop and using the tools of the trade for maintenance of a machine are comparable no matter what the capacity of the motor cycle. John Thorpe's vast experience of the two-wheeler world makes itself apparent in this informative book about how to 'Be Your Own Motor Cycle Mechanic'.

When the bike just stops working, the motor goes silent and you coast to a halt, where is the first point to look for trouble? If you don't know, then buy the book, read it and understand why those 'old timers' won Isle of Man Tourist Trophy races even after roadside repairs. Electrical faults are always difficult to diagnose, but the fault-finding guides on electrics, carburation, engines and gearboxes contained within this volume are clearly understandable by even the most inexperienced newcomer to the two-wheeled world.

Two-strokes, four-strokes with one, two, three, four or more cylinders are all part of the modern motor cycle scene. With service and labour costs soaring to unprecedented levels, it pays to learn about the bike you ride and be able to service or repair it yourself. John Thorpe's diy guide to motor cycle maintenance is compiled from years of practical experience and will prove of value to both the novice and the experienced rider. The intricacies of engine internals are clearly explained and the information relating to the methods of tackling specific tasks make this book just as essential in a workshop as a good set of tools.

Charles E. Deane   Editor *Motor Cycling*

Introduction

With garage labour charges running at astronomical rates, the question really ought to be why everybody doesn't undertake his own motor cycle maintenance and repairs. At one time, a bike was a cheap option as personal transport, but increasing mechanical complication and ever-rising costs for spares and materials have eaten into the bike's financial advantages.

Doing-it-yourself reverses the trend. With the simplest bikes – petroil-lubricated, single-cylinder two-strokes – maintenance is so simple that even novice riders can undertake it. The essentials are a good basic tool kit, a working knowledge of its use and reliable data on the bike. That does not usually mean buying an 'official' workshop manual. Most of those currently sold by the major concessionaires are useless for do-it-yourself work. They are designed as memory refreshers for professional mechanics who have already gone through a 'works' training course, and who have at their disposal a battery of special tools designed to speed up the work. For home mechanics, it is better (and much cheaper!) to buy one of the specially written bike manuals designed for the do-it-yourself rider. Several monthly magazines also carry regular servicing features on specific bikes, and it's worth writing to the editorial offices to check whether they have carried an article on your model and, if so, whether a back number can be obtained.

Lifting a Suzuki two-stroke twin engine

There is no need to be put off if your bike happens to be more complicated than usual. You do not need to be four times as skilled a mechanic to work on a four-cylinder engine, rather than a 'single'. Basically, all engines are just multiples of a single-cylinder four-stroke or two-stroke. It will take longer to do all the work, since there may be sixteen valves to adjust rather than two. However, if you can adjust one valve, you can adjust them all. If you can decoke one piston, you can decoke three. And you can comfort yourself with the thought that you are saving three or four times as much money.

Start being your own mechanic, though, with simple operations such as routine servicing. Given the tools, you can do all the work yourself. In practice, you may not think it worthwhile investing in some of the more exotic equipment, in which case you can do most of the routine jobs yourself and then take the bike to your local dealer only for jobs such as multi-carb tuning, or resetting the timing.

While the manufacturer's elapsed-mileage servicing schedule has to be the basis on which you work, it's advisable to keep a running check on the bike. The first essential may seem odd, but it is one which big bike fleet users like the police regard as the most vital part of servicing. Clean the bike regularly – every week, if possible. The idea is not just to keep the machine looking smart – although that's a big enough bonus when, eventually, you do wish to sell it – but to ensure that there is no part of the bike with which you are not completely familiar, nor any part that you do not physically touch and check at least once a month. This aspect is dealt with in detail in the Routine Maintenance chapter, p. 46.

Cleaning the bike, start from the front and work methodically to the rear. Check the tension of every spoke. The easiest method here is to grasp a pair of spokes at the interlacing point, and press them together; any appreciable movement shows that one of them is loose. Shine a torch onto the disc pads, and satisfy yourself that they are not dangerously worn. Check the security of the wheel spindle, the oiltightness of the fork seals and the tension of every nut and bolt.

Working back past the engine unit, look for oil leaks, or smudges of discoloured light alloy that tell a mute tale of loose fastenings allowing mating faces to work on each other, grinding away the metal. Check every cable for fractured strands and rust. Examine the numerous electrical sockets and connectors which are used on modern bikes. A loose lead could blow your main fuse, and leave you stranded in fast traffic with no motor and no lights.

Behind the engine, unless you're lucky enough to have shaft drive, is the chain. This is the most vulnerable and cost-provoking item on the whole bike, for it and its two sprockets really need to be renewed together, unless you want to waste money with old teeth chewing into new chain links. If the chain has been removed at regular intervals – it's a job to be recommended three or four times a year – for thorough cleaning in a paraffin bath, and then immersion in molten grease, it may need only inspection and adjustment, but if it looks dry then it should come off again for cleaning and lubrication. The exception is a sealed-link chain, which can be lubricated without removal, using an aerosol lubricant.

While servicing the chain, examine the sprocket teeth individually. None must be chipped, and if any are adopting a hooked shape you must fit a new chain and new sprockets; there are no short cuts. Incidentally, leave the re-installation of the chain until the washing-down, hosing and drying of the bike is finished. There's no point in greasing the chain if you then wash it over with detergent.

It is also a good idea to follow another police practice and check round the bike before riding away on each and every trip. It needn't be a fetish; all that is needed is a quick visual inspection to ensure that everything looks in order, plus a check on lights, brakes and horn before moving off. Many people make a point of strolling round the bike while waiting for the tank to be filled, just checking that there are no obvious loose fastenings, or missing split pins in the spindle nuts, or disconnected leads. You can even check your mixture at a glance, just by looking at the exhaust tail pipes. If one is black and sooty, and another is burned a harsh white, then you've got a rich mixture on one or more cylinders and a weak one on the rest.

Routine maintenance, using these regular checks together with the recommended services, makes up the main part of do-it-yourself money saving. The other part comes from the very substantial costs you can avoid when an overhaul is necessary. However, the beauty of do-it-yourself routine maintenance is that it puts off any need for overhauls by many thousands of miles. Overhauls are needed only when components wear and components wear quickly only when they are working under unfavourable conditions. Bad luck or accident damage apart, the better you maintain your bike by doing the minor jobs thoroughly, the less need you will have to tackle major work. And – a word of warning – there is no point whatsoever in stripping components that are already working well. A rider who pulls his engine apart every winter, having covered perhaps no more than 10,000 miles since the last strip-down, isn't clever. Mechanically speaking, he is illiterate, because every working surface on that motor will then have to bed-in again, and the unit will just about have reached efficiency by the next strip-down.

Most of the overhaul work needed on bikes can be confined to the top end, and the most commonly required job is a decoke. With two-strokes, clean up the piston crown, the ring grooves and rings, the ports and the exhaust system. With four-strokes, add checking the valves and guides, lapping-in valves and renewing valve springs.

Bottom-end overhauls are rarely needed on bikes that have ball or roller bearings, which are generally good for 100,000 miles or more. Four-stroke multis with plain bearings can usually manage about 30,000 miles before new shells are required, although if scrupulous attention has been paid to oil and filter changing that mileage could easily be doubled.

Accidental damage is another matter. Here, you may want to make as big a saving as you can – in the time that the bike is off the road, forcing you to use expensive public transport, in the actual cost of repairs and in your valuable no-claims bonus. You have two choices from the do-it-yourself point of view. You can take the bike into your own workshop, strip it yourself, and be faced with a bill for nothing but the spares, or you can show a substantial saving by stripping-out the damaged units and then taking them to a dealer for the rest of the job to be done. It's worth remembering that it can cost a considerable amount just to take an engine out and put it back again – yet it is work that's easy enough to tackle at home with a very minimum of tools.

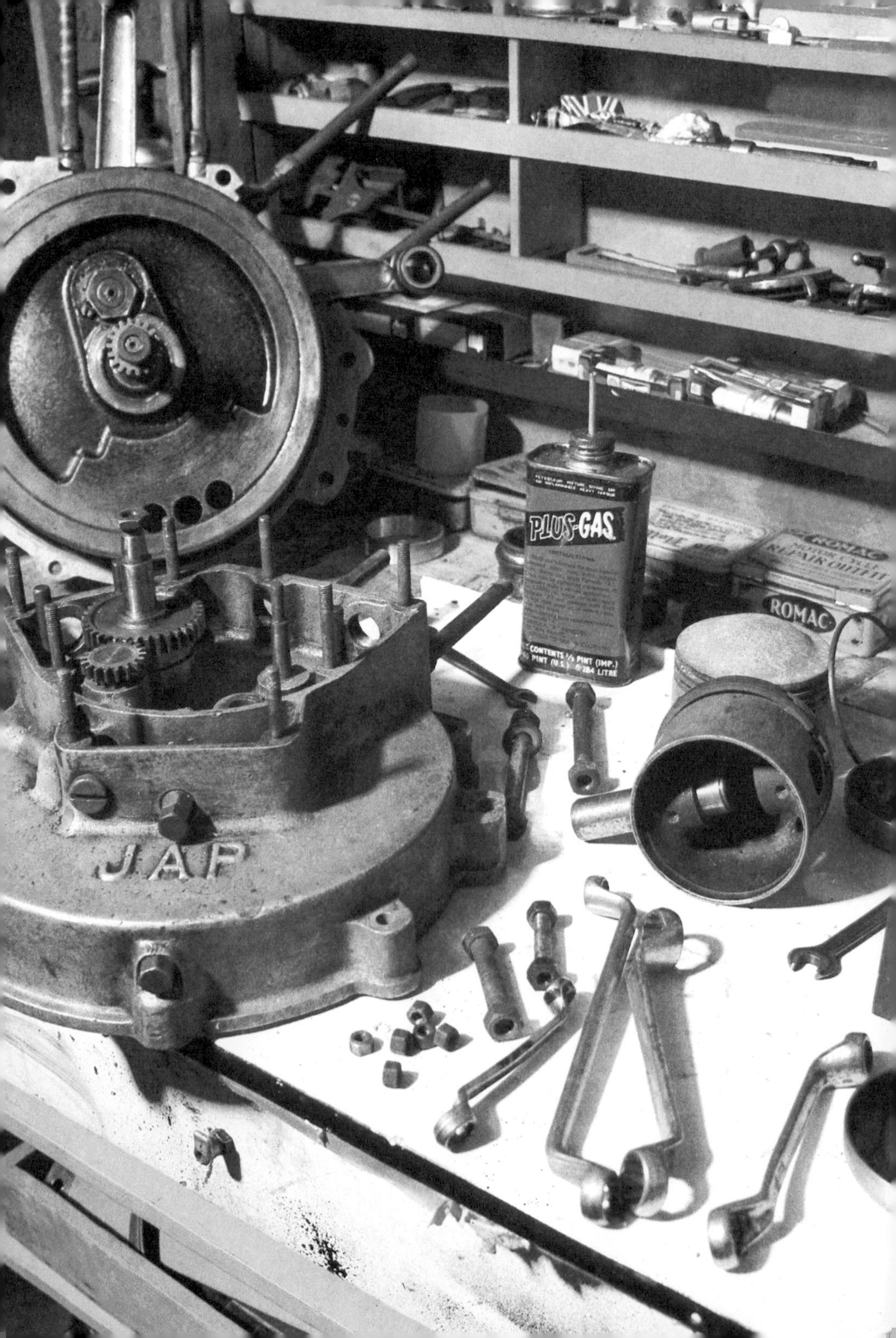
PLUS-GAS
ROMAC
MOTOR CYCLE REPAIR OUTFIT
ROMAC
JAP

Inside the Workshop

Given the chance to see inside a top-class motor cycle workshop, a casual visitor is usually impressed, most of all, by the overall cleanliness. The days of back-street garages with oily floors and cluttered benches, if not gone, are certainly passing. Bikes are now big business, and the major factories demand standards of servicing that not so long ago were reserved for their own development or racing departments.

So, the professional mechanic now works on a bench that is skinned over with sheet metal to keep it clean and free from oil stains. For servicing, the bike stands on a ramp. The flooring is still of concrete, but sealed and painted to prevent it shedding dust. The whole area is illuminated by shadow-free fluorescent tubes, with wanderleads to take light into awkward corners.

Every mechanic has his own tool chest, which often takes the form of a wheeled trolley, so that every commonly used piece of equipment is within easy reach. Special tools are accommodated on peg-boarding set round the walls with the outline of each tool painted in so that anybody can see at a glance if it is not in its proper place.

Vintage engine or modern multi, the workbench still needs to be clean and tidy

On a smaller scale, this is the ideal to aim at for home maintenance and overhauls. Most garages have concrete floors, and it's a simple job to make these as oil-resistant as those in the professional workshop. Any builders merchant can supply a suitable sealant which can be brushed on. When dry, this provides a tough and shiny surface that solves the dust problem once and for all, and which needs little more than wiping over with a mop to keep it clean.

After the floor has been sealed, decide where the work bench is to go. Until that's settled, the positioning of lights and power points cannot be finalised. A four-foot fluorescent tube should go over the bench itself, and there should be a five-foot tube to give general illumination for the rest of the workshop. If possible, set the bench next to a window to get the advantage of daylight as well.

For power, at least two 13-amp sockets are needed. One should be handy for the bench: the other for the general working area. That way, the lead-lengths can be minimised.

It's best to have the necessary wiring done professionally, especially if an external electricity supply needs to be installed. Mains voltage supplies can kill, and no risks should be taken by attempting to economise on what is normally a fairly moderate cost. Where it's impossible to obtain a supply of electricity, gas lighting is a reasonable alternative. In this case, however, it is out of the question for petrol to be taken into the workshop. Even an empty petrol tank contains enough vapour to blow up the building (just one cupful of petrol has the same explosive potential as a stick of TNT) and gas lighting is a form of open flame. Wherever such lighting is used, the bike must have its tank and float chambers removed before it is wheeled into the workshop.

Gas lighting in itself is efficient. A lamp running on the smallest 190-gram butane cartridge gives illumination equivalent to an 80-watt bulb and will burn for six hours at a time. As the gas mantle is fragile, the lamp should be positioned fairly high, out of the way of knocks. It should not be set too close to woodwork, however, since the heat thrown out is considerable.

Gas lanterns cannot be used for close-up work on the bike. Here, a battery-operated lantern can stand in for a wander-lamp. For short jobs, an inspection light powered by the bike's own battery can be used, but anything above an hour's continuous lighting may discharge the battery unacceptably.

With lighting and power laid on, the next consideration is the bench. For bike work, it needn't be very big – a surface 1.25 metres long by about half a metre wide is enough. Rough-sawn timber around 100x50mm (what used to be called 'four by two') bolted together for a box-type frame, with a covering of old floorboards about 20mm thick, is sufficient. Even an old door can be used as a top.

Skin the bench with sheet aluminium of around 18-gauge. Hammer it down round the edges, and then drill countersunk holes in the down-turn to take fixing screws. If two or more sheets of alloy have to be used to cover the bench make a butt-joint and, again, use countersunk screws to keep the surface flush. Complete the job by installing, if possible, a full-size shelf about halfway down the legs and covering this with sheet vinyl. It will form a clean and handy storage space for big components.

A ramp can be constructed in much the same way. Use sturdier timber, as it will have to support the weight of a bike, and make it about half a metre high. Industrial-grade vinyl flooring makes a good covering material for this application.

Line the walls of your workshop with peg-boarding set on light wood framing pinned in place; paint it with light-reflecting washable emulsion and you are now ready to start equipping your workshop with tools.

Spanners

Traditionally, a professional mechanic provides his own tools, and his kit contains such a wealth of spanners that being held up for the right tool is a pretty rare occurrence for him. Luckily – since that kit has probably cost upwards of £300 – a home mechanic doesn't need to emulate him. A quite modest kit will suffice, providing it covers the range of types and sizes needed for the particular bike.

The most familiar spanners are the open-enders. Slim, and with their heads set at an angle to permit the tool being reversed to obtain fresh purchase, these are the all-rounders of your kit. An open-ended spanner can be slipped into awkward spaces (although for even more confined quarters it's possible to obtain specially shaped obstruction spanners) where rings and sockets simply cannot operate.

As versatile as they may be, open-enders have their disadvantages. Each spanner is designed to give a set leverage, which is appropriate to the torque usually needed for the size of bolt it fits. Applying greater force than that can cause the spanner to slip off the nut; it may also damage the spanner itself by springing the jaws apart. It needs only a slight distortion to turn the spanner from a precision tool into an instrument that might have been specially designed to round off the corners of any fastener to which it is applied. So, make it a rule *never* to apply anything but standard leverage and arm pressure through an open-ender. Even the fairly common practice of tapping the free end with a soft-faced mallet can cause jaw distortion – and there are other ways of freeing overtightened nuts and bolts.

Discounting box spanners – which are generally too flimsy for serious workshop use – the next step up is the ring spanner, in which the heads are closed rings designed to grip the fastening at each corner, instead of exerting pressure just on two of the flats as the open-ender does.

The ring spanner, like the open-ender, is designed basically to give a set amount of leverage and no more. It will often free a nut on which the open-ender has failed, partly because it has a better grip and partly because it applies its thrust at six points all round the fastener. Most ring spanners, however, are cranked, which inhibits their use in confined spaces, and they have an inherent shortcoming in having a radiussed lead-in which means that they rarely seat for the full depth of the fastener. They do tend, therefore, to shear off the upper section of the fastener's angles, in just the same way as might an ill-fitting open-ender. For that reason, you will often find that a professional mechanic has ground away the lower surface of the ring, leaving it completely flat – a technique that can also be applied to socket spanners.

With socket sets, you add versatility to your workshop. The basis of a socket set is the bar on which the drive is mounted. By arranging the drive so that it can be slid along the bar, it is possible to get varying degrees of leverage to suit the job in progress. For a stubborn nut, the full length of the bar can be used. Alternatively, the drive can be centralised, and one hand placed on each side of the bar to bring your whole strength to bear.

The single drive (the half-inch size is the one most generally used) is employed with a whole range of sockets, which means, of course, that you need to employ its power with caution. The force that may safely be used on a 22mm fastener would simply snap the head off an 8mm bolt. With sockets, however, there is plenty of 'feel', thanks to the rigidity of the bar and the close fit of the socket itself on the fastener.

A good-quality socket set includes more 'goodies'. Almost certainly, there will be long and short extensions to enable the sockets to reach nuts buried deep in components. Some sets also include a universal drive, with which the actual angle of approach can be varied. You can't *quite* operate the socket round a corner, but it is almost possible! Work is eased considerably if a ratchet drive is used in conjunction with sockets. Ratchets are reversible – or have a reverse catch – so that undoing or fastening a nut or bolt becomes a simple matter of oscillating the handle. This again is particularly advantageous where working space is limited. The rigid bar may need an arc of a foot or more in which to operate: a ratchet drive can ease a bolt undone using only a few inches of movement.

Perhaps not so useful for bikes, the speedbrace is the third type of drive often supplied with a socket set. It looks remarkably like a streamlined version of the brace-and-bit of one's schoolday woodwork classes and it operates on just the same principle. Fit a socket to it, apply it to the fastener and twirl the speedbrace. The nut is spun off in a fraction of the time needed with other hand tools.

Tools for virtually every eventuality

A socket set offers yet another possibility – use of a torque wrench. This may look like a refined tommy bar or a larger ratchet bar. In fact, it's a precision tool that enables you to apply exactly the amount of torque to a fastener that the makers specify. Two types are in general use. The cheaper version consists of a squared drive attached to a long springy handle. This handle carries a scale,

and welded to the drive is a fixed pointer. As pressure is applied to the handle, the arm deflects and moves the scale relative to the pointer. To apply the required torque, just keep pressing until the appropriate mark is indicated on the scale. More expensive, the ratchet type can be preset so that when the torque you have dialled up is reached, the ratchet slips and no further pressure can be applied. Adhering to torque settings prevents damage to both fasteners and components – and it also ensures that you can undo the nuts and bolts again later on!

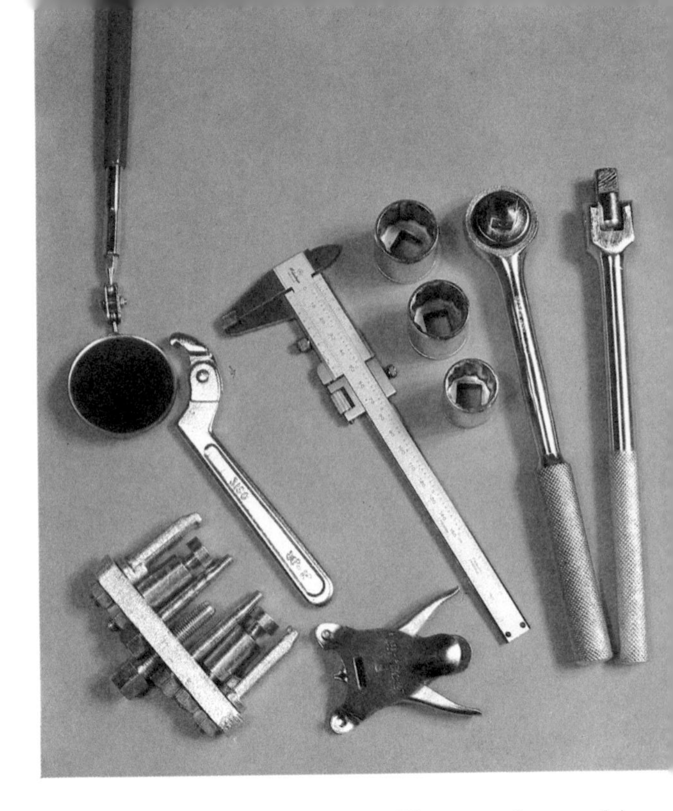

A handy mirror, a universal puller, a C-spanner, a piston ring expander, a vernier gauge and some sockets

Also working on the ratchet principle, ratchet spanners are a development of rings. Here, the head is a hexagon, which slips over the fastener and fits it perfectly. Working the ratchet handle to and fro loosens or tightens the fastener. This type of spanner is expensive, but it combines to a large extent the virtues of both open-enders and rings, so it's worthwhile investing in a few for special applications.

Currently assuming greater importance, as the major Japanese manufacturers steadily retreat from the unpopular cross-headed screws which once figured overmuch on their machines, are Allen keys. Despite the name, they *are* a form of spanner – basically a cranked hexagonal bar designed to fit socket-headed screws. They can be used in two ways. For undoing socket-heads, the shorter arm of the key is inserted into the socket screw, and the longer arm is used as a lever to turn it. When assembling, the socket screw is placed on the longer arm, and the key is twirled by its shank to take the screw up to finger tightness. The key is then re-engaged with the longer shank free, for the final tightening. Some mechanics make up their own useful Allen keys by setting a length of hexagonal bar, about 25mm long, into a bolt head. This can then be engaged in an appropriate-sized socket and used with the various drives from the socket set.

Other spanners that may be required for specific jobs include C-spanners, peg spanners and castellated drives. C-spanners are used for tightening and loosening ring nuts, the most typical application being on the steering head bearing adjuster. The C-spanner supplied in bike tool kits for adjusting rear suspension unit settings is *not* usually suitable for any other purpose.

Peg spanners have pegs of steel projecting from the face of the spanner to engage in holes drilled in the flush surface of a round fastener. The screw rings used in the tops of fork sliders on some models, for example, cannot be undone without damage save by use of the correct peg spanner. It is unusual to find fastenings of this type on engines or gearboxes, but one exception is the castellated ring nut used on certain Honda clutches and centrifugal oil filters. A socket with castellations formed on its face has to be used to undo these, and more than one mechanic has made up his own simply by filing the necessary 'pegs' on to an old, damaged, plain socket. This takes time, but it saves money.

The most familiar of the specialist spanners is probably the plug spanner – a tool for which there is usually no possible substitute, with today's deeply recessed plug locations. It is basically a box spanner, turned by applying a tommy bar through holes drilled in the spanner body. It is possible to obtain more sophisticated plug spanners that have a flexible insert which will lock the plug into the spanner, and which may have a ball drive with an inbuilt tommy bar.

Professional workshops often use a rather similar plug spanner as part of a socket set, but a home mechanic might regard that as a bit of a luxury, more especially since it lacks portability. With these heavier plug spanners, it is also easy to overtighten the plug into the head, either distorting the plug body, or stripping the threads.

Which spanners should you buy? That depends entirely upon your bike, but as a generalisation you will rarely need a spanner smaller than 8mm, and most routine work can be done without going beyond 17mm. The most usual sizes across the flats, for fastenings on the Japanese and European bikes that make up 99 per cent of the market, are 10, 11, 12, 14 and 17mm. Beyond that, it becomes a matter of buying spanners specially for a particular application, as and when it arises. It's often overlooked that individual spanners and sockets can be bought at tool shops, and that a comprehensive toolkit can be built up quite painlessly over a matter of twelve months or so.

There may be a temptation to short-circuit matters by investing in adjustable spanners. Don't do this; an adjustable in the bike's portable toolkit may be a useful stand-by for a roadside emergency, but it is not, and never will be, a viable workshop tool. The easiest way to ruin nuts and bolts is to attack them with an adjustable – unless, that is, you happen to believe that pliers are for gripping nuts.

Screwdrivers

Were you to judge it solely by its appearance, you'd think that an impact screwdriver is too heavy for normal work on alloy castings. Don't believe it! If you have a motor cycle on which the engine covers and crankcases are joined by screws, you are going to need an impact screwdriver, and you'll bless the day you bought it.

It's a daunting-looking tool, the cylindrical body carries a square drive at one end and has a face at the other. Separate screwdriver bits are supplied with it, and these push into a special socket which fits on to the drive. Engage a suitable bit into the screw, give the face of the impact driver a sharp blow with a hammer and almost miraculously, the screw immediately loosens. For the rest, just rotate the body of the impact driver. Sometimes, an impact driver will work *without* the hammer blow, its thick, stubby body giving your hand a really good grip to get purchase on to the screw and turn it.

The alternative to an impact driver is a T-handled screwdriver, but this will not free really stubborn screws. Neither can you use a T-handled driver in the way that you can employ the bits and socket from an impact driver – in combination with the speedbrace from a socket set for quickly spinning up all types of screws. With the T-handle – although it *can* be spun – you need one T-handled driver for each type of screw.

Ordinary handyman-type screwdrivers are useful for light applications – the screws on spring clamps, for example – but they are almost useless for overhaul work. For these light applications, however, the T-handled driver is equally

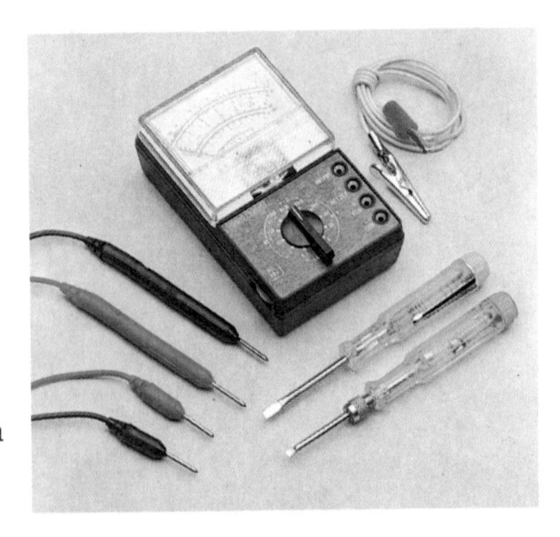

A test meter and a pair of electrical screwdrivers

suitable providing it is long enough to clear any obstructions.

Most of the screws found on a modern motor cycle are of the cross-headed type; slotted screws are comparative rarities, but you have to be prepared to meet them. For instance, they crop up on some contact-breaker points plates, on carburettor jets and in some types of clutch push-rod adjusters. A few machines have slotted tappet adjusters too, so several types of bladed screwdriver may be needed. Start off with a general-purpose driver, with a $\frac{3}{16}$in blade, and add to the collection as you go along.

One special driver that can be very handy indeed is a small electrical type, whose handle incorporates a tiny neon bulb which glows when the blade is placed on a live contact. These are available for battery voltages (6/12v) and for mains voltages (220/240v) and the two are totally different. You need the 6/12v

A selection of pliers and cutters, an adjustable spanner and a self-grip wrench

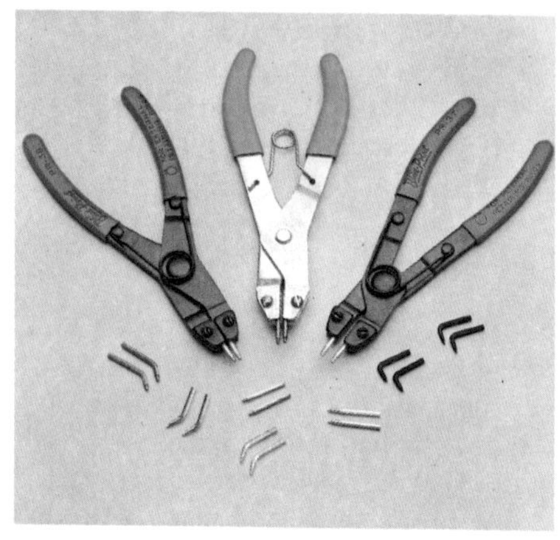

Various types of circlip pliers with interchangeable noses

type and it must *never* be used to check out a mains system.

Pliers

Apart from the odd circlip, or split pin, there are few items which require pliers to grip. If you employ wire cutters and strippers for electrical work, in fact, your pliers will come in for very little use, so don't over-equip yourself with these tools. One pair of conventional pliers with insulated handles, one pair of snipe-nose pliers, again, insulated, and for versatility a pair of adjustable pliers of the type car mechanics use for water-pump glands will meet your requirements perfectly. For serious dismantling, however, you will also certainly need circlip pliers.

These have peg-type noses so that the pliers can be engaged with the holes in the circlip tongues and used to spring the circlip from its slot. Two types are needed – one for circlips that have to be expanded for removal and one for those that have to be compressed. Modern Japanese engines make considerable use of both types of circlip. Besides locating the gudgeon pins, circlips lock some clutch bodies, secure oil-pump shafts, prevent sideways movement on gear-selector shafts, hold kickstarter mechanisms and position gearbox pinions.

Self-grip wrenches

Looking like a large set of pliers, a self-grip wrench is a versatile tool that can be used almost as a third hand, with jaws that can be adjusted to grip over spans ranging from zero up to 30 or 40mm. It works on the over-centre principle, and the jaws are heavily serrated to ensure that work units held by them cannot slip. Because of this, however, it is essential to set the span accurately. Forcing the wrench closed on a component that is even fractionally too large can result in heavy surface damage. Used properly, a self-locking wrench is an invaluable workshop tool and its versatility can be improved by use of a special clamp, which enables it to be locked to a workbench and employed as a light vice.

Vices

For serious work, something more substantial than a self-grip wrench is needed. The answer is a bench vice – the bigger the better. A minimum size for bike work would be one with 125mm jaws. It should be securely through-bolted to the workbench and positioned over one of the legs with the inner stationary jaw in line with the edge of the worktop. Set like this, it enables long components to be accommodated by 'underhanging' them.

A vice is a powerful tool – it can even be used as a form of press – and in standard form it is delivered with serrated, hardened-steel jaws. Locking a delicate bike component between these would cause extensive surface damage, so an essential addition to the vice is a pair of soft pads which can be inserted when vulnerable items need to be gripped. At their simplest, these can be home-made from offcuts of light alloy sheet, hammered round the jaws to form removable pads. Even hardwood strips can be interposed as a makeshift measure, although the professional answer is interchangeable jaw packings for specific jobs. An ancillary application of a well-made vice is as an anvil for hammering and rivetting. Indeed, some vices have a special anvil built in.

Hammers

Properly used, hammers are among the handiest tools in any workshop. An engineer's hammer normally has a 2½lb head, with a hardened striking face at one end and a ball pein, for metalworking, at the other. This is a reasonable weight for general use. The smaller 1½-pounder lacks the weight needed to minimise the number of blows given to a workpiece: while a 4lb club (a stubby, double-faced tool rather like a miniature sledge hammer) is needed only for really heavy work of the sort more likely to apply to cars than to bikes.

A home mechanic's tool kit must, however, include several of the variants for specialised work. A copper- or fibre-headed mallet is essential for use where force has to be applied without risk of surface damage, while for sterner stuff (freeing a light-alloy cylinder block whose gasket has fused for example) the only possible tool is a rubber mallet. Some mallets are produced with screw-in interchangeable fibre and rubber faces. One of these can act as a dual-purpose tool.

Punches and cold chisels

Ancillaries of the hammer, a selection of punches and chisels is a necessity. Punches can be sharp tools, used for dot-marking components or staking together mating surfaces (for example, the vertical faces of a nut and its shaft), blunt-ended or shouldered, for transferring force from the hammer to a specific component area. Punches of the latter type are more properly called 'drifts'. Every workshop needs a selection – at least one hardened-steel centre punch for staking, drifts in several sizes and lengths, for driving out bearings etc and an equal number of soft-metal drifts for use on non-hardened components.

Cold chisels are for cutting, and they have fewer applications on motor cycles than in cars, where there is more sheet metal. A chisel can still be the handiest tool, though, for such jobs as easing the tang of a tab washer away from a nut, or for cutting a control cable inner wire providing the strands have first been secured with solder. That done, a sharp blow with a hammer and cold chisel, operating on an anvil, provides a cleaner cut than snips can.

Drills

Where power is laid on, a two-speed electric drill with a ³⁄₈in chuck capacity provides the basis for a major extension of the workshop's range.

The most obvious use of a drill is that of making holes. For that, interchangeable drill bits are required. These are of several types, with quite separate uses. High-speed carbon steel drills are for use on hard metals. They are best used on the low-speed setting – usually 900rpm – to avoid overheating at the tip. They are also relatively brittle, and will snap easily if misused. For lighter work, in soft metals, ordinary, mild steel drill bits are satisfactory.

Every major drill manufacturer also markets accessories which adapt the drill to offer some of the facilities of a power workshop. A pillar drill conversion gives absolute accuracy by enabling the drill to be mounted in a stand perpendicular to the workpiece, and delicacy of touch through a lever-operated control system. A horizontal bench stand allows the drill to be used as a power grinder, or to be fitted with an abrasive disc to form a rotary cutter. Flexible extension drives, used with special cutters and wire brushes, enable the power drill to profile and polish exhaust and inlet ports – a job where the higher speed of 2400rpm is invaluable. With ordinary rotary wire brushes, cleaning carbon from piston crowns and valve stems is reduced to a few moments' work.

Less practical, but welcome where a mains drill cannot be used, battery-powered drills have the obvious advantage of total portability, and can carry out most of the work of which the 240v drill is capable. The obvious restriction is that dictated by the capacity of the battery. Where a heavy-duty car battery is available, one of the drills designed to work off extension leads could be a better answer than a self-contained unit, with its lower-capacity power source.

The other solution is a breast drill – a hand-powered tool, but one capable of tackling most of the basic jobs although at a much lower speed. It pays to select a breast drill that has a two-speed gearbox, the lower speed being used to multiply the applied torque for heavy work.

Files

Basically, in the motor cycle workshop, files are simply tools for finishing off a job already roughly done. The most useful files for a biker are one with a medium cut, for general work, and two or three different sizes of fine file for detail jobs such as squaring-off contact-breaker points faces or plug electrodes, or carefully opening up piston ring gaps. A typical application of the heavier file would be for smoothing-off the end of a bolt that has been cut to size. For opening up holes in, for example, fairings or top boxes one should use a triangular, rather than a rat-tail, file and finish the job with an abrasive paper.

Most files terminate in pointed metal tangs. It is essential, for safety's sake, to fit handles to any such files in the workshop. Were the file to snag while being used with any force, the tang could inflict a very serious wound.

Saws

Two types of saw are useful in a biker's workshop – a hacksaw and a pad saw. A hacksaw is for cutting metal, using renewable blades in a 'horseshoe' frame, set up with a screw-tensioner. The saw is designed to cut on the outward stroke only. Two hacksaws – one large general-purpose saw, and a small 'Junior' saw for light work – are ample, but keep an adequate supply of blades for each; they *are* rather vulnerable.

A pad saw is basically a handle with a securing screw to take a variety of blades. Unlike the hacksaw, a pad saw has a blade fixed at only one end and it can therefore be used to cut through, rather than across, a workpiece. Special pad-saw blades are available for use in differing materials, and most home mechanics also save broken hacksaw blades for use in the pad saw where the material to be dealt with is relatively soft.

Sawn edges are invariably rough, and should be finished off with an appropriate file before the workpiece is used.

Splitters

As an alternative to hacksawing in half-nuts that refuse to budge, a nut splitter offers a quicker and easier solution. It is basically an open 'anvil' that slips over the nut, with a screw-type cutting blade that is forced through the nut on being tightened with a spanner. On some versions, a fixed blade on the anvil looks after the other side of the nut.

A screw action is also used on chain splitters. These have spring-loaded claws that enable the tool to be locked on to the chain link. When the splitter is positioned, its screw-type punch is brought to bear on the chain rivet, which is easily pressed out to break the chain. This type of splitter works well on all chains with normal rivets, but may not cope with the specially strong rivets used in one-piece superbike chains, for which a manufacturer's tool is usually required.

Stud extractors

Basically hardened steel tapers, equipped with a left-handed quickthread, the 'Easyout' type of stud extractor is the one most applicable to bike work. It is designed to be screwed into a hole drilled in the broken fastening. When

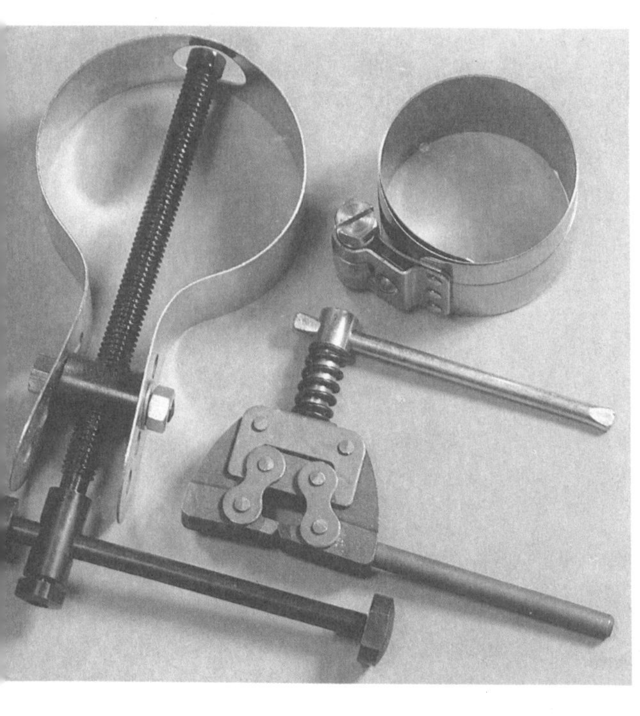

A gudgeon pin remover, a chain splitter and a piston ring compressor

it has penetrated deeply enough to lock solidly into the stump, further turning unscrews the extractor and stud together.

Extractors of this type are sold in sets, suitable for a range of stud sizes.

Compressors

Save for a few heavy-duty applications – removal of the transmission shaft damper spring on the CX500, for example (for which a one-off tool is needed) – the only generally used spring compressor is that required for valve removal. It comprises a U-frame, with a pair of feet or a ring at one end and a hand screw at the other. The feet are engaged on the valve cap, and the end of the screw on the valve head. Tightening the screw compresses the valve spring and pushes the valve cap clear of the stem so that the collets can be removed. It is used in the same way for refitting valves.

The limiting factor with valve spring compressors is, of course, the distance between the feet. What is suitable for a 50cc bike will be too small for the valves of an 850 twin, and vice versa. Some 'universal' compressors can be adapted within a reasonable range of machines, but a well equipped workshop really needs two or three compressors to cope with more than one bike.

With some machines, a special compressor is also required for removal of the springs from the rear spring/damper units, but this is not a universal requirement. The usual type of compressor for the job comprises a lower clamp to fit round the damper body, and an intermediate pressure plate sliding on rods set into the clamp base. A hand screw set in an upper plate forces down the pressure plate until the suspension spring is sufficiently compressed to enable the securing collets to be removed.

Compressed suspension springs can be lethally powerful, and where a compressor is not being used it is advisable to lock the spring with three steel hooks set at 120° around it before releasing the cap.

Valve grinders and cutters

Most four-stroke poppet valves require the use of a suction-type valve tool for grinding-in. This is merely a suction cap set on the end of a wooden rod. The sucker is pressed on to the head of the valve and used to oscillate and lift it during the lapping-in process which is the final stage of reseating valves.

Grinding-in used at one time to be the full process in itself, but with modern engines its place has been taken by cutting and refacing the seats on the valve inserts and on the valve. The cutters used on the seats are basically rotary hand-operated reamers, and up to three may be required for each seat, depending upon the designed seating angles. This is a job normally entrusted to a professional workshop. Where valve head face truing is specified, it is done on an angled grinder – again, a professional operation.

The correct cutters for any specific engine are listed in the maker's workshop manual and are usually obtainable as special tools through the appropriate main dealers.

It is normal practice to use a reamer to finish to size a newly-installed valve guide. Again, the reamers required are specific to the model, and these too are listed as special tools by the various makers.

The correct use of reamers – especially for valve-seat cutting – calls for good judgment. Too heavy a cut on a seat, for example, may set the valve so high in the head that it is impossible to bring the valve clearances within the prescribed limits. Any home mechanic planning to use tools of this type should practice on scrap components first.

Measuring tools

The basic measuring outfit is a millimetre rule which can double as a straight-edge (an engineer's rule made of steel, not a boxwood schooldays ruler) backed up by a set of feeler gauges.

The rule can be used for checking lengths (although a vernier calliper is much better for the job) and the gauges for measuring gaps. In some applications, the two are combined. If the straight-edge is placed vertically across a plane surface, for instance, any gap that can be seen beneath it is warpage, which can then be measured with the feelers.

Metric feelers are calibrated in millimetres; imperial gauges in thousandths of an inch. Nowadays, metric gauges are more useful, since at least ninety per cent of the bikes on the market have all settings and clearances in metric units and

A spark plug gapping tool, a feeler gauge set, a tyre pressure gauge and a dial gauge and stand

the stated imperial equivalents are just approximations.

Feeler gauges are accurately machined strips of spring steel. Using them requires a knack – soon gained – of judging when the blade slides in a gap with just a hint of friction. Too easy a movement means the gap is too wide; too 'sticky' a movement means that the blade is being forced into a gap that is marginally narrow.

One stage up in measuring tools, the vernier calliper has two sets of jaws – one for measuring external lengths and diameters, a second for internal dimensions. Most callipers also have a sliding rod for checking depths.

Each calliper has two measuring scales. The graduations on the vernier (secondary) scale are used to sub-divide those on the main scale, making it possible to read down to very fine limits. To take a measurement, the cursor is moved until the jaws fit snugly over the workpiece, at which point it is then locked with a knurled thumbscrew to hold the reading. This is first taken at the 'zero' mark on the main scale; the vernier is then examined to see which of its graduations is aligned exactly with one of the graduations on the main scale. Each division equals a tenth of a millimetre, so this second reading gives the fraction that is to be added to the initial reading to complete the measurement.

For even greater accuracy, dial gauges or micrometers are required. These are, however, not really necessary in a home workshop, where the only need for measurement beyond that possible with feelers is to determine where a component falls outside the very wide limits of tolerance used to define whether it is still serviceable or not. For this, a vernier calliper is quite accurate enough.

Not all measurements connected with the bike are linear. In several instances, pressures have to be determined with accuracy. The most familiar is the checking of tyre pressures with a gauge. While the simple plunger-type tyre pressure gauge is a reasonable guide, accurate pressures can be better obtained with a dial-type gauge. These are usually calibrated in imperial (lb/sq in) or metric (kg/sq cm). Some, however, are marked in atmospheres – 'bars' – so many times normal atmospheric pressure. This is almost (Kut not quite) the same as kg/sq cm, 0.98 kg sq/cm being equal to one 'bar'.

Cylinder compression is measured by a similar but heavier-duty gauge. Again, the simplest is a 'jumbo' size plunger gauge which screws into the cylinder head in place of the plug. Spinning the engine on the starter with the throttle open, thrusts the plunger out of the gauge body, and the pressure reading is taken as with the tyre gauge at the point where the plunger graduations line up with the body rim. Dial gauges are more accurate. They are not normally screwed into the head, but have a neoprene or rubber taper seal that must be held hard down against the edges of the plug hole while the motor is being spun. Compression pressures are an excellent guide to internal engine condition, since all makers quote a standard pressure which should be reached in each cylinder, and a maximum permissible difference between cylinders. A compression gauge is therefore a far more useful workshop tool than is much of the more abstruse, if more glamorous, equipment.

Half-brother to a pressure gauge is a vacuum gauge, whose job is to measure the depression in the induction tract. Most carburettor adjustment on multi-cylinder machines is now done with the aid of vacuum gauges – usually one gauge to each cylinder. For home workshop purposes, however, it is possible to do the same job – though much more slowly – using a single gauge. This is linked to each inlet in turn, most machines having a blanked-off hole in the stub specially for the gauge to be attached – and the warmed-up engine is run at idling speed while the gauge reading is checked. It should fall within the limits set by the factory. Each carb is checked in turn, the gauge being used to equalise the vacuum in each inlet. With all pilot screws properly set, the gauge is removed and the idling adjusted on the machine's own tachometer.

One further essential measuring

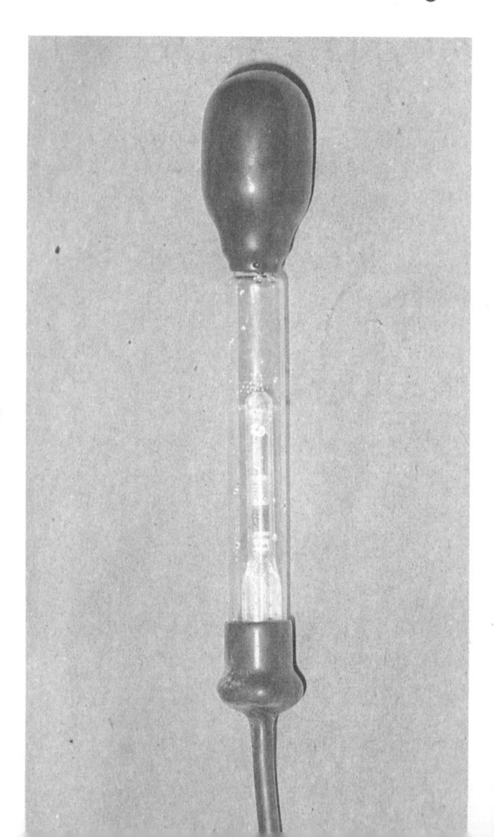

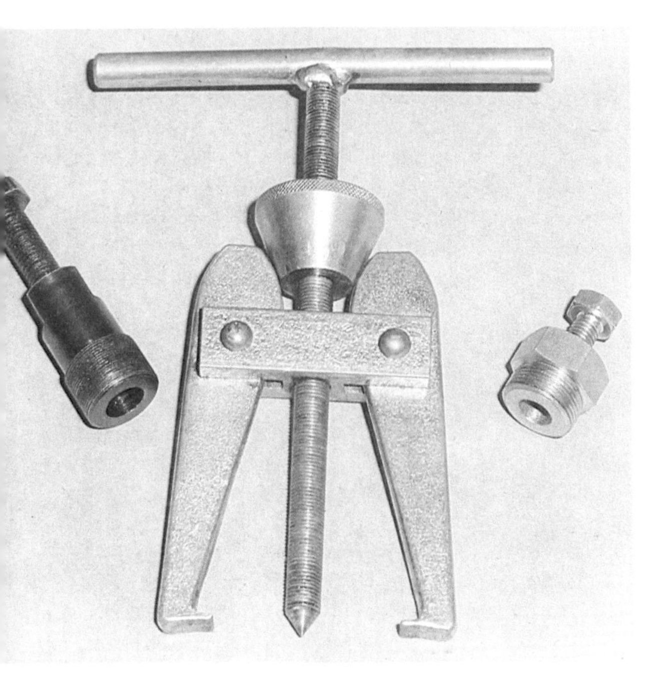

Opposite page, below: A typical hydrometer
Left: A selection of pullers and extractors

instrument is also one of the cheapest – a hydrometer, which indicates the specific gravity of the battery electrolyte. The hydrometer consists of a transparent tube with a pick-up pipe at one end, and a rubber bulb at the other. Inside the tube is a graduated float. Electrolyte from each battery cell is sucked up by pinching and releasing the bulb, and the specific gravity is determined by the point to which the float submerges. A fully charged battery, at 60°F should give a reading of 1.260/1.280. Anything higher suggests an internal short; anything lower, partial discharge.

Pullers

Not now as widely used as in the past, pullers may be required for some specific jobs. They may vary from the simple screwed rod needed to draw off the alternator rotor on some Honda models (for which a front wheel spindle is an acceptable substitute) to a complicated double puller required to split the crankcases on some Suzuki two-strokes. Universal pullers – a misnomer, since they are usually restricted to components with a fairly narrow range of diameters – consist of two or more legs equipped with claws which engage behind the part to be extracted, and a centre screw to bear on the fixed component and so draw the other away. A common application is withdrawal of a flywheel magneto rotor, held to a shaft by a taper and Woodruff key. For this type of unit, a variant is a centre-piece that screws in to the rotor, carrying a screw to engage on the end of the shaft. Holding the body of the extractor with a spanner, and using a second spanner to turn the screw, winds the rotor from the shaft.

An alternative is a slide hammer. This is basically a cylindrical weight drilled through the centre, which is free to slide on a long shaft with an abutment at its upper end. The lower end carries a cross-piece which can be bolted to the component that is to be removed. Sliding the weight smartly along the shaft so that it strikes the abutment sharply, is equivalent to hammering-off the unit. Expanding extractors are occasionally used to withdraw parts such as BMW steering head bearing tracks, which are not easily driven out by drifts. Another type of extractor – basically, a lever with an eccentrically mounted free-swinging jaw – can be used to grip projecting broken studs, though for home workshop use, a Mole-type grip is often an acceptable substitute.

Locking tools and strap wrenches

Professional workshops often contain special tools for preventing units revolving when shaft nuts are being undone. One method is to use a strap or chain wrench – a handle carrying a length of chain or a flexible strap which can be wound round the circumference of a rotor or clutch body, so that the wrench jams and provides a lever by which the unit can be held still. An alternative for clutches is a handle brazed to an old clutch plate, which can be inserted to lock the centre. For flywheel rotors, a peg spanner with two abutments to engage in the face slots is sometimes employed.

A different type of locking tool is the piston base block, set between the piston and the crankcase mouth so that the crankshaft cannot rotate. Two blocks of hardwood about 20mm thick make an acceptable home-workshop substitute. Another improvisation is simply a pad of rag inserted between the driving and driven teeth of a gear-type primary transmission.

Also a form of locking tool – and one that is extremely useful when multi-cylinder bikes are being worked on – is the piston ring clamp. These are sold as special tools: but can equally well be improvised from thin sheet steel with a couple of nuts and bolts to close them. The clamps are placed around the piston, and as each ring is closed up in its correct position the clamp is slipped up to hold it. With all the rings secured, the block is lowered into place, the clamp being slipped down the piston only as each ring enters the bore. When all rings are safely home, the ring clamps are slipped off. The same procedure can be used on motors such as that of the CX500, where the pistons and rods are inserted through the tops of the bores. Here, of course, the clamp is slipped up the piston, rather than down it, as the rings are fed home.

Timing tools

Aids to timing the spark can be visual (a test lamp or, more sophisticated, a stroboscope) or audible (a buzzer, or a transistor radio).

A basic timing rig is simply a bulb set in a holder, or a buzzer, linked to two wires, each equipped with a crocodile clip. One clip goes on to the contact-breaker spring blade; the other to a good earth, such as the crankcase. Depending on the particular type of ignition system used, the bulb will either light up or extinguish as the points break. With the audible type, the buzzer sounds instead.

A transistor radio set to a frequency between two stations – and placed just under the contact-breaker housing will give a distinct click as the points open. However, the most accurate method of setting ignition is with the aid of a stroboscope, which is a flashing lamp that 'freezes' the timing marks on the motor while it is actually running.

The cheapest strobes use a neon tube connected in series with the HT feed to the sparking plug. They tend to be weak, and need to be used in a darkened workshop. Where possible, it is better to buy the more expensive power stroboscope, equipped with a Xenon tube. This type connects to the battery, as well as the HT system, and gives a powerful white light that clearly illuminates the timing marks, even in full daylight.

Wiring tools

Two basic tools suffice for work on the wiring. A wire stripper is the key to clean removal of insulation – the gap between its jaws is adjustable to accommodate different gauges of cable so accurately that just a sharp pull removes a length of insulation, leaving the internal conductor untouched. Wire strippers also incorporate cutting jaws to make a clean incision through stranded cable – the sort of job where the wire cutters or pliers tend to crush instead of cut.

Once the conductor has been

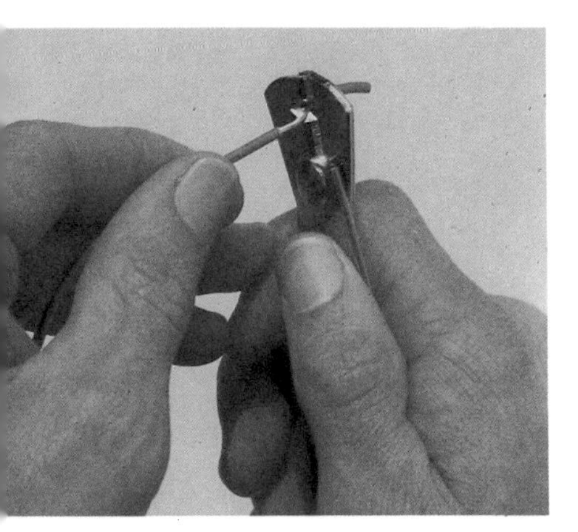

To fit a new connector, first bare the end of the wire

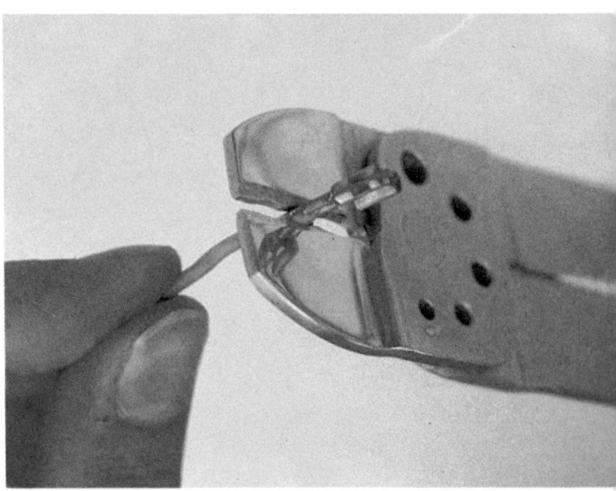

Fix the new connector to the wire by using crimping pliers

stripped, the modern way is to crimp on a terminal. For this, a crimping tool is required. It is designed to crush the terminal round the conductor in such a way that there is complete electrical contact between them, without the need for soldering. Crimping tools are usually sold with a supply of terminals, as a set.

Lifting tools

Necessary only when working on a few bikes with ultra-heavyweight components – for example, when removing the engine from a Honda 'Gold Wing' – lifting tools can be of two main types.

A jack, of the type used to raise small cars – can be either a simple screw-operated scissors jack, or a bottle jack with hydraulic operation. The jack is inserted under the component to be raised, usually with a wooden pad interposed to obviate damage to the castings. The jack is then extended until it is bearing securely on the component, subsequent extension forcing it upwards.

An alternative is one of the midget hoists – basically, a multi-sheave rope tackle – which can be slung from a garage roof beam (if the structure is robust enough to take the weight) or from a tripod formed from scaffold poles. The free end of the hoist is then secured to a sling placed round the component that is to be lifted, and the hoist operated to lift it clear.

Fixing tools

In this context, 'fixing' includes soldering, brazing, and welding – all of which are well within the home mechanic's compass. For soldering, several sizes of electric iron can be needed – too small a bit can lose its heat so quickly, when placed against the workpiece, that efficient soldering becomes impossible. The solution is, ideally, to purchase an electric soldering gun supplied with different sizes of bit, which can be changed according to the nature of the work involved.

For small jobs, quite effective battery-powered irons are available. The batteries fitted to bikes in the over-250cc classes should be able to cope with the drain of one of these irons providing its use is not prolonged, but for constant use in a non-mains-power workshop it is necessary to have either a car battery, or else rely on a gas-heated iron.

Here, again, the size of iron has to be related to the job in hand. A small iron sold for electrical work cannot hold enough heat to solder sheet metal, for example. In this case, there is no alternative to having a range of irons for the different jobs likely to be undertaken. For heating up, a small single-burner camping stove is ideal. It is even possible to buy a soldering-bit attachment for butane gas torches; these are very handy.

Brazing is a form of hard soldering, using bronze rod instead of solder. It demands the use of a large, propane-burning gas torch fed from an $8\frac{1}{2}$lb LPG container; plus a brazing hearth which can be constructed from old firebricks. It is, however, an expensive process and on balance it is probably cheaper to

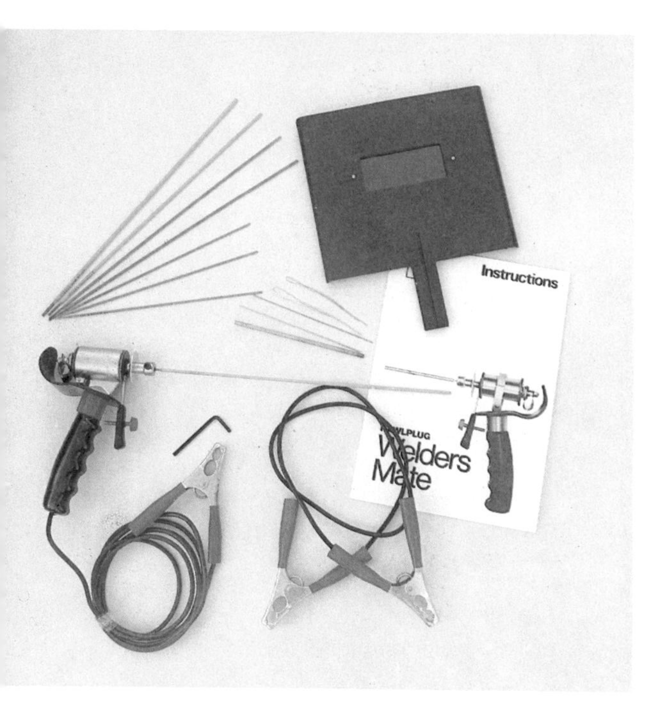

A portable arc-welding set

take components to a professional workshop for brazing, or braze with an electric welder instead.

Home welders are quite a practical proposition providing the workshop has one or two 12-volt car batteries. Gas sets *are* available, but they are relatively costly, and gas welding unless very carefully done can badly weaken the parts being joined.

Electric sets for battery operation are of two main types. For 12-volt operation, there is a carbon-contact torch in which current from one battery terminal is led to a carbon rod clamped to the torch, while a return is arranged by connecting the other battery terminal direct to the workpiece. Touching the carbon rod to the work produces a white-hot short circuit which is hot enough to melt and fuse the two metal surfaces, while more molten metal is fed in from a filler rod also held against the carbon tip.

With two car batteries connected in series, to provide a 24-volt power source, an arc welder can be used instead. This is much like a professional mains kit, using flux-coated welding rod in the torch. When touched on the workpiece, this produces a fierce arc, which melts the rod and deposits it on the workpiece, which itself melts.

If a solenoid is incorporated to control the current, a battery-powered arc welder can be used on metal as thin as 20-gauge without blowing holes in it, making it ideal for fabricating 'one-off' accessories for the bike.

Using the Tools

Proper handling of tools is ninety per cent 'feel' and ten per cent technique. Only practice can develop your manual skills, and the more you use your tools the better mechanic you will become.

Spanners

Start by mastering the very simplest technique – the correct use of spanners. Since practising on the bike might be expensive, it's a good idea to pick up some written-off components from a scrapyard or a breaker, and use those as your earliest test-pieces.

We saw, in the previous chapter, that every spanner apart from a socket is designed so that hand pressure applied to one end gives adequate torque for tightening the size of bolt for which that spanner is used; but what *is* hand pressure?

Basically, it is the pressure that can be applied if the wrist is flexed as the spanner is turned. Lock the wrist solid, and what is then being applied is arm pressure – too high a loading for fastenings in the under-14mm range. Too much pressure, initially, puts an excessive shearing strain on the mating threads of the nut and bolt. Continue to exert it, and one of two things must happen. Either the threads will give way – it's called 'stripping' – and the nut will then turn uselessly on the bolt, or the threads will hold and the strain will be transferred to the metal of the bolt. Excessive pressure on the spanner will then distort, or snap, the shank.

Teaching yourself how to feel when a nut and bolt are approaching their limit is a slow business, but one that can be speeded up if you also have a torque wrench. Check, in the workshop manual, typical torque settings for the bolts on your machine. Then, on the test-piece, try tightening the appropriately-sized bolt to its recommended setting, using an open-ended or ring spanner and working simply by feel. Check your estimate by undoing it with a socket on the torque wrench, noting the reading on the wrench needed to get the nut turning. That is the torque you applied when tightening the fastener.

Where an open-ended spanner is being used in a confined space, the offset of its jaws enables it to be reversed on every other movement, so obtaining a fresh purchase where it would not otherwise be possible to do so. Apart from special obstruction spanners, open-enders are the only type that offer this facility, although a ring spanner can be reset on a fastener at 60° intervals providing there is room to accommodate it.

Usually, only an open-ender will reach really awkward areas.

The exception, of course, is a fastener that is recessed into a component. Here, the socket set should be used. With sockets, it is advisable to use the shortest extension that will enable the spanner to reach the fastener, and to employ the stiffest tommy bar. If there is room to use the ratchet handle, do so. Choosing the stoutest combination open to you means that you bring the greatest power to bear – whippy tommy bars use up an inordinate amount of the effort fed into them – and reduces to a minimum any tendency for the socket to ride up the hexagon. Ideally, pressure should be applied over the whole depth of the head of the bolt or the nut. If a socket lifts, the pressure becomes concentrated over too small an area, and the angles of the flats can then be torn away.

Freeing fasteners

Never be tempted to apply excessive pressure to a fastener that has locked solid. It is feasible, of course, to slip a length of piping over the tommy bar of a socket set, and so produce two or three times the leverage. The likeliest result, however, is that the fastener will snap or – worse – be so strained that it may fail on the road later on.

Freeing nuts and bolts calls for care and patience. Where the trouble is rust on the threads, frequent applications of penetrating oil will eventually loosen them up. But it does take time – perhaps a week or more of applying the fluid, and leaving it to soak in overnight. A more immediate method is to apply local heat, providing it can be done safely. This presupposes that there is no petrol or oil in the vicinity, that the fastener is not on a painted or lacquered part and that all loose rust

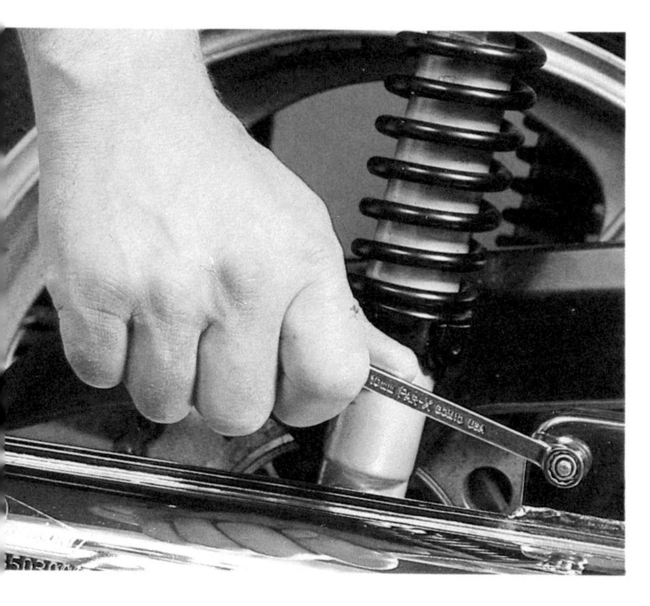

Use only hand pressure on a spanner

can be cleared away from the exposed threads before you begin. There is little point in 'starting' a nut only for it to jam again on a new section of rusted thread.

Where an open flame can be used – on rusted exhaust system fastenings, for example – play the flame on the nut and bolt until both have become too hot to touch. Then turn off the torch, and apply the spanner. A steady strong pressure should start the fastener turning.

An alternative to an open flame is an electric soldering iron held in contact with the end of the bolt. This technique is useful when a bolt has 'welded' itself to the threads in a light-alloy component. In the absence of an electric soldering iron, heat can be applied by wringing out rags in hot water and placing them over the area. It takes little more than a minute for the hot rags to expand the light alloy, and so loosen the grip of the threads.

Where the fastener is a screw, the simplest method of freeing it is to use the impact driver. Select the appropriate bit, and insert it into the screwdriver socket. Check that the driver is set to turn anti-clockwise, and engage the bit closely in the screw head. One sharp blow with a 2½lb hammer on the driver will jar the threads and, at the same time, spin the bit to start unscrewing the fastener. Thereafter, the impact driver is used as a normal screw-driver.

Too much enthusiasm with powerful hand tools can snap the fastening, as we've already seen. The remedy is to use a stud extractor; or to drill the broken fastener away, and then retap the hole.

A drill is needed, in any case, for the stud extractor. Select a drill bit that will put a hole down the centre of the fastener, yet still leave some 'meat' around it on which the extractor can grip. Using 900rpm on a two-speed electric drill – or the lower gear on a hand-operated breast drill – put a hole as deep as possible into the broken section. To avoid the drill skidding off across the surface as you start it up, first centre-punch a deep dimple to act as a guide.

Now insert the extractor, and lock it down anti-clockwise. Its quickthread will bite into the fastener, and once it is locked solid it will start to unscrew it.

If you have a fastener that is really jammed, however, even the extractor may fail. The only solution, then, is to drill the fastener out. Having made the pilot hole, switch to the next size of bit up and drill away still more of the centre. Repeat the process until the hole comes very close to the threads. Then, using a needle punch, the remnants can be tapped inwards, towards the now-empty centre. It may then be possible to insert snipe-nosed pliers to draw out the remains. If the remaining steel 'wall' is very thin, even a bradawl from your woodworking kit – or a stout darning needle – will suffice to pick away the rest, clear of the threads.

It's quite possible, unfortunately, to misjudge matters and take out the blind hole threads during drilling. There are then two possible repairs.

One is to drill the hole cleanly, tap it oversize and use a larger fastener in that particular hole. Alternatively, the hole can be drilled and tapped to take a special insert, formed from a hardened steel coil, which will restore it to its designed size. Although do-it-yourself insert kits are available they are expensive, and it is usually more economical to have the hole rebushed professionally.

Hammers

Jarring tight threads can be effective even without an impact driver, but considerable care is needed to avoid damaging the components if light alloy is involved. Against the head of the fastener, abut a stout steel drift. Holding it hard against the screwhead, give the free end a sharp blow with your hammer. Engage a T-handled screwdriver, and the fastener should undo with no further trouble.

While use of a hammer in these applications is legitimate, it is a technique that calls for the right touch. As a general rule, always use the heaviest hammer that can be operated in the available space; and always give one sharp blow in preference to a series of light taps. The sudden shock will often spring jammed components apart, where light hammer blows will simply cause burring and damage.

Some types of extractor work on hammering principles. There is one, for breaking tapers, which is screwed into place on, say, a flywheel magneto rotor, and which is then given a smart hammer blow to free the taper fixing. An alternative is the slide-hammer extractor – basically, a screw-in rod on which is a freesliding weight. When the weight is slid up the rod, to hit hard against an abutment at the end, it literally hammers the rod and whatever it is attached to straight off its mountings. A tool like this can be made at home from an old front-wheel spindle and a cylindrical steel billet, providing a local workshop will drill the billet to take the rod.

Scrapers

Any engine overhaul work eventually demands use of a scraper. There is the obvious application of removing carbon from piston crowns and combustion chambers: but some form of scraper is usually essential, too, whenever a casing with an interposed gasket is removed. Unless you are very lucky, the gasket won't come away cleanly, and little areas of gasket material will adhere to one surface or the other. Unless all of this is cleaned away, an oiltight seal will be impossible. The tool that does the trick is a scraper.

Though scrapers *can* be bought, 99 per cent are home-made. Many professional mechanics swear by a miniature scraper that consists simply of a piece of broken hacksaw blade, the end of which has been ground to a chisel shape. Very effective in the right hands, but as with all hard-metal scrapers only light pressure must be applied. Otherwise, the scraper will dig into the delicate light alloy surfaces being cleaned, and cause damage that can only be rectified by grinding the faces flat again on a milling machine or, laboriously, with compound on a sheet of plate glass.

For do-it-yourself work, the safer bet is to make a scraper out of a small strip of hardwood, or a stick of hard solder. Cut or file the end to chisel profile, and you have a scraper that is effective, but one that will not dig in to soft metal.

With this type of scraper, surfaces can be cleaned up most easily by dousing them in petrol, paraffin or meths and then using the scraper to chip away any adhering gasket.

The same requirement for a scraper that will not gouge soft metal is applicable to decarbonising. The smoother the surfaces exposed to combustion are, the less 'key' they give for carbon to grip. The scraper is therefore used sparingly on piston and head, the final cleaning-up being with rotary wire brushes and – if a mechanic is super-scrupulous – with fine wire wool moistened with metal polish.

About eighty per cent of the carbon area can be cleaned off with the scraper, used with a 'back and forth' motion all the time, but constantly changing the direction of cut.

Files

The file comes into its own when the mechanic has to start improvising. You may need a bolt 50mm long, when the only one to hand is half as long again. The obvious solution is to cut it; sawing off the odd 20mm is easy enough, but were the sawn bolt then to be offered up 'raw' it would be likely to remove the threads into which it was being screwed. A file is used for smoothing metal in just such an instance. With the bolt mounted firmly in a vice, a few strokes with a medium-cut file will remove the jagged edges left by the saw, and a little delicate chamfering around the bolt with a fine file will give it a clean lead-in.

A file is designed to cut in one direction only, and there is nothing to be gained by grinding it back and forth across the workpiece. Hold the file by its handle, place the thumb of the other hand on the end, and guide it smoothly and firmly across the surface. After one full stroke lift it, return it to its starting position, and make another cutting stroke. Continue this 'cut, lift, return' sequence until the desired amount of metal has been removed. Use of a file requires practice – it's not as easy as it looks – and the technique of making a good square cut is best acquired by practising on scrap material first.

Valve grinding

The valves are accurately matched to their seats – providing pitting is not severe, in which case they must be recut – by use of the grinding tool. It comprises a rubber sucker, which is stuck to the head of the valve, and a wooden handle which can be spun between your hands. After cleaning the valve and seat, the valve head is smeared with fine grinding paste, the sucker is attached, and the valve is dropped home. Holding it lightly down on its seat, oscillate the valve tool back and forth through an arc of about 120–180 degrees a dozen times. Then lift the

A special tool with a rubber sucker is used for grinding in the valves

tool – with the valve still attached – and turn it through 90 degrees. Keep repeating the process until both the valve head and the seat have a continuous matt grey line around them. Really fastidious mechanics finish the job with further lapping-in using a mixture of fine paste and paraffin: cunning ones slip the grinding tool's rubber sucker on to a speed brace and do the whole job with a fraction of the effort! Both, afterwards, wash all traces of paste off the components with paraffin.

Diagnostic equipment

Make it a rule never to dismantle components unless it is strictly necessary. That's where diagnostic equipment comes in. With the help of machinery such as this, you can isolate a trouble-spot before reaching for the spanners.

Electrical faults are the most difficult to trace, yet they can usually be pinpointed using one of the simplest of instruments – a test lamp. The best type to buy is one shaped rather like a screwdriver, with a sharp probe where the blade would be, a small neon bulb in the handle and a crocodile clip and cable for earthing.

However, it's easy to make up your own lamp by soldering a cable to each side cap of a festoon bulb of the same voltage as the bike battery. Fix a crocodile clip to one cable and a sharply-pointed needle to the other.

The test-lamp is used to check for the presence of power in a circuit. Suppose, for instance that the stop-lamp won't work, but that the bulb seems satisfactory.

First, check the bulb by connecting the crocodile clip to a bright metal part of the frame and putting the probe on the live terminal in the centre of the bulb holder. Preferably find a helper to operate the brake pedal with the ignition on. The test lamp bulb should light. If it doesn't, move on to the switch.

First, check that current is being fed to it by connecting the tester from the switch feed wire to earth. The bulb should light with the ignition on. If it doesn't, check the feed wire back to its power source. If the lamp does light, connect the tester between the switch output terminal and earth.

With the ignition on, operate the brake pedal. If it lights, the trouble is between the switch and tail lamp. If it doesn't, the switch is faulty.

If you suspect the battery isn't pulling its weight, you can test it with a hydrometer – a glass tube with a squeeze-bulb at one end and a calibrated float inside. Remove the battery caps and draw a sample of electrolyte into the tube. The calibration on the float will show the specific gravity of the electrolyte and indicate the state of charge of the battery. A high specific gravity indicates a well charged battery. At 60°F a fully charged battery will have a specific gravity of 1.260 to 1.280. All cells should be checked, and all should give the same reading. Consistently low specific gravity readings after a daytime ride suggest that the charging system needs checking. If the battery indicates a high specific gravity shortly after a run, but loses its charge when under cover overnight, it needs renewing.

A fully charged battery should give a hydrometer reading of 1.260 to 1.280

Professionals use electronic equipment to diagnose engine trouble. Unfortunately this is expensive, and is not practicable for home workshop use. There is a fairly inexpensive way of looking right into the combustion chamber of a four-stroke while the engine is running, however. It's a device called a Gunson Colortune.

To use it, remove the spark plug and fit, in its place, the Colortune plug, which has a transparent insulator. Start the engine. If it's cold and the choke is in use, you should see orange flashes through the transparent section as the plug ignites the rich mixture. As the engine warms up, the mixture at steady speeds should burn with a bunsen-blue flame. If it is very pale blue or almost white the mixture is too weak, and if it is orange, it's too rich. As you snap open the throttle, the mixture should momentarily richen – an orange flame – before reverting to bunsen-blue when the engine revs are held steady.

A compression tester will tell you if a four-stroke multi needs a top

A cigarette paper can be used to judge when the points break

A test lamp and battery offers a more accurate guide than paper

overhaul. Simply remove the plugs, fit the tester into each plug-hole in turn and crank the engine on the starter with the throttle open. Readings should not vary by more than 15 lb per sq in. If they do, the low-compression cylinders are suffering from piston bore wear or a leaking valve.

You can check which it is without lifting the head if you put a squirt of engine oil through each plug hole and test the compressions again. If the low readings improve, it's the bores that are worn, because the injected oil has improved the piston seal. If the readings *don't* improve, suspect a poorly seating valve or a blown head gasket.

Ignition timing

Sooner or later you'll need to check the ignition timing, and depending on whether the machine is an elderly four-stroke, a modern multi-cylinder four-stroke superbike, or a fairly new two-stroke the equipment you need varies from a slip of cigarette paper or a test lamp to a stroboscope, dial gauge and buzzer.

Four-strokes have timing marks on the generator rotor and stator, or on something attached to the crankshaft, adjacent to the contact breakers, and a nearby casting. The aim is to get the contact-breaker points *just* opening when the moving and fixed timing marks align – the handbook will give exact details relating to your individual machine.

It's the moment that the points begin to open that is difficult to judge. If you sandwich a cigarette paper between the contacts (clean them first) and slowly rotate the engine, you should just be able to withdraw the paper in one piece as the marks align. Similarly, if you connect a test lamp (12v or 6v depending on the system) between the contact-breaker spring blade and the crankcase, the bulb should just begin to light (ignition on) as the timing marks align.

This becomes much easier on a four-stroke if you have a stroboscope. Its flashing light freezes the timing marks so that you can see their respective positions with the engine running.

Although the cigarette-paper method can be used on two-strokes, modern engines really need more accurate ignition timing if they are to give their peak performance. Two-stroke timing is generally checked by ensuring that the contact-breaker points are just opening when the piston is a measured distance down the bore before top dead centre (tdc). On the Suzuki GT 250 for instance, this distance is quoted as 2.03mm before tdc, and this sort of measurement can only be taken with a dial gauge. Screw it into the spark plug hole, turn the engine, and adjust the gauge to show zero with the piston at tdc.

A dial gauge in use to measure piston travel

To indicate when the points open, Suzuki recommend a buzzer. Connected between the contact-breaker spring and earth it emits a steady buzz when the points are closed with the ignition on. When the points are about to separate, the tone of the buzz alters.

So, to check the ignition timing on a Suzuki multi, for instance, switch on the ignition, turn the engine in its normal direction of rotation until the dial gauge registers the appropriate piston travel and, with luck, the note from the buzzer will just begin to alter at this instant!

Carburettor adjustment

It's possible, on a twin-cylinder machine, to adjust carburettors individually after removing the spark plug from the other cylinder, but you can't do this on a four-cylinder engine with four carburettors – or on a six with six!

On the bigger multis you need a set of vacuum gauges. Honda use a nest of four identical gauges to set up the carburation on their four-cylinder machines. Each gauge is connected by its vacuum pipe to a stub on the inlet of each carburettor. With these gauges hooked up, it's possible to adjust all carburettors individually with the engine running using the pilot air screws and the throttle slide screws until they all give an identical vacuum reading.

Soldering

If you have a soldering iron which requires external heat, the first job is to tin the bit so that solder flows freely on and off it. Clean the copper until it is bright, using glasspaper, then heat it in the flame until you notice the flame around the copper turn green. Make sure you have a stick of flux-cored solder handy. Keep heating the bit until the green flame begins to turn orange. This is the stage when you remove it and apply a little cored solder to the tip. The solder will flow freely on to the copper and give it a tinned coating. You can now start work.

The sorts of item needing a touch of solder are cable connectors – particularly 'bullet' terminals – and terminal tags. You can, of course, obtain crimp-on terminals, but since the appropriate crimping tool is rarely to hand, these are often loosely fitted and make a poor connection. If a bullet connector is to be fitted, bare the end of the cable and if necessary scrape the wires clean with a penknife blade. Heat the iron as before, or plug in the electric iron, and bring the bit of the iron, when heated, and the end of the solder into contact with the bared wires. You really do need three hands here, so hold the wire in the vice, a self-grip wrench, or even a clothes peg before you start. If you've done things right the iron will melt the solder, which will run into the cables. Once this has happened, remove the bit before the heat melts the insulation. The next step is to poke the tinned wire inside the bullet connector so that it sticks through the hole in the end. Heat the iron again, put a blob of solder on the bit, take the cable and dip the end of the

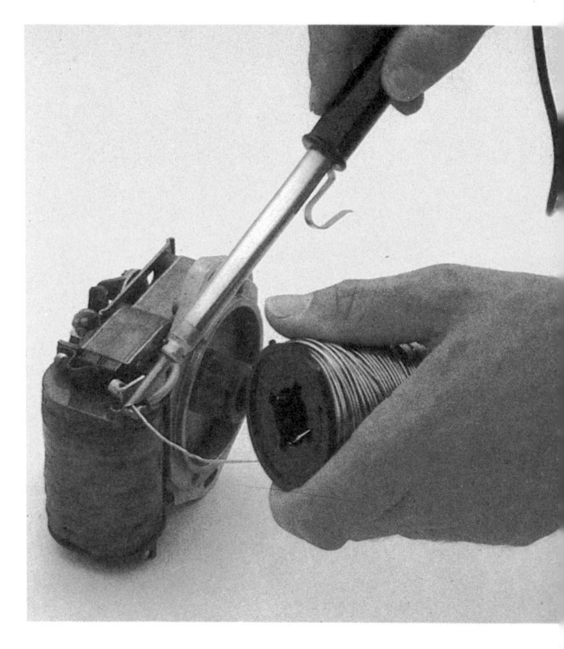

Use resin-cored solder and an electric soldering iron for delicate jobs

connector in the molten solder. Capillary action will draw solder into the connector and fuse it to the wire.

Brazing

Small components can be brazed and there will be more chance of retaining sufficient heat for this if you set up a brazing hearth made from pieces of old firebrick, as mentioned in Chapter Two. As with soldering, you need a flux to prevent oxides forming on the metal being heated and to encourage the filler metal – in this case usually bronze rod – to flow into the joint. Brazing flux is usually borax, which is supplied as powder but can also be mixed as a paste.

This is what's involved. First, clean the joint to be brazed down to bare metal and coat it with flux. It helps if you bind the joint together – soft iron wire is ideal as it is malleable and won't conduct much heat. Light up the torch and apply it to the joint. When the joint is red hot, heat the end of the bronze rod briefly and dip it into the flux powder to coat it. Put it back into the flame until it melts and runs into the joint. Allow the work to cool before grinding off any surplus bronze and flux with a power sander.

Welding

In theory, welding involves heating two pieces of like metal to melting point and fusing them, although it's usual to add a little extra metal from a filler rod to bridge any gaps. It is beyond the compass of this book to give a full welding course, but it's worth looking at some of the do-it-yourself cut-price alternatives to the expensive oxy-acetylene equipment that the professionals use. The cheapest are battery powered and there are two main types – carbon contact torches, or arc welders.

The carbon-contact arrangement uses a holder with a heavy-duty cable at the handle end and a carbon rod clamped in the business end. The cable is connected to one terminal of a 12-volt battery (preferably from a car) and the other battery terminal is cable-connected to the metal being welded. If you are working on a complete machine, disconnect the alternator to prevent any damage to the diodes when using a battery welder.

To use the carbon contact torch, simply touch the tip of the carbon rod on the workpiece. The short-circuit will make it glow white hot, and once the hot carbon has heated the metal to the appropriate temperature it will begin to fuse together at which stage you can feed in metal from the filler rod and move the carbon tip along the joint in a series of tiny circles.

Although it will weld, the average carbon contact torch takes so much power from a 12-volt battery in bringing the metal to melting point that it's better to use it for brazing, which does not require such high temperatures. Tinted goggles are supplied with carbon contact kits and should be worn when welding or brazing.

The arc welder needs more than 12 volts for all but the thinnest rod and the lightest metal, so two car batteries connected in series will provide the answer, giving 24 volts. Like a mains arc welder, the battery unit uses a flux-coated welding rod which is gripped in a holder. The electrical hook-up, with an additional battery, is the same as for a carbon-contact system, but when the welding rod is touched on the workpiece a fierce arc is produced, melting the work and the rod, which deposits itself on the joint. A full facemask *must* be used to prevent eye damage.

Adhesives

You may think there is not a lot that you need to stick on the average machine, but into the adhesive category fall the special fluids, such as Loctite Stud and Bearing Fit, which ensure that parts, once tightened, don't come loose, and the range of silicone-base gasket materials which come in useful for such jobs as sealing the crankcases of two-strokes on re-assembly. But ensure that the liquid gasket material is petrol and temperature resistant.

Glassfibre

Glassfibre is used to make top boxes, fairings and panniers. It is a handy material, but if it suffers a hard knock, it's likely to shatter.

Make sure that the resin is worked thoroughly into the matting when carrying out glassfibre repairs

Providing you can collect all the bits and pieces together, however, you've a very good chance of making the damage look as good as new – for the broken pieces will retain their original shape (although surface 'crazing' may be very difficult to eradicate). All you need is a glassfibre and resin kit – the sort that accessory shops sell for patching holes in rusty cars – and some body filler paste.

First, fit together the damaged section, sticking it (on the outside) with something like carpet tape to make it rigid. Mix resin and hardener as detailed in the kit instructions and use an old paintbrush to stipple strips of glass mat behind each of the breaks. Use plenty of resin and put on at least two laminations of mat.

Once the resin has cured – the initial process takes about twenty minutes at 60°F – peel off the carpet tape, mix up the body filler, and knife this into the exposed joins. Once this has set, rough-shape the filler with a coarse file, then rub it down with progressively finer grades of wet-or-dry abrasive paper used wet. Start with something like 120 grit and finish with 400 grit. Once the surface has dried, fill any pin-holes with a skim coat of filler, finish this with 400 grit paper dipped in soapy water, and the repaired item will be ready for priming and painting.

Routine Maintenance

Some of the most important tools for maintaining a bike are a bucket, a stiff brush, and some rags. This is because the weekly cleaning routine is regarded by many experienced riders – including police patrolmen – as the key to keeping the bike roadworthy.

Cleaning thoroughly means that there is no part of the exterior which is not regularly handled or examined. It's a first-class way of ensuring that faults don't get overlooked in their early stages.

It is not essential to get out the hose and polish to carry out a stem-to-stern examination, but doing so will ensure that the vulnerable chrome and paint (perhaps the least reliable parts of any motor cycle) will also last that much longer.

For best results, use a stiff bristle brush to work grease solvent into all the nooks and crannies around the forks, the engine, and the rear suspension. Let it soak into the dirt, and then give it a preliminary hosing to blast away the worst deposits. That done, do the rest of the job by hand, using well wetted rag and plenty of water, with a dash of car shampoo as a solvent.

Front tyre

Wipe over the front tyre, examining it for damage as you do so. Here, you will be looking for cuts or bubbles in the sidewalls (which are *very* dangerous – scrap a tyre in that state) and for stones trapped in the tread grooves. Winkle them out before they can be driven through the rubber. Look for any other damage to the tread area, and measure the wear. Renew the tyre when it's down to 2mm of tread.

At the point where the bead of the tyre meets the rim, look for telltale signs of rust that could be caused by

Replacing a faulty valve core

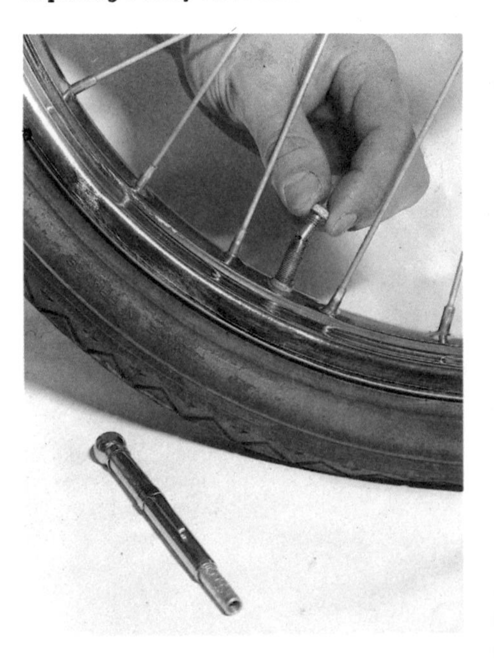

corrosion on an exposed bead wire – check the fitting line all the way round the tyre. It should be concentric with the rim, and evenly set all the way round. If this is not the case, deflate the tyre and correct the fault.

Examine the valve. Test it by removing the cap and wiping a little soapy water across the top. It should stay there in a film. If it becomes a bubble, you have a leaky valve. It may just be dirt under the seal, or it may be a faulty core. Press the valve pin and let a blast of air come out, then repeat the check. The bubbling should have ceased, since the air under pressure will dislodge any loose dirt. If you still have a bubble, fit a new valve core. Most pressure gauges have a core removal tool screwed into the plunger base. Unscrew the core, fit a new one and pump the tyre up to the recommended pressure.

If the valve is in order, simply check the front tyre pressure and then refit the valve cap. Don't omit this. It may look insignificant, but that cap is your lifeline. It prevents the tyre deflating with a rush if the valve fails, and it is essential that it should be screwed on and that its internal seal should be in good condition.

Another point to check is that the valve lockring is tight. A loose ring – or locknut, on some valves – will allow the valve to sit at an angle. If there is any tendency for the inner tube to creep, the valve could be pulled out, in which case the tyre would flatten without warning.

Hopefully, other makers may follow the Honda lead – set on two excellent machines, the CBX and the CX500 twin – and use tubeless tyres. Until then, it's down to Honda owners alone to make sure that their tubeless tyre valves are still seating properly in the rim. They snap into place and are locked by the internal pressure, but accidents can happen and a partly dislodged valve could cause a steady loss of air.

Front wheel

Bikers lucky enough to have Comstar wheels, or the cast-alloy equivalents, are spared one of the most weary of chores – cleaning a multiplicity of spokes, and the awkward areas of rim around them. Put the time spent on this clean-up to good use by checking that each spoke is sound, and that it is tight. The easiest way is to press two spokes towards each other just below the point at which they interlace. The most you should feel is a slight springiness. Neither should actually move. If it does, it needs to be tightened before the wheel goes out of true. Up to one turn of the nipple can usually be given without any danger of the spoke piercing the inner tube. However, it is always a good idea to remove the tyre and make sure that the spoke is not protruding beneath the rim tape. In this way, each spoke can be tightened as much as is necessary and any excess removed with a grinding wheel spun in a power drill.

Those with a musical ear can check spokes, incidentally, by tapping them with the end of a spanner. A correctly tensioned spoke will ring.

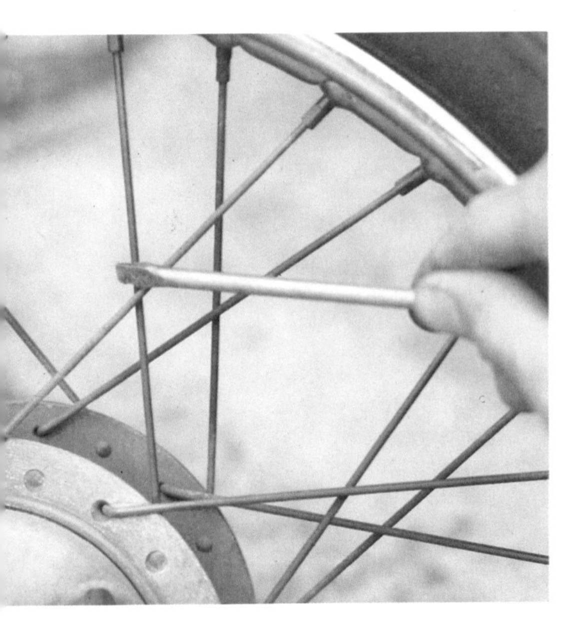

Noise from the spoke reveals its tension

Adjusting spoke tension

A loose spoke will produce just a dull thud.

Check the wheel bearings by lifting the front wheel and grasping it top and bottom, then trying to rock it around the spindle. No movement should be felt. If the wheel moves under this test, however, cornering will exaggerate this movement markedly.

If you feel movement, investigate its source. It may be due to loose spindle nuts, or the bearings may be worn. Close inspection should tell you which is the case. If the spindle is staying still while the wheel rocks, then it has to be the bearings which are at fault.

Steering head

Since the wheel is off the ground, now is the logical time to check the steering head bearings for adjustment. First, set the forks centrally and tap one end of the bars with a finger. The forks should turn on to full lock under their own weight. Recentralise them and repeat the procedure for the other lock. To some extent you have to interpret what you find, since a stout wiring harness may slow up movement one way or another. Stiff operation in both directions, however, means that the head bearings are too tight.

The opposite fault – loose bearings – is checked by placing a finger at the upper bearing/head gap and then rocking the forks backwards and forwards. There should be no obvious movement, and you should feel no play.

Rectification of either fault is exactly the same – the adjustable upper bearing has to be reset. Getting at the adjustment is tricky on some bikes, easy on others. The most common method is to screw the upper bearing track closer to its lower track to reduce play, or to ease it away from the lower track to increase play. On some bikes, this can be done simply by freeing a locknut and turning the adjuster nut clockwise to tighten the bearing or anticlockwise to loosen it. On other machines, it may be necessary to remove the handlebars and a bearing cap or shroud before it is possible to get a spanner on to the adjuster. The locknut and the adjuster may be a pair of hexagons, a hexagon and a lockring or two lockrings. Lockrings require the use of a C-spanner and not all bike tool kits contain one. It is possible, however, to tap the ring round with a soft-metal drift and a hammer where no suitable spanner can be found. Take great care over this adjustment. Follow the handbook or manual instructions to the letter and be absolutely certain that the bearing is not overtightened.

Fork sliders

Still with the wheel off the ground, check the fork sliders for play on the stanchions. Grasp the spindle at each side and alternately try to pull it towards you and then push it away. You should not be able to feel any movement.

Adjusting the steering head bearings is a simple affair on most bikes

If the lower ends of the forks tend to rock, either there is wear in the slider bushes – an overhaul job – or the stanchions themselves are moving in the yokes. Check the security of the fixings at the upper and lower yokes. If the bolts are tightened to the correct torque – or are hand tight when tested with the appropriate ring spanner – the likelihood is that the movement is caused by bushes that have become oval.

Front brake
Examine the front brake. If it's a disc unit, this is the time to check pad wear. Most pads are marked with red wear warning lines, and if these lines are about to contact the disc then the pads are due for renewal. If the lines never existed – or, worse, have disappeared – measure the amount of meat remaining on the pad. The minimum permissible is 1.5mm.

Examine the hose connections. They should be tight, with no tell-tale damp patches around them – damp means fluid leakage. Check the lines themselves for cracking or abrasion. With sliding callipers, make sure that they can move freely. On drum-brake bikes, check the amount of wear on the shoes by noting the position of the brake arm when the lever is operated. It should form less than a right angle with the operating cable. Examine the cable too. Its exposed areas must be free from rust, with no broken strands. Once a single strand breaks, the rest will quickly follow, so any damaged cable must be renewed without delay.

Pad wear is checked with a vernier

Front mudguard
Check that the inside of the guard has been hosed free of all mud deposits that might snag the wheel. This is a hazard to watch for, particularly if the bike has been used on unmade road surfaces. Ensure that all mudguard stays are unbroken and that their securing bolts are properly fastened.

Headlamp
An accurate headlamp check can only be made on a beam setter. At this stage, just ensure that the beam is not obviously deflected up or down, or to either side, and that the lamp is securely fastened. Check that the wiring loom is not trapped, and that there is no abrasion at the

point where it enters the lamp.

Examine the lens for damage, and look through it at the reflector. When discoloration begins, the reflector must be replaced with a new one. Only a mirror-like 'as new' reflector will give the bright concentrated light beam necessary for safe riding at night and in bad visibility.

Front flashers

Check that each flasher operates. Examine the lens for damage or for any sign that it is losing its coloration. A faded lens should be renewed. Look for water trapped in the lamp body. Release any that's there, and dry out the lamp with

Only an approximate adjustment can be made without a beam setter

mutton cloth. Get rid of the last vestiges with a hair dryer, and then fit a new lens gasket to weatherproof the lamp.

Handlebar controls

Check that each control is properly positioned and that its fastenings are tight. Check the locknuts on mirror stems, so that the mirror cannot be misaligned by wind pressure.

Examine all exposed cables for damage and lubricate them. Check that the nipples turn freely, without snagging, in the levers. Test all switchgear and run a little electrical lubricant into each. Check the electrical cables for damage.

Make sure that the handlebar clamps are secure, and that the handgrip rubbers are not damaged. The grips must not be free to move on the bars. If a grip – or even half a grip – can twist, remove it and reseat it using a suitable adhesive.

Ensure that the stoplamp switch, coupled to the front brake lever, is working properly. If not, and the lamp itself is serviceable, ascertain which type of switch it is. A pressure switch installed in the hydraulic lines is better serviced by a dealer, but a microswitch screwed into a recess under the front brake lever is usually held only by a single screw and two leads with snap connectors. This type can be removed for checking. Undo the screw, drop the switch out and turn on the ignition. The stoplamp should light. If it does not, try depressing and releasing the microswitch plunger several times. If the lamp still refuses to come on, detach the two connectors and roll back their rubber insulators. Press the connectors together with the ignition on. The lamp should now light. If it does, the microswitch is faulty; if not, there is a wiring fault to be traced.

Power unit

Look for any signs of leakage, particularly in a position where oil could be thrown on to the rear tyre. If leakage is found, investigate it and cure it.

Exhaust system

Put a spanner on all accessible nuts and bolts, and check all accessible socket screws or crossheads. Look for signs of blow-by at exhaust pipe joints, and check that if the silencer has water escape holes in its lower surface they are still clear.

Fuel system

Examine the carburettor, fuel leads and fuel tap for stains that show fuel leakage has taken place. Look for split or perished pipes, loose float chamber securing screws and sloppy operation of the tap. Many taps can be adjusted by tightening up the screws securing the outer plate.

Fuel tank

Check the underside of the tank for leakage at the seams. Examine the tank mountings and check that the anti-vibration rubbers are sound. Examine the fuel tap unions and test them for security with a spanner. Check any pipes linking the two tank cheeks on 'split' designs. If corrosion is noted on the underside of the tank, neutralise it and then prime and paint it to prevent a leak developing.

Where a separate oil tank is used, carry out similar checks.

Main frame

Examine the tubes and joints for cracks or rust. Neutralise rust patches. Use the appropriate spanners to test the security of all engine mountings. Examine the footrest hangers and pillion rests for damage and renew any worn rubbers.

Raise the rear wheel clear of the ground and test the rear fork pivot by pressing from side to side at the rear wheel spindle. No side play should be noted. If the fork can deflect, there is wear in the pivot bearings and they should be stripped for examination and renewal of faulty parts. If there is only slight play, check the security of the pivot spindle.

Check springs for secure location

20mm is about the average permissible deflection for transmission chains

Correct alignment of the wheels is essential and adjusters each side are provided

Subframe

With bolted-on subframes, run a spanner over the fastenings to check that they are tight. Examine saddle mountings and the attachment brackets for pillion footrests, the rear brake hydraulic cylinder, the stop lamp switch, and any other fittings to the subframe for security.

Rear spring units

Check that both units are on the same spring setting. Ensure that the upper and lower mountings are tight and that the rubber bushes are sound.

Rear tyre

Carry out all the checks detailed for the front tyre.

Rear wheel and chain

Carry out all the checks detailed for the front wheel. With chain-drive bikes, include an examination of the chain and the sprockets. Test the chain for tension. A maximum up and down movement of 20mm at the midway point of the lowest run is average. Test this with the wheel turned through 90 degrees, three times, until the tightest spot on the chain is found. Make any adjustment so that play is correct at this point, otherwise the chain will be too tight. Make a note that a new chain and sprockets will be required before the next routine maintenance period expires.

Carry out the adjustment as described in the manual for your bike. Where drawbolts are used, first ensure that the wheel is properly aligned. Then mark one flat on each of the adjuster nuts, and note its position. Choose a flat that is either uppermost, or pointing outwards. Free the spindle nut, and turn the adjuster nuts one flat at a time on each side until the correct play is obtained in the chain. Tighten the spindle nut, and then recheck the chain tension. Lastly, test for wheel alignment by placing a long straight board across the front and back wheels. If they are evenly aligned in the frame, the board will touch both rims at two points. If it contacts only the front of the rear wheel, the left-hand adjuster has been overtightened. If it contacts only the rear section of the rim, the right-hand adjuster has been overtightened. Loosen the spindle nut, and slacken the overtight adjuster by one flat. If the chain loosens, take up an equal amount on the other adjuster. By varying the two settings, an equal amount at a time, the correct chain tension and an accurate wheel alignment will be obtained.

Rear lamp and rear indicators
Check these in the same way as for the headlamp and the front indicators. It is common for the rear lamp to be flexibly mounted, so ensure that the rubber 'cushions' are in good repair.

General
Remove the appropriate side panel, and check the battery electrolyte level. Ensure that all battery connections are clean and tight, and that the battery vent pipe is clear. These often tend to become blocked by road dirt at the bottom, or to be kinked where they are led past frame members.

Ensure that all fuses are sound and that electrical leads from them are not trapped or kinked.

Check the speedometer and tachometer cables. The outers must be undamaged – this includes the impervious outer skin, which must be repaired with pvc tape if it has been abraded – and must run in as smooth a curve as possible from the instrument to the take-off point on the power unit, or to the separate gearbox on the front or rear spindle.

Check the attachments at the instrument ends. If the cables are to be lubricated, undo the attachments, pull the drive out of the instrument, and then draw out the complete inner cable, leaving the outer casing in place.

The drive cables must be lubricated *only* with grease. If oil is used, the rotating drive cable will act as a pump and force it into the instrument movement. This usually causes irreparable damage. At best, the instruments will need to be sent to a specialist for cleaning and repair.

The battery vent pipe can be blocked

Safety

Before finishing this part of the routine maintenance inspection, double-check that every nut or bolt that is intended to have a security fitting in fact possesses one.

The most usual types are spring clips or split pins inserted in the front and rear wheel spindles. Spring clips can be refitted, but once a split pin has been used it should be discarded. Straightening it out for removal weakens it to such an extent that it may fracture on the road.

Mileage-based maintenance

The major tasks that come naturally under a mileage-covered basis are oil changes and tappet checks on four-strokes, plug and points checks on both two-strokes and four-strokes and periodic attention to the hydraulic systems of the brakes and the front forks where applicable. All other items should be dealt with as running maintenance, picked up during the weekly checks.

Spring clips often secure fastenings, as on this rear wheel

Oil changes

Taken as a general rule, the smaller the sump the more frequently the oil has to be changed if internal wear is to be kept within reasonable bounds. However, this is not invariable. Big, highly stressed, air-cooled engines such as those of the Kawasaki 1000 or the Suzuki GS750 have reasonably large sump capacities, but they still demand oil changes at 2000/3000-mile intervals. That is not significantly different from the 1500-mile interval demanded by small-sumped bikes such as Honda's CB400F or CB100N.

The water-cooled CX500, however, can go 7200 miles between oil changes. So, refer to the handbook for your own bike to ensure that your motor gets its fresh oil when it needs it – not too early, but most definitely not too late.

Oil is best changed after the bike has had a few miles running to warm it up. That way, it will flow more easily and drain clear of the oilways. The faster the oil flow when the drain plug is removed, the greater the flushing action. That means that sludge and swarf will be cleared, instead of remaining in the sump.

Have ready an old 1-gallon (5-litre) oil can, with one side cut away. That makes an excellent drain tray. You'll need a new filter element, unless your bike uses a centrifugal arrangement, and on Hondas you must be certain to have a socket or ring spanner that is an exact fit on the centre bolt on the oil filter housing. This has a small hexagon – deliberately, to ensure that the crankcase threads cannot be stripped by too much force being applied on assembly – which means that the spanner must sit right down on the hexagon to apply its full power. An open-ended spanner will *not* do the job.

The new oil filter element should come complete with all necessary seals, but check this before removing the old one.

Put the bike on its stand, remove the oil filler cap to ensure that there is no internal suction and then unscrew the oil drain plug. Keep pressing up on it when it is fingertight, as you turn it, so that as it clears its threads you can whip it smartly out to release the oil. It will be hot, remember, so *don't* leave your hand in the way.

Leave the oil to drain, helping the last drops out by turning the motor a few times on the kickstarter. Then wipe the drain plug clean – if it's a magnetic plug, it will probably have a 'beard' of small metallic particles, but it should *not* have metal chips adhering – and replace it. Although it is not essential, using a new washer will ensure an absolutely oiltight seal.

Now move the drain tray under the filter housing. On some bikes, this housing may be incorporated in the sump drain. On Moto Guzzis, it is in the sump pan itself and the whole pan has to be removed by freeing its ring of securing bolts. More frequently, however, it is bolted externally to the crankcase.

Undo the securing bolt, and detach the bolt, housing and element as a unit. Drain any oil from the housing and set it aside; scrap the element.

You can, if you're ultra-particular about these things, now analyse the oil to see what, if anything, has broken or worn inside your motor. Shine a lamp beam on the surface of the oil, at an angle, and you can pick out the little silver specks that were once parts of pistons and the gold ones that used to be bushes. You can test with a magnet to see which are non-ferrous (light alloy, or soft metal such as phosphor bronze) and which are ferrous (shavings from rotating parts such as gears, or sliding parts like selectors).

In general, though, there is no need to worry unless you find large metal remains in the oil. A gear tooth, or a piece of curved bushing, means big trouble inside the motor which will *have* to be dismantled without delay. Never take a chance with anything like that. It can lead to seizure without warning, and if it's the transmission that locks up instead of the engine there is no way of freeing the rear wheel.

Fit a new oil seal to the centre bolt and renew the filter housing O-rings

Some bikes have the oil filter casing set in the sump base

New seals should be used when renewing the filter

where applicable. Install the new element and offer up the unit to the bike. Tighten it to the specified torque. Now fill up with oil to the upper mark on the dipstick, refit the cap and run the engine for a few minutes. Remove the dipstick, wipe it, and then check the oil level again. You will probably find that it has dropped, since some of the oil will have passed into the oilways and even more into the filter housing. Top up again to the 'full' mark and the job's over for another couple of thousand miles.

Owners of bikes with no dipsticks, but with a little window instead, will have to do their best to check the level visually.

Setting the tappets

Tappet adjustment – more accurately valve clearance adjustment – is of two basic types.

There is the familiar screw-type adjuster, in which the effective length of the rocker tip or the push-rod is varied, and there are bucket tappets, which require the use of special shims and complex mathematics.

First, it is essential to know whether the clearances specified by the factory are to be applied to a hot or a cold engine. Usually, with alloy motors, it is a cold setting, which means that the motor should not have been run for at least the previous twelve hours.

Left: tdc is almost invariably stamped on the rotor or flywheel
Below: the valve covers are removed prior to adjusting valve clearances
Bottom: the correct feeler should fit with just a hint of friction

Most manufacturers make the job easy, these days, by stamping accurate tdc marks on the rotor, or the flywheel, and providing a fixed pointer on the case so that the guesswork can be taken away. Check where the tdc marks are, and bare them. Remove the plugs and, in the case of most fours and some twins, the tank as well, the latter to give reasonable access. Remove the valve covers and turn the engine until the tdc mark for the first cylinder is aligned with the pointer. Check that the valves are 'on the rock' (the inlet and the exhaust valve rockers will move a little if tapped like Morse keys). If either valve is under pressure you have tdc on the exhaust stroke, rather than on compression, and the crankshaft will have to be given one full turn to obtain the right setting.

Select a feeler gauge of the exact size for the recommended inlet valve clearance, and offer it up. This may involve a bit of jockeying for

position; where access is a real problem, it is often easier to use a feeler that has been cut down to a half or a third of its normal width, and detached from the nest. The correct size of feeler should enter the gap and slide with just a trace of sticking. If it is an easy fit, the gap is likely to be too wide. Check this by trying the next feeler up in size. It should refuse to enter.

To adjust the clearance, free the locknut and turn the adjuster clockwise to reduce the clearance, anticlockwise to increase it. Often, the adjuster is slotted to take a screwdriver. If so, use a ring spanner on the nut and have it just loose enough to allow the adjuster to turn. Leave the spanner in place while you operate the adjuster, and when you think the feeler is just a sliding fit hold the adjuster with a little reverse pressure on the screwdriver while you nip up the locknut.

Some machines have squared adjusters that nothing in the toolkit will fit. For these, you should have a special key, but fingers will usually turn the adjuster, and an adjustable spanner will hold it while the locknut is tightened.

Having locked the nut, test the setting again. The correct feeler should enter, the larger one should not. When the setting is right, repeat the procedure on the exhaust valve. Then turn the motor to tdc on the next cylinder and continue adjusting it until all tappets have been brought within limits.

Refit the valve caps, smearing the O-rings lightly with oil, but don't refit the cover over the timing marks, or the plugs, if the ignition timing is to be checked or the plugs cleaned and serviced. Otherwise, install them.

Shim tappet adjustments

Typical of the procedure for this type of adjustment is that required on the double-overhead-camshaft Suzuki twins and fours. Remove the fuel tank and detach the valve cover. Remove the contact-breaker cover so that the engine can be turned over by using a spanner on the centre bolt. Remove the sparking plugs.

Now turn the crankshaft until two exhaust valve bucket tappets have the heels of the cams bearing on them, with the peaks pointing obliquely upwards. Check the clearance between each cam and bucket. If it is outside the specified limits, it must be adjusted by removing the shim and substituting a thinner one, to correct too fine a clearance, or a thicker one, to reduce too large a gap. Suzuki have a range

The peak of the cam is in the correct position to measure the cam-bucket clearance

of 20 adjusting shims, varying from 2.15 to 3.10mm in thickness in 0.05mm steps. Kawasaki's range runs from 2.00 to 3.20mm, again in 0.05mm steps.

To calculate the size of shim needed, first write down the actual clearance that has been measured. Then write down the desired clearance. If this is larger than the actual clearance, subtract the actual clearance from the desired clearance to obtain the difference. You will need a shim thinner by that amount. If the desired clearance is smaller than the actual clearance, subtract it from the actual clearance to obtain the difference. You need a shim thicker by that amount.

You now have to remove the existing shim to find out what thickness it is. This is done by use of a special tappet lifting tool – which, oddly enough, actually presses the tappet down. This is slipped in to place to depress the bucket tappet so that the shim can be grasped with a pair of tweezers and lifted out. It

Different shims are needed if the valve clearance is wrong

will be marked with its size. Add to that size the difference you have worked out if the shim needs to be thicker, or subtract it if it needs to be thinner, and select as a replacement the standard shim that comes nearest to the figure you have calculated. Insert it, remove the lifting tool, and recheck the tappet clearance just to make certain that you got your sums right. Repeat this procedure with all the other valves.

This sounds complicated and is, compared with the procedure for screw adjusters. However, bucket-type tappets, once set, rarely lose their adjustment between top overhauls and no more than the feeler gauge check is usually necessary.

If a valve has become pocketed its stem may project so far that it is impossible to obtain the correct clearance. In such a case, it is usually permissible to remove the valve and grind a little from the top of the stem. Just how much varies from bike to bike, but with the GS400/425E, for example, the valve can be ground until the depth of the stem above the retaining collets is 4mm.

Eccentric adjustments

A few bikes, such as the Honda CB350 and the Kawasaki Z400, have used eccentric tappet adjusters. With these, the valve clearance is measured in the usual way and the adjustment carried out by freeing the locknut that holds the eccentric and turning the shaft by inserting a screwdriver into the slot. The direction is indicated by + and — marks stamped on the casting, and on the Z400 the shafts have punch marks which must always be kept facing towards the inner side.

Sparking plug settings

Start maintenance of the plugs with one thought uppermost – should they simply be discarded in favour of new ones? The short answer is that any plug that has covered more than 5000 miles in an air-cooled engine or 7500 miles in a water-cooled one is almost certainly past its best. Renewal at this stage should pay dividends in improved acceleration and reduced fuel consumption.

With new plugs, maintenance is simple enough. Use a feeler gauge to set the gap accurately – don't assume that it must be right just because the plug is new. It takes only a few knocks during delivery to jar the very fine gap further closed.

To reset a gap, the side electrode must be bent towards the centre electrode or away from it. One is often advised to use a plug gapping tool for the job, but most of these seem to have been designed to deal only with 14mm short-nosed plugs. Long-nosed plugs make it a tricky operation, which can often lead to a cracked insulator on a brand new plug. It's permissible, where the gap must be widened, to ease the side electrode away from the centre either with a very thin screwdriver, or by grasping it squarely with a pair of pliers and exerting a steady hand pressure.

It is best to lift the electrode enough to widen the gap to just over the setting that is wanted and to complete the job by tapping the side

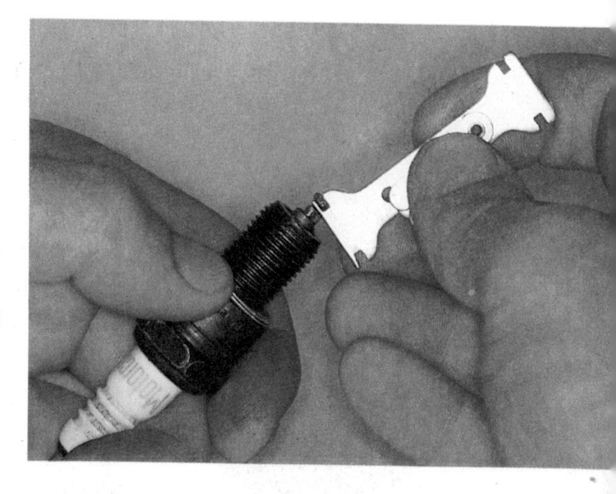

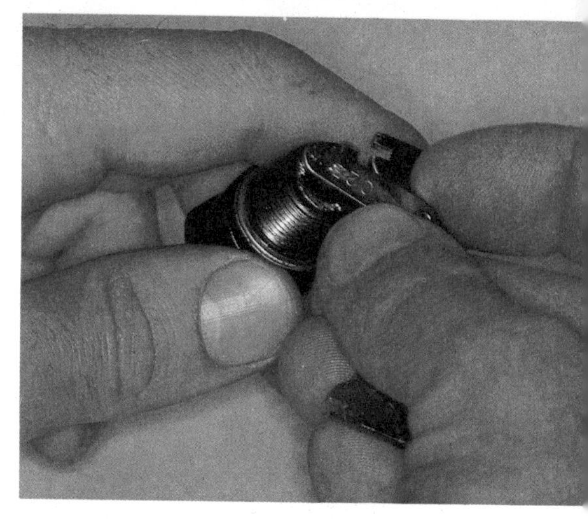

Top: here the proper plug gapping tool is being used
Above: the gap is checked once more

electrode gently with the flat of a smallish (12 or 14mm) open-ended spanner. After each tap, try the gauge until you obtain a close fit. Check the gap with the next-higher feeler, which should not enter.

When installing a new plug, tighten it down, by hand only, until the

Plugs in various conditions: 1 good condition, 2 fouled by carbon deposits caused by an over-rich mixture, 3 damaged by overheating, 4 damaged by pre-ignition, 5 oil-fouled, 6 with heavy carbon deposits, 7 insulation broken, 8 central electrode damaged by excessive abrasive cleaning

washer is just trapped between the plug body and the head. Then use the plug spanner to give it a turn through no more than 120 degrees. A quarter to a third of a turn is sufficient to seal the washer by gently crushing it, without flattening it completely. This is important, since a flattened washer doesn't necessarily make a very good seal, and over-tightening the plug can tear the threads in the head and can also distort the plug body. If that happens, an air leak can open up.

Plug fouling

You can tell from your old plugs what's going on inside the cylinder. A plug that's been in an engine that is running at working temperature on the proper mixture, without burning excessive oil, has its nose coated with a deposit that is roughly the colour of milky coffee. The electrodes look nicely squared-off, too, not eroded. If the plug still looks newish, but is black, try wiping the deposit off. You'll probably find that it will just rub away on your thumb. A soft, soot-black deposit is found only in engines which are running over-rich. This not only wastes fuel, but it makes the motor run too cool for efficiency and tends to wash the oil film off the bores, so that ring and bore wear accelerates.

Also black, but very different to look at, is a plug fouled by oil. You'll know what carbon looks like, so you should have no difficulty recognising it on your plugs. It has the same unattractive scaly, semi-shiny appearance. There may be a thin oily film on the nose as well. In a two-stroke, it suggests that the oil pump setting may be wrong, or that too much oil is being mixed with the petrol when you fill up. On a four-stroke, it means worn guides, faulty oil seals, or worn rings/bores.

The exact opposite – although equally unpleasant to look at – is the ashy whiteness of a plug that is slowly being cooked through overheating. This condition usually eats the electrodes as well. The likeliest cause is too weak a mixture, through fuel starvation, incorrect jetting or an air leak into the combustion chamber. The last of these might be caused by a tight inlet valve tappet or by a faulty head gasket. A second cause of plug burning is the wrong grade of plug.

If the engine has been 'pinking' (detonating or firing too early), be prepared to find that the plugs have suffered almost total erosion of the electrodes. Pinking is usually caused by the use of too low a grade of fuel, too high a compression ratio or too much ignition advance. The plug is almost certainly the victim of the condition, not the cause of it.

Lead fouling is less common. It gives the plugs a rather greenish look and means that your favourite fuel is over-endowed with tetra-ethyl lead. Try changing your brand.

Fouled plugs can be cleaned. Worn ones are not worth saving, even though you can have them sand-blasted to remove the fouling and then use a fine file to square off the electrodes. Concentrate, however, on cleaning-up the really serviceable plugs. Use a stiff-bristled brush to remove the deposits. Don't use a wire brush, since this can leave metallic traces on the insulator nose and so cause some of the current to track to earth instead of helping to produce a fat spark at the plug gap. Use another bristle to pick away deposits down in the nose or, if possible, immerse the end of the plug overnight in a weak acid such as ordinary household vinegar. That softens the carbon, and this can then be easily scraped away with a sliver of wood. Try a toothpick for this job. Cheap, do-it-yourself bead blasters have become available and these make plug cleaning easier and more effective. File the electrodes square before setting the gap.

New plugs

Don't experiment with plug grades. Stick to the maker's recommendation

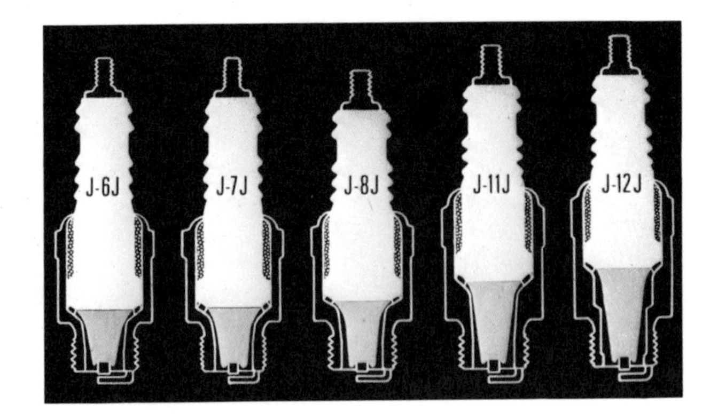

A series of plugs with heat ranges from cold, on the left, to hot, on the right

– or, if the standard grade is unsatisfactory, consult the plug manufacturer's table of permissible variations for your bike. If you do a lot of motorway running, and very little town work, you may want a colder plug. If you do most of your mileage in city streets, with only the odd gentle cruise along the open road, you may need a hotter plug.

Don't be misled by these terms. A 'hot' plug is not an easy option for tuning the engine; it simply denotes a plug that has a nose that is designed to absorb heat instead of transmitting it. It is therefore able to burn off deposits as they form. However, since it *is* hot running, it can retain so much heat that it causes a hot spot and the result is a hole burned neatly through the piston. This can happen inside a few miles, so great care is needed if experimenting with plugs.

A 'cold' plug is one that retains less heat within its own nose. Therefore, it cannot burn off fouling as easily as can a 'hot' plug. Instead, it is able to withstand constant hot running without breaking down or damaging the piston. The general rule is that a hot-running engine needs a 'cold' plug and a cool-running engine needs a 'hot' one. These plug grades are sometimes known as 'hard' and 'soft' respectively.

When fitting new plugs, the second point to consider is the reach. This is basically the length of the threaded portion. The longer it is, the more the plug nose projects into the combustion chamber. Most plugs are of a standard reach, but some engine designs demand longer or – more rarely – shorter reaches.

Long-reach plugs must not be fitted to an engine designed to take standard-reach or short-reach units. Apart from the obvious danger that the extra projection of the nose will be struck by the piston the first time the motor is cranked, if there *is* sufficient clearance and the plug stays in for any length of time the exposed threads will get choked by carbon, which may mean removing the head and cleaning off this carbon in order to unscrew the plug.

Something rather similar can happen if one of the commonest of mistakes has been made and the plug threads have been oiled or greased before fitting. Far from making it easier to take the plug out next time, the lubricant turns to carbon under heat and welds the two threads together. Plugs must *always* be fitted dry or with a little graphite on their threads. Just rubbing a soft pencil over the threads is sufficient.

Cleaning plug holes

The easiest way of dealing with choked sparking plug hole threads is to run in a suitably sized tap. The 'diy' equivalent is an old plug in which a hacksaw cut has been made, vertically, for the full depth of the threads just to one side of the centre electrode. This acts as a cutter and scours away any fouling. Used without a plug washer, it should be deep enough to clear the whole threaded area. It must itself be cleaned before each application, to avoid depositing swarf into the combustion chambers.

Insulator check

It isn't just the electrode end of the plug that needs to be serviced. In use, the insulator tends to collect a surface film of conductive matter that can lead to current leakage. Just wiping it with a rag doesn't remove all the deposit, while using petrol simply leaves another residue in its place. When refitting a used plug, wipe the insulator carefully with rag moistened with methylated spirits. The residue will evaporate completely, leaving a perfectly clean insulator.

Plug terminal check

Some plug caps are designed to slip on to plugs that have the terminals removed – you'll have noticed that a plug is usually supplied with the terminal loose in the box – so where the other type is used on your bike you need to fit the terminal yourself. It goes on the plug with the rounded end upwards, and should be screwed down fingertight, then given a further nip up – less than a quarter of a turn – with pliers to ensure that it stays put. A terminal that has jiggled itself loose so that it makes only intermittent contact with the plug is often the cause of an annoying misfire.

Points check

A chore denied to those who have electronic ignition systems, points checking and adjusting is a two-fold operation. First, examine the points by opening up the gap – simply lift the moving arm as far as it will go, against the resistance of its spring – and checking the condition of the contact surfaces. They should be clean, with no pitting, and with plenty of 'meat' left on them.

At one time, it was considered essential that the points should be filed so that they were absolutely square to each other. Now, it is no longer easy to be dogmatic, since electrical manufacturers have developed points profiles with curved contact areas, and it is difficult to tell at a glance whether your asymmetric points are there by accident or design.

If the points seem to be in reasonable condition, with a well defined contact patch, do *not* dress them. Instead, merely clean them and then check the gap. On older bikes, where one is pretty certain that the points were originally square-cut, they can be dressed in place with a points file or removed for squaring-up on a fine oilstone.

Pitted points

Electrical sparking at the points eventually pits the surfaces. It is common for one point to develop a small crater, while a matching pip builds on the other where the eroded material has fused. In practice, the crater has no effect and can be disregarded. The pip, however, makes it impossible to obtain an accurate points setting, so it must be removed.

The easy way, with a good eye and a steady hand, is to use a very fine file to cut the pip away without taking the arm off the backplate. The job is done using the very minimum of pressure, so that the main body of the point does not become bevelled. When the pip has been removed, clean the points.

Cleaning points

A folded slip of rag dipped in meths is used for initial cleaning of the points. This will remove any slight grease film that may have built up. Wrap the cloth round a feeler gauge, moisten it with the solvent, open the points and saw away half a dozen times to bring off the dirt.

Now finish the job by taking a clean strip of writing paper and inserting it into the gap. Turn the crankshaft so that the points just loosely grip the paper and draw the strip out. It will be dirty. Insert a fresh strip and repeat the operation. Continue this until the paper comes away clean.

Adjusting points

An average points gap is 0.35mm (0.014in), although exact settings for each bike will be specified in the handbook. On some of the simpler machines, varying the points gap is the only method of adjusting the ignition timing, so it is essential to refer back to base information before altering a gap that may seem too small or too wide. Reducing the points gap effectively retards the ignition; increasing the gap advances it.

To reset the gap, turn the crankshaft until the heel of the moving points arm is right on the peak of the cam. This is the position in which the points are fully open. Insert the appropriate feeler gauge, which should just slide in. As with the tappets, if it fits double-check by trying the next size up. If your set of feelers gives too wide a jump, gently turn the engine and note by how much the heel moves off the peak before the points grip the feeler. This should happen virtually at once. If so, the gap is correct; otherwise it needs to be narrowed a little.

Position the heel accurately on the peak again and insert the feeler. Loosen the screw that locks the points arm, and operate the adjuster. This may be an eccentric screw, set in an elongated hole in the plate carrying the arm, or it may simply be a slot and fulcrum into which a screwdriver blade has to be inserted and twisted. Make sure that the securing screw has been freed only

The points gap should be checked when the points are in the fully open position

The appropriate size feeler should just fit between the points

enough to let the plate move against resistance, and slowly alter the gap, sliding the feeler in and out as you do so. The moment you feel the points grip the feeler, hold the adjuster steady and retighten the securing screw.

If you have chosen a points gap that is midway between the narrowest and widest settings recommended by the makers, the points should now be accurately set. The only check to make is that a feeler of the narrowest dimension is

These points are adjusted by a screwdriver blade using the slot and fulcrum provided

a loose fit, while the wider one won't enter at all.

Contact-breaker lubrication

Some contact-breaker mechanisms have a felt pad incorporated to act as a miniature oil tank for constant lubrication. With this type, dribble a miserly ration of thin oil on to the felt, until it is just damp. It must *not* be so wetted that it starts to exude drops of oil.

However, just one drop of oil may be applied to each moving-arm post, and where there is no felt pad to do the job the surface of the cam can be given a very thin film of grease. This must not be overdone, or it may find its way on to the points. A blob of grease half the size of a match head, wiped evenly round the cam, is sufficient.

Weatherproofing points

Water in the contact breakers can bring the bike to a standstill almost as fast as applying the brakes. It is therefore a good idea to treat the mechanism with a water-displacing spray, such as Rocket WD 40, before refitting the cover.

Clutch adjustments

It is common practice for clutches to have as many as three separate means of adjustment. They are, in effect, two methods of altering the relative inner/outer cable lengths; and one of varying the throw of the actual operating mechanism in the transmission.

Clutch play is usually stated as the amount of free movement at the handlebar lever. It may be given as the distance that the end of the lever travels before the clutch starts to free – usually around 15-20mm – or as the gap between the edge of the lever and the fixed mounting on the bars, where a movement of about 5mm would be average.

Minor adjustments are made by screwing the cable adjuster in or out until the correct play is obtained. Most bikes have a knurled adjuster on the clutch control itself, enabling this operation to be done on the road without tools. Just free the lock-ring, turn the adjuster inwards to increase play or outwards to reduce it, and then lock the ring again. There is often a second and larger adjuster where the cable enters the transmission casing. It may be covered by a rubber shroud, but it operates in just the same way, although it normally has hexagons instead of knurled rings.

When all the cable adjustment has been taken up, the third adjuster can be used. First, free off both adjusters completely by screwing them fully home. Then operate the release mechanism adjuster. This usually takes the form of a screw or a quick-thread bearing on the operating rod. With this type, the securing locknut or lockscrew is released, and the adjuster is turned until resistance is felt. This shows that all play has been taken up. The adjuster is then backed off by a quarter-turn to restore some free play, and the locknut is tightened.

Now, the lower cable adjuster is used (where two cable adjusters are fitted) to obtain the correct play at the lever, any fine adjustment being made on the lever-end adjuster once the locknut of the lower one has been tightened.

Brake bleeding/fluid change

Air can enter the hydraulic braking system only if the fluid level in the reservoir has been allowed to fall

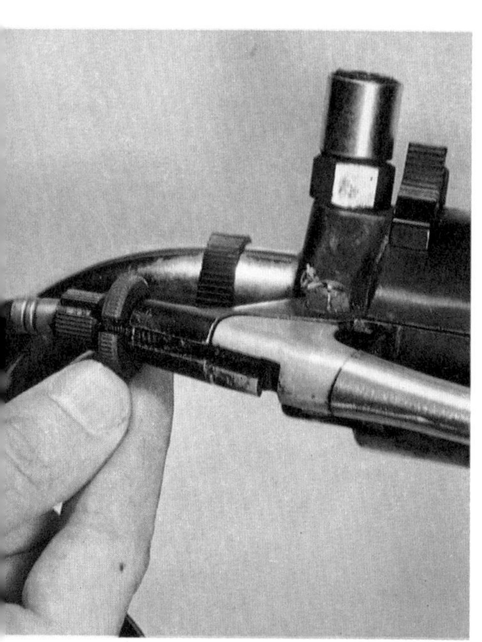

This knurled adjuster makes it possible to adjust the clutch cable without tools

The clutch cable adjuster at the engine end will need spanners

below the danger level, or if a union has been loosened. However, water can, and often does, find its way into the system.

Hydraulic fluid is able to absorb water vapour from the air that enters through the vent hole, which is one reason why a diaphragm is often used. Harmless in itself, this water can boil under the heat of braking, releasing not only steam, but air as well. Unlike a liquid – brake fluid, or water itself – air and steam are compressible. The result is a spongy feel to the system and less effective braking.

At least once every two years, the hydraulic system should be drained and fresh fluid added. In the interim, the brakes should be bled if there is any deterioration in efficiency.

The two operations are similar. For both, all that is required is a supply of fresh fluid, an old jam jar to act as a container for the expelled fluid, a length of plastic hose small enough in bore to fit the bleed nipple and long enough to reach the ground and a spanner for the nipple.

Remove the rubber cap from the nipple – if there isn't one, buy a replacement – and attach the hose. Put the other end in the jar, open the bleed nipple, and remove the reservoir cap and diaphragm. Operate the brake lever, squeezing and releasing it until all fluid in the system has been expelled.

It is permissible to flush the system through with methylated spirits if the expelled fluid shows signs of severe contamination, but usually this is unnecessary. Just close the bleed valve and top up the system. Then open the valve again and, keeping the reservoir level steady by adding more fresh fluid, operate the lever until the fluid leaving the valve is a clean natural colour.

Bleeding to expel the air is then carried out. Usually, you are advised to have a helper for the job, although it can be done single-handed. Have enough fluid in the bottom of the jar to keep the end of the hose immersed, acting as an air lock. With the hose firmly attached to the nipple, and the reservoir full, open the bleed valve with one hand and, with the other, give the brake lever a long slow pull. Just as the stroke is coming to an end, close the nipple. Let the lever return slowly. Then open the bleed again, give another stroke, and again close the bleed before the lever reaches its stop. Between strokes, keep an eye on the level in the reservoir and top up well before it falls to the minimum level mark.

Continue bleeding until the fluid being pumped into the jar is completely free of air bubbles, then close the bleed screw firmly and top up the reservoir to the maximum level mark. Refit the diaphragm, screw the cap down firmly, and if necessary repeat the operation on the rear brake.

Here again, it is relatively easy to carry out the job single-handed by kneeling beside the bike and pressing the brake pedal with one hand while operating the bleed with the other.

Any difficulty with single-handed bleeding can, of course, be overcome by using one of the special devices sold for car-brake bleeding.

Drum brake adjustment

Raise the front of the bike by inserting a block under the crankcase so that the front wheel can be turned easily. Spin the wheel, and check that it is turning freely. Operate the brake, and note the amount of lever travel required to bring the shoes into rubbing contact with the drum. If it exceeds 20mm travel at the end of the lever, loosen the locknut on the cable adjuster, and screw the adjuster outwards until the correct play is obtained. Then retighten the adjuster.

Where the cable has adjusters at the brake plate and at the lever, free the lockring at the lever end and screw the lever adjuster fully home first, then take up the play on the main adjuster, reserving the range of adjustment at the lever for fine on-the-road settings.

With twin-leading-shoe brakes, all necessary adjustment is done in the same way. The connecting rod between the twin operating arms should *not* be reset unless the brake shoes have been changed.

Rear brake cable adjustment is carried out in the same way. However, it is more usual for the method of operation to be by rod, which is even more simple to set. The rod is spring-loaded through a clevis pin, on the outer end of which is a click adjuster nut. This locks itself against the clevis pin every half turn.

Keep turning the rear wheel, while taking up the play with half-

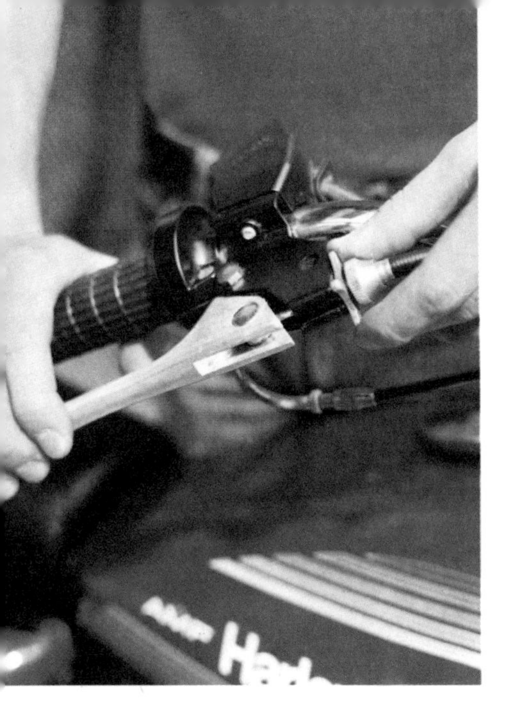

Adjust a cable-operated brake if the lever moves more than 20mm before the brake bites

Rear brake adjustment is simplicity itself with rod-operated systems

turns of the adjuster. As soon as the brake shoes begin to rub on the drum, back off the adjuster by half a turn and check the play at the brake pedal. If the brake is too fierce – and it is unwise to set it with less than 20mm free pedal play, since drum rear brakes are notorious for locking – back off the adjuster by half a turn at a time until the end of the brake pedal moves 20–30mm before the shoes begin to bite.

Pedal adjustment

It's surprising how few riders realise that the actual position of the rear brake pedal can often be adjusted to bring it neatly under the foot. The usual method is by a combination of splines on the spindle and a screw stop somewhere near the fulcrum. If you are having to lift your foot off the rest to reach your pedal, it could be that a few minutes spent resetting the control would make operation easier and safer.

Stoplamp adjustment

After resetting the brake adjustment, check that the stoplamp lights and extinguishes properly. It can be reset by holding the body of the switch steady and screwing the mounting nut up or down. The more the switch body is raised, the earlier the stoplamp operates.

After adjustment, check operation several times to make certain that the adjuster has settled down into its mounting.

If either brake or gear pedals do not fall easily to the foot, they can be relocated on their splined shafts

Fault Finding

Tracking down troubles requires a painstaking process of elimination from an amateur mechanic, eliminating possible causes of a problem until the guilty party is exposed. A professional often has the advantage of modern electronic diagnosis equipment that can virtually explore the inside of an engine, thus simplifying his job, but as a do-it-yourselfer, you will have to rely more on old-fashioned brainwork. Probably ninety per cent of faults that will cause a breakdown will be in the engine unit, this being the major part of a motor cycle.

Sudden engine failure

1 A complete and sudden engine failure unaccompanied by seizure is almost certainly electrical in origin. Nothing else will cause an engine to stop without warning if it will still turn over freely. Before the bike has rolled to a halt, you can start making your checks. The obvious one is to glance at the ignition switch to make sure it is still on; also check the engine kill-switch – a gloved hand can easily knock it into the 'Off' position.

2 Although the engine has stopped, are other electrical circuits operating normally? Is the ignition light on? Do the flashers operate? Have the lights gone out? If so, you have a total failure of the electrical system. The most likely cause of this is that the master fuse has blown. You now know that you need to look for an electrical fault severe enough to burn out the 15 amp master fuse – the only one on the bike that serves both lighting and ignition circuits. Resist the temptation to fit the new fuse and start up. Fuses blow only when they are overloaded, not because they deteriorate. The fault that burned out the original fuse will simply burn out the replacement too. Did you operate any electrical equipment just before the engine stopped? If so, the fault is probably in the circuit serving it. Suspect, also, any electrical equipment which has recently been worked on, or any electrical accessories that have recently been fitted. Before spending time checking their circuits, however, make two simple checks. Ensure that the battery leads are firmly fitted to the battery itself, and that the other end of the battery earth lead is securely bolted to the frame. An earth lead adrift will deaden the whole electrical system. If the leads appear good, check the master fuse. Where it is burned out, you have a major wiring check to make.

3 Has the engine alone been affected? Here, the fault must clearly be in the ignition circuit. Check by removing the sparking plugs so that the unit can be turned over easily. With the HT leads connected, earth each plug in turn on the cylinder head and switch on the ignition. Spin the engine – use the kickstarter, rather than the starter button, to conserve battery power – and see if you have a spark. If there's no spark, try substituting a new plug – especially if your engine is a two-stroke.

With a multi-cylinder engine, it is unlikely that a fault in the HT circuit will cause a complete engine failure, and since the contact-breakers are normally also duplicated the inference is that the fault must lie between the contact breakers and the battery. Check back along the wiring to find the reason. A snap connector may have come adrift; or there may be a fracture in the wire. A rough-and-ready circuit tester can be improvised from a short length of electrical cable, a turn of insulating tape and one of the indicator bulbs. Bare the ends of the wire and tape one to the bulb cap. Hold the bulb terminal against the connector on the lead you want to check, earth the other end of your test-lamp wire, and switch on the current. The bulb will light if current is reaching that point. If not, remake the connection and, using the colour-coding as a guide, move down the lead to the next connector and check again. Eventually, you'll find one that is live. The obvious inference is that between that connector and the previous one tested there's a break in the wiring. Where the lead is accessible, the position of the

A home-made test lamp facilitates the tracing of a circuit break

fracture can often be pinpointed by moving down the lead, a couple of inches at a time, alternately pushing and pulling on the insulation with the cable gripped between the thumb and forefinger of each hand. Where the conductor is broken, the insulation will stretch as you pull it.

Most electrical leads are gathered into looms, and it is unlikely that a fracture will occur inside the loom. Single leads, therefore, are suspect. If moisture can reach connectors they may corrode and fracture. The conductor may also break at the point at which it is crimped to the connector, especially if it is subjected to vibration.

Engine misfires and stops

1 Failure of this type can be due to electrical, fuel, or mechanical faults. An electrical fault is likelier than the other two to show itself, initially, as an intermittent misfire. A fuel fault gives the motor a 'strangled' feel, and it can often be identified with the bike still on the move by closing the choke, either fully or partially. If the motor picks up as this is done, the problem is almost certainly fuel starvation. Mechanical faults are usually signalled to the rider in advance by noises that are not usual. Tapping noises suggest trouble in the valve gear, pistons, or small ends. Knocks can be caused by big-end bearings failing. Rumbles suggest trouble in the mains. Any tendency for the bike to slow with the throttle open, coupled with an increasing noise level, suggests imminent seizure due to overheating or lubrication system failure. If this is allowed to develop, the engine will lock up.

2 Follow the same procedure as before where an electrical fault is suspected.

3 For fuel faults, start with the obvious one of checking that there is fuel in the tank and that the tap is switched on. Even if the level is high, it is worth trying a restart after switching to reserve. This opens an extra feed pipe into the tap. Check that fuel is reaching the carburettors by detaching the feed pipe at the float chamber end. If there is no flow, carry out the same check at the fuel tap. No flow there indicates blocked filters or dirt in the tank cap vent. If air cannot enter the tank, suction prevents fuel leaving it.

A blocked fuel tap can cause a breakdown

Except on the 'Gold Wing' Honda – currently the only motor cycle equipped with a fuel pump – no other fault is possible in the fuel-feed system. On a multi, with more than one carburettor, only one fuel fault will cause complete engine failure if petrol is reaching the float chambers – water contamination of the petrol. All garage fuel pumps deliver a certain amount of water, although this is not normally enough to be significant. Filling up at an open pump on a very wet day, however, can cause water to build up in the bottom of the tank, and if this enters the fuel system it can block the jets.

Two-strokes using petroil lubrication can suffer their own particular form of oil pollution if too much lubricant is added to the fuel.

If the engine starts at all, the trouble becomes only too obvious as a huge cloud of smoke issues from the exhaust pipe. Since the jets cannot pass the same quantity of this 'thick' fuel, this fault has the unexpected side-effect of causing overheating as well, as the mixture tends to be weak. The cure is to drain the tank and refill with petroil in the correct proportions. On pump-lubricated motors, incorrect oil pump settings will produce the same cloud of smoke, but not the overheating, since the oil is normally injected into the inlet tract between the carburettor and the inlet port. Instead, the pump-fed motor will rapidly oil up its plugs. With petroil-lubricated machines, it is possible for some of the petrol to evaporate, leaving an artificially oil-rich mixture, if the machine is left standing for long periods. The result can be a thickish oil deposit in the base of the float chamber, which blocks the jets. Where a petroil-lubricated two-stroke refuses to start after a lay-up, check this possibility. Better still, run the machine to a stop with the fuel switched off *before* storing it.

Too much fuel is as bad as too little – worse, in fact, since with over-flooding there is always a risk of the bike catching fire. This fault is usually a result of dirt evading the filters and becoming lodged under the carburettor's needle valve. It is the motion of the bike that disturbs sediment in the tank and float chambers, so over-flooding is likelier to develop with the machine on the move, rather than at start-up. Since the motor is using up at least

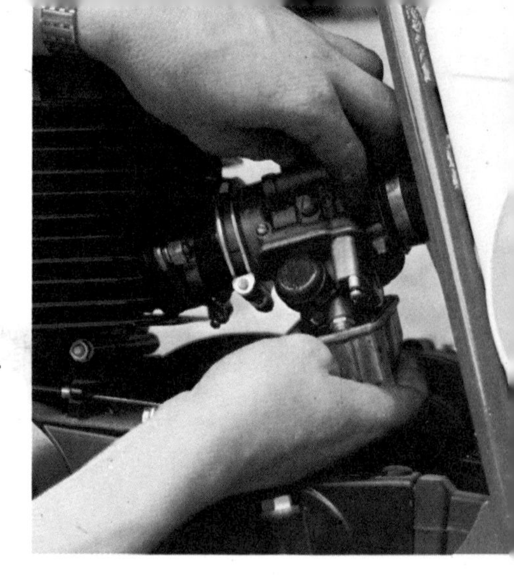

If the needle valve sticks, remove the float chamber to deal with the fault

part of the excess fuel, the symptoms tend to be suppressed as long as the engine speed is relatively high. From the saddle, you can feel that the motor is not running normally and you may see the tachometer needle fluctuating a little. The power delivery may have a 'grumbly' feel to it, which becomes more and more pronounced as engine speed drops and the mixture progressively richens.

Stop immediately, to minimise the amount of fuel escaping from the float chamber. Better still, switch off the fuel as soon as flooding is suspected and open up in an intermediate gear to use up what remains in the float chamber. With the bike stationary, you can then remove the float chamber and swill out the needle valve assembly to remove the dirt. If you cannot reach the float-chamber securing screws – on some multis it's a difficult road-side job, on others its impossible –

try turning on the fuel and rocking the machine from side to side on its centre stand. The series of jolts, combined with the flow of fuel past the valve, often dislodges the dirt. You can then drain and flush the tank, fuel lines and float chambers in your workshop – a necessary task, if recurrence is to be avoided.

4 Sudden mechanical failures are rare, but not unknown. Perhaps the commonest – total loss of compression on a two-stroke, caused by a hole in the piston crown – is really a result of an electrical fault. Similarly, bearing failure on a four-stroke usually results from cumulative wear and, perhaps, from neglect of oil and filter changes.

Mechanical faults affecting the running of the machine are usually confined to the ignition components, the valve gear, or the clutch. Again, only the valve gear is likely to develop a fault that cannot be traced to cumulative wear that *should* have been noted and rectified during routine maintenance.

Revving beyond the red sector on the tachometer is the likeliest cause of valve trouble. A missed gear-change, for example, can speed up the engine beyond the point at which the valve springs can respond. The valves then oscillate, and a valve head may collide with a piston crown. This can damage both components. The valve stem can be bent or broken and the piston holed. Unless the engine is stopped immediately, the internal damage may escalate beyond repair.

Signs of valve damage are a loss of compression, showing itself in reduced performance, and misfiring. Where the engine spits back through the carburettor, the inlet valve is at fault. It is not seating properly, therefore mixture or hot gas is being driven through the induction system on the compression and ignition strokes.

Backfiring and banging in the exhaust system shows that either the exhaust valve is not seating properly, or that ignition is incomplete and that unburned fuel is being expelled into the silencers and igniting there.

With any of these symptoms, stop as soon as you can and carry out a visual check to locate the source of the trouble. With multis, the faulty cylinder can sometimes be determined simply by holding a hand close to each exhaust pipe, near the port. One that is significantly hotter or colder than the rest suggests that it is that cylinder at fault. With multiple-silencer systems, the tail-pipe can also give a clue. The end will be a matt grey if the exhaust gases are normally constituted. A scaly black deposit shows that oil is being burned, a sooty one, an over-rich mixture and cold running; a white-ash deposit suggests a weak mixture and over-heating. The same tell-tale signs can be read from the deposits on the noses of the plugs, when those are removed.

5 Of the ignition components that could cause misfiring, the likeliest are the contact-breaker assemblies. In most current designs, the ignition timing is set by rotating the base plate carrying the contact breakers, and locking the setting with screws. If these loosen, it is possible for the

The contact-breaker baseplate has slotted mounting holes to permit timing adjustment

The auto-advance springs may break and cause a loss of power

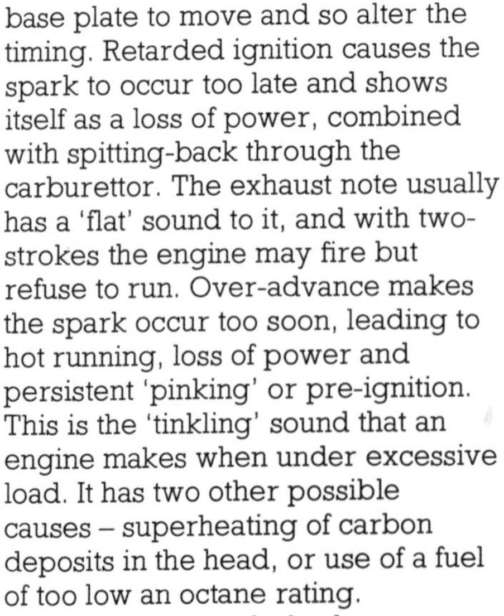

base plate to move and so alter the timing. Retarded ignition causes the spark to occur too late and shows itself as a loss of power, combined with spitting-back through the carburettor. The exhaust note usually has a 'flat' sound to it, and with two-strokes the engine may fire but refuse to run. Over-advance makes the spark occur too soon, leading to hot running, loss of power and persistent 'pinking' or pre-ignition. This is the 'tinkling' sound that an engine makes when under excessive load. It has two other possible causes – superheating of carbon deposits in the head, or use of a fuel of too low an octane rating.

Further ignition faults that may develop on the road include weakening or fracture of one or both springs on the auto-advance mechanism – causing the motor to over-advance at low revs. Almost certainly, you will hear the two centrifugal weights rattling if this has happened. The contact-breaker spring may weaken or snap, although this is rare, or condenser failure could result in excessive burning of the points.

6 Only one clutch trouble can have an effect on engine performance – clutch slip. This is indicated when the engine revs rise rapidly on opening the throttle without the machine gaining much speed. The cause may be faulty adjustment of the clutch operating mechanism, which must always have free play if slip is to be prevented. The exact play varies, but a movement of around 15mm at the end of the handlebar lever should be reasonable. Wear in the clutch friction plates or faulty tensioning of the clutch springs are the only other likely causes of slip.

Wet-weather misfiring

Pure water does not conduct electricity, but rainwater always contains dissolved salts which change this. As much of the motorcycle's ignition system is exposed, misfiring under wet conditions can almost invariably be put down to water somewhere in the system.

Some machines with metal-shrouded plug caps have suffered badly from this fault – but not for the obvious reason. Metal-shrouded caps in themselves are not noticeably inferior to all-plastic caps. They were found, however, to cause hair cracks in the plug insulators, due apparently to their expansion when hot and their subsequent contraction when cooling. The cure for wet-weather misfiring, therefore, is to change to new all-plastic caps. It is not sufficient just to remove the metal screening from the existing caps.

Wet ignition leads, plug insulators and contact-breaker assemblies can be 'dried out' with water-displacing sprays. These also have a preventive role. Spray the ignition system, and it will be safeguarded against condensation, which can have the same effect as flooding of the electrics.

On some machines a particularly puzzling wet-weather problem can occur. This is a persistent misfire, which seems to have all the symptoms of plug trouble, but which does not respond to drying out of the ignition.

This may be due to water entering the carburettors through the air filters. Often, these filters are set in a compartment under the dual seat, and water can reach them either by penetration around the nose of the seat or by being absorbed by the sponge-like seat filling and then pressed out by the weight of the rider. As a temporary cure, the filter element can be removed. Permanent rectification may involve some do-it-yourself water sealing around the filter housing.

Water-logging of the filter element can also result from operation of the engine's anti-pollution devices. Here, regular filter replacement is the only cure.

Starting problems

There is no basic difference in diagnosis techniques for poor starting, and much the same sequences can be applied as for misfiring or engine failure.

If the engine was running satisfactorily before the bike was stopped, and it then refuses to start, this is a clear pointer to electrical or fuel trouble, rather than anything mechanical.

The likeliest cause is a poor spark. This suggests a battery or plug problem – one compounded nowadays by an increasing reliance on the starter motor.

Where a machine does not start up within a few presses of the button, it is essential to discontinue use of the starter and to revert to kick starting (if your machine has such a device). Even during the initial attempts to start, a breathing space of about 20 seconds should be allowed between dabs on the starter button to give the battery time to recover.

The electrical current needed to provide a good spark is relatively small – even a torch battery wired into the low-tension system provides enough to energise the coil for kick starting. A starter motor, on the other hand, is virtually the equivalent of shorting the battery direct to earth, with a locked-rotor drain of up to 320 amps. That is enough to flatten the average motor cycle battery within two minutes; hence the need to revert to kick starting before too great a drain occurs.

A series of routine checks should be carried out as set out below.

1 Check that the ignition is on and that the engine kill switch is set to 'Run'.

2 Ascertain that there is sufficient fuel in the tank and that it is reaching the carburettors.

3 Check that the choke is operative.

4 Remove a plug and examine it. Clean the electrodes and check the gap. With a plug in poor condition, try closing the gap to 0.020in. Remember that plugs in air-cooled engines have a useful life of only 5000 miles for top efficiency and that a wider gap often develops due to erosion of the electrodes. Where in doubt, fit new plugs.

5 Check the plug insulators and the spark plug caps. Wipe them with a rag, preferably meths-soaked, to remove road dirt. This usually contains metallic traces that can leak current to earth and so weaken the spark.

6 Check the contact-breaker points on machines that have them. Dirt on the contact faces, burning of the faces and incorrect gaps are all spark-weakening factors.

7 Check the specific gravity of the battery cells: a reading of 1.260/1.280 should be obtained. A higher reading suggests an internal short circuit, reducing battery capacity. A lower reading indicates under-charging – again, meaning that the battery is not delivering its full potential.

8 Check the fuses and wiring if all other checks have failed to locate the cause of the problem.

9 Try connecting a second battery. Note, however, that if the electric starter is to be used proper booster cables must be employed for the connection, since a heavy current drain is involved. Where the second battery is to be fitted only to increase the capacity available for kick starting, normal electrical cable can be used instead. Connection must be made in parallel – connect the positive terminal of one battery to the positive of the other and negative to negative.

10 In cold conditions, battery capacity is reduced and the engine is harder to turn because of oil drag. Atomisation of the fuel is affected too. Under these circumstances, it is permissible to use an easy-starting spray. These usually contain ether, which has a very low flashpoint. Injected into the air intake, such a spray gives an easily-fired mixture in the cylinder. An alternative is to remove a plug and inject ether direct into the cylinder, or to use an injection of lighter fuel.

Shrouding the engine, carbs and battery with plastic sheeting and blowing in hot air from a hair drier or fan heater is another effective expedient. It takes about twenty minutes to create a 'summer's day' ambient temperature around the engine. Where this means is used, however, it is essential to ensure that the power cables and mains-voltage electrical equipment are not allowed to get wet.

What's that noise?

Few troubles occur without warning. Most faults give advance notice that they are developing, either in the 'feel' of the response or by noise.

No book can tell a reader how to sense that an engine is no longer running with its accustomed sweetness: but noises are fairly distinctive. Note, though, that there are extraneous factors that have to be taken into account. Even a change of helmet can alter your aural perception. With a full-face on, you effectively block out noises that would be perfectly audible to a man wearing an open-face helmet. Noise transmission even differs between helmets of like type, so you have to learn just what the effect of your particular gear is. Road surfaces, too, can produce or accentuate noises, and eliminating such factors is part of the art of diagnosis.

Some noises tend to disappear when the bike is at a standstill and the engine is not under load; others do not. In the workshop, noises can be pinpointed with considerable accuracy by use of a stethoscope or a listening stick. The stethoscope is the same device as a doctor uses to sound your chest. Plug the earpieces in, place the probe against the motor and you can hear precisely what's going on inside. A cheaper alternative is to use a long screwdriver. Put the handle to your ear, block off the other ear, and apply the point of the driver to the engine. The cacophony will surprise you, but with practice you'll find you can isolate the source of virtually every noise you hear.

The commonest noises are those associated with the operation of the engine. Some are basically non-mechanical. The persistent metallic tinkling sound heard under load or on acceleration is 'pinking' or pre-ignition. This is caused by the mixture igniting ahead of time. It can indicate that the fuel being used is of too low an octane rating – eg two-star instead of four-star – but, it can equally mean that there is carbon in the combustion chambers, which is becoming incandescent and igniting the charge prematurely, or that the ignition timing is over-advanced.

Backfiring is the other side of the coin. Here, fuel is being pushed out of the exhaust port unburned. It collects in the silencer and is then ignited by the hot gas passing through. Too rich a mixture is one answer. A damaged exhaust valve seat – or even an overtight tappet – is another. Spitting back through the carburettors is caused by gas forcing its way past the inlet valve seat. A tight inlet tappet, a damaged inlet valve or seat or grossly over-retarded ignition timing are all possibilities.

Rattles from the engine are usually associated with the pistons, bores, or rods. Piston slap, caused by excessive piston skirt/bore clearances or by worn rings, is a regular sound that changes its frequency according to engine speed. It can also be associated with worn small-end bearings, and in such cases it rapidly becomes an insistent clank as the gudgeon pin oscillates in its increasingly loose bush.

Rustling or tapping noises are usually in the valve gear, though the primary drive and clutch can also be the culprits. The listening stick will soon decide between them. A rumbling sound, however, suggests trouble in the lower end of the motor – with faulty main bearings as prime suspects. A knock from the bottom end is frequently associated with big-end failure.

High-frequency noises – whines or screeches – indicate clutch or gear trouble. As pinions wear, their teeth become noisy and the gearbox whines continually. Constant screeching means that a rotating part – perhaps the clutch body – is in contact with other metal and that the oil film between them has broken down. Severe wear is taking place, and you should stop instantly. One other possibility is a whirring sound that tells you that the kickstarter ratchet is failing to disengage.

The rolling chassis, too, can produce its quota of noise. Squeals from a disc brake indicate high spots on the pads, or glazing on their surfaces. In drum brakes, it suggests dust on the linings.

No smoke without fire?

With four-stroke engines, the smoke emitted from the exhaust pipe is a guide to the internal condition of the motor. White or grey smoke indicates that oil is being burned – which also shows that in some way it is entering the combustion chamber. The cause may be nothing worse than overfilling the sump – something not to be recommended, since the excess oil can also be forced out of the breathing system or through crankcase joints.

Where the oil level is correct, there are several possible faults that can be suspected. If the condition has developed gradually it probably stems from a worn bore or worn inlet valve guide. Sudden smoking – especially if associated with lost or reduced compression – means broken or seized piston rings.

Black smoke is caused by excessive fuel being burned. Possibly the fuel level in the float chambers is too high, either through maladjustment or because the float needle has stuck. A main jet may have been working loose and finally dropped into the chamber, or on bikes with a cold-start device rather than a choke the plunger could be stuck in the open position. With choke-type carbs the flap may not be opening properly (in either of these cases the engine will also be 'hunting' quite badly); and there is the final possibility of an obstruction in the air cleaner cutting down the amount of air being drawn in.

Brown smoke indicates a weak mixture. Fuel starvation, caused by low fuel levels, clogging in the fuel pipes or obstruction in the main jet, is the most likely cause, but mixtures can also be weakened by too much air being admitted, possibly due to the carbs coming loose on their stubs, or through leakage occurring around the air filter hose or element seals.

Top-End Overhauls

Although the most familiar service operation performed by diy mechanics, the top overhaul – a 'decoke' – is also one of the least understood. It is not an instant method of restoring lost performance and it is often carried out far too frequently. Even on two-strokes – which are notoriously fussy about carbon formation in the exhaust port and tail-pipe – a full top overhaul is necessary only at very wide time intervals. It is enough just to clear carbon from the exhaust port and from the detachable tailpipe at the end of the silencer. With four-strokes, carbon formation on the piston crown and the combustion chamber surfaces is very light. It takes several years of average use for these deposits to reach a level at which they *must* be removed and the engine will be all the better for remaining undisturbed. Good maintenance is minimal maintenance – but minimal maintenance strictly carried out.

What *must* be done, periodically, is to check the four-stroke's compression – accurately, with a gauge – and then to remove the head to reseat the valves immediately this test shows that leakage is occurring. It is usually a wise move to take the chance of renewing the valve springs and any oil seals in the guides at the same time. Since the head is off, the carbon deposits can also be cleaned off – not as the main purpose of the overhaul, but as an incidental operation that just happens to be convenient.

Not all carbon is harmful. With older motors, the build-up on the edges of the piston and at the top of the bore often acts as a secondary oil seal between the bottom half of the motor and the combustion chamber. Remove it, and up goes the oil consumption. Lubricant that had previously been confined to its proper place and job is pumped, instead, into the combustion chamber and burned. It then forms carbon.

A cutaway of a typical two-stroke engine, a 125cc Morini

The trick is to clean up the piston crown, but to leave a ring of carbon a few millimetres wide around the edge. This is too far from the hot-running centre of the piston to cause pre-ignition, and it can continue to do a useful job keeping the oil where it belongs.

Top overhaul preparations
Start by assembling in advance all the tools and materials that will be needed for the job. Although, obviously, these will differ in detail from make to make, and from bike to bike, a minimum requirement will be common to all.

Materials
Decoke set (new gaskets for head, rocker box, exhaust pipe joint; oil seals for valve guides or stems; oil seals for internal passages)
Wet-or-dry paper (fine grade) for polishing piston crown, combustion chamber and valve stems
Grinding paste (fine) for lapping-in valves
Jointing compound
Metal polish
Paraffin (2 litres minimum) for cleaning components
Valve springs
Wire wool

Tools
Bristle brush
Feeler gauges
Scraper with blunt edges
Screwdriver, flat-bladed
Screwdriver, cross-head – or socket-screw keys, as appropriate
Spanners for all nuts and bolts
Torque wrench
Tray and old paintbrush for cleaning parts
Valve grinding tool
Wire brush (or rotary brushes for use with drill)

Work facilities
Where possible, always leave the engine in the frame. This provides the best and steadiest of workbenches. Unfortunately, there are many bikes on which this cannot be done, for the very good reason that there is insufficient clearance between the underside of the frame tubes and the top of the cylinder head to allow the head to be lifted.

To make it easier to handle the motor on the bench, an engine stand can be made up from scrap wood. A couple of metres of stout timber from a demolition site – it will need to be about 60mm x 40mm section – and a few nails are all the material needed.

Cut four rails about 400mm long, and two crosspieces 300mm long. Nail together, in pairs, the longer sections to form two bearers 60mm wide by 80mm deep. These form the sides of the stand. Nail a cross-piece at each end. You now have an engine stand with raised side rails which will support the motor in a number of different positions and prevent it rolling about on the bench.

'Short' decoke, two-strokes
Unless there is evidence that the rings need attention, it is quite permissible to reduce the work on a two-stroke engine to little more than lifting the head and removing the exhaust pipe.

Remove the exhaust pipe first

Next, remove the head fastenings

The technique is a simple one. Free the exhaust system – usually, this is held by nuts on the exhaust flange studs, and by a single bolt on the silencer – and remove it from the bike. It may be necessary to jar the pipe slightly with the heel of your hand to break the seal at the flange.

Next, undo the head fastenings. These may be nuts fitting on to long studs that hold both head and barrel, or individual bolts holding the head on to the cylinder itself. Again, the joint may need to be jarred before the head will part company with the engine. This is best done with a rubber mallet. Otherwise, use a block of wood. Sometimes, it is possible to unseat a sticky head simply by turning the engine over, either on the starter motor or on the kickstarter. Providing the sparking plug has been left in place, compression will lift the head from inside. Take care, if this technique is used, not to disturb the barrel. The best technique is to refit the head fastenings temporarily, but to leave them a few millimetres away from the head. They then act as stops.

Separate short studs may fix the cylinder head to the barrel

With the head off, turn the motor to bring the piston to tdc, then scrape away the carbon from the piston crown. Switch to wire wool to remove the remaining traces and follow this with a final rub over with fine wet-or-dry (silicone carbide) paper moistened with metal polish. Wash the crown with paraffin to remove any lingering trace of abrasive, and dab it dry.

Now spread a film of grease over the crown, and turn the motor over until the piston is at bdc. Lightly grease the exposed surfaces of the cylinder bore.

You can now clean up the exhaust port, working from the outside. Chip away the carbon with a scraper, and finish off with – if possible – a polish from a rotary wire brush used with a drill and flexible drive. Periodically, it helps to suck out any loose carbon, using a vacuum cleaner hose. Failing that, flick it out of the port with a small, dry paintbrush.

Inevitably, some carbon chips will enter the cylinder. These, however, will simply adhere to the grease spread on the walls of the bore and the piston crown. When the port is clear, it's an easy job to bring the piston slowly back to tdc, pushing the grease and carbon debris in front of it. Wipe it away once the piston is again at tdc, and give the piston crown another quick wash with paraffin. Then decarbonise the head in the normal way, scraping off the worst of the carbon and then polishing off the rest with a rotary wire brush. Finish, again, with wire wool and/or polish-moistened wet-or-dry.

With its fastening removed, the tailpipe can be drawn from the silencer

Be particular about the plughole threads, where any residual hard carbon trapped in the lower section could become incandescent and cause pre-ignition. Careful picking with a darning needle is usually an effective method of dealing with this.

Complete your short decoke by removing the silencer tailpipe and freeing it completely from hard carbon deposits. These tend to block the perforations, and here an ordinary gimlet is as effective a tool as any to use as a probe. Thoroughly wire-brush the baffle, to clear surface carbon, and then refit it.

Where decokes have been neglected in the past, the tailpipe may be very difficult to remove. Jarring it with a block of softwood – if done carefully – will usually free it. Where it has a bar across it, hooking on a piece of stout wire and locking the free ends in a self-grip wrench forms a diy extractor.

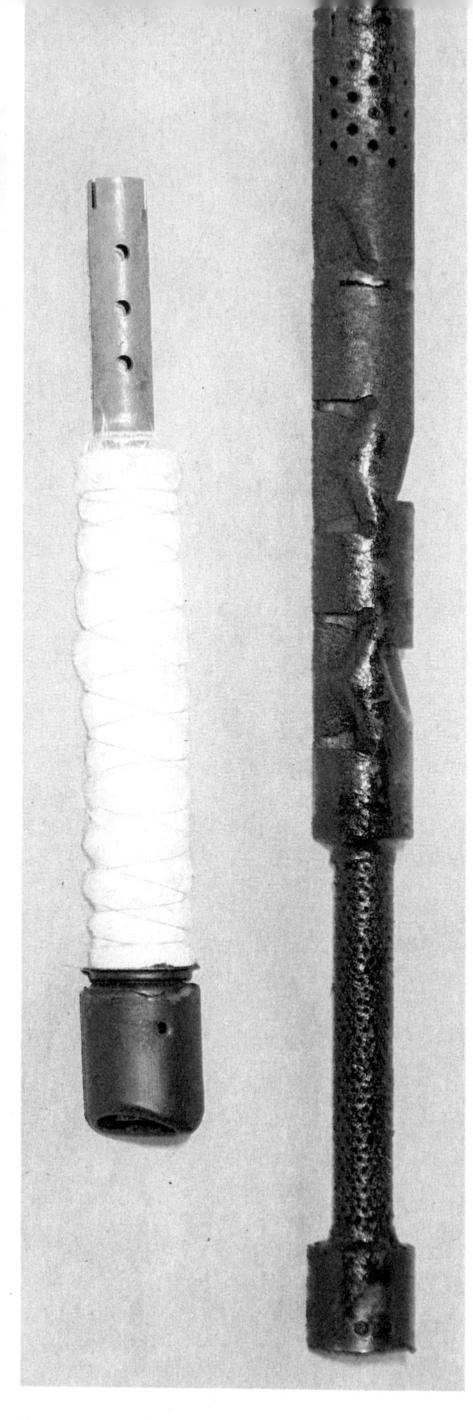

Two-stroke silencer internals, old and new

Complete the short decoke by refitting the head and exhaust system. Tighten the head fastenings in the recommended order and in stages and use new gaskets or packings where appropriate.

The entire job can be completed, on a single-cylinder engine, in half an hour.

Full top overhaul, two-strokes

Where the short overhaul technique is inappropriate, simply extend it into a full top overhaul by lifting the barrel as well. Usually, the barrel is held to the crankcase by the nuts that secure the head, sandwiching it between the head and crankcase on long studs. Sometimes, however, the barrel may be fixed by its own short studs, with nuts bearing on a flange at its base.

With multis, it is common practice for each cylinder to have its own individual head and barrel, but this is not invariable. The Suzuki GT 250A range, for example, has a common head for two separate barrels. Some of the older twin two-strokes used a single block containing both barrels.

When removing two-stroke barrels, it is a good idea to set the piston to mid-stroke so that one hand can be slipped under it as the skirt starts to clear the mouth of the barrel. That way, you can make sure that it doesn't flop on to the studs or any other obstruction. This is an important point, since the working faces of the piston are quite delicate. However, there's no general rule about it and some mechanics prefer to put the piston at tdc so that the barrel clears

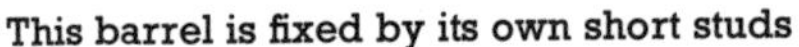

This barrel is fixed by its own short studs

Remove the barrel with great care

piston and studs at the same time. Either method works; just remember that the object is to avoid tapping the piston thrust face against any other part of the motor.

With the barrel off, the piston itself can be removed. First, always check that the crown is marked to show which way round the piston has to be fitted. Usually, an arrow will be stamped on it, pointing to the front. This may be obscured by carbon, so as a precaution it's quite permissible to scratch your own light mark either on the crown, or just *inside* – not outside – the piston skirt. Since the piston may look symmetrical, you might think this is a bit pedantic. However, things aren't always what they seem and in some cases – on the Kawasaki triples, for example – the gudgeon pin holes are in fact slightly offset to prevent piston slap. Other strokers have piston porting and simply won't work with the piston reversed. Even a piston which was symmetrical when new will have bedded-down in its cylinder and won't operate so efficiently if it is unfeelingly switched into a different working environment. For this last reason, it is also essential to ensure that the piston is marked to show to which cylinder it belongs as well.

Once satisfied on this point, cover the crankcase mouth with clean rag or crumpled-up newspaper and winkle out the circlips holding the gudgeon pin. These may be simple wire circlips, or spring-steel snap rings. Wire clips can be eased out with the aid of a screwdriver, but snap rings demand the use of a pair of circlip pliers. Insert the pliers' prongs into the two small holes in the snap ring, squeeze the pliers, and the ring will be contracted sufficiently to enable it to be lifted straight out.

Mechanics with labour-saving ideas, incidentally, usually remove only one snap ring unless the gudgeon pin is so tight a fit that it

Remove the gudgeon pin circlips

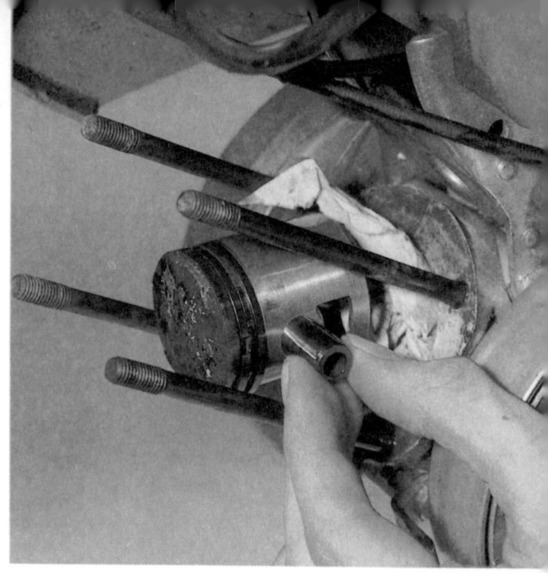

The gudgeon pin may slide out easily

needs to be pressed out. Some gudgeon pins slide easily enough when pressed. Some are a closer fit, and need to be tapped out. Insert a soft-metal drift slightly smaller in diameter than the pin; cup your hand round the piston to support it – you'll find you can still hold the drift between thumb and forefinger – and lightly tap the end of the drift with a hammer. Once the pin starts to move, change your grip to get your hand clear. If the pin is really tight, don't resort to hammering to shift it. The connecting rod/piston assembly is not designed to take that type of side load. Simply expand the light alloy piston until it releases its grip on the steel pin. Light alloy expands faster than steel, so local heating of the piston will open up the gudgeon pin hole faster than the pin can expand. That heating can be provided by using a small gas torch or – providing you are careful not to scald yourself – merely by wringing out rag in hot

A drift may be required for the more stubborn pins

water and wrapping it round the piston. Give it a minute to do its job, unwind it, and the pin should move freely. If not, repeat the process until it does.

Removal of the piston rings is a tricky job, since rings are brittle and sit in deep grooves. There is always a risk of breakage during this operation, so make certain that you either have some spare rings handy, or that you have time to visit your dealer to get them. With a secondhand bike, you'll need to check the piston crown first, since the motor may have been rebored and an oversize piston fitted. If so, you'll need oversize rings too. It is normal for the oversize to be stamped on the piston crown and on the upper surface of each piston ring. Typically, the markings would be '50', '100', or something similar. These indicate, respectively, pistons that are 0.5mm and 1.0mm oversize. It is also common for rings to carry a letter on the upper surface. This is not an indication of size, but simply a maker's code. A ring marked 'N', for instance, was made by Nihon, one marked 'T' is a Teikoku product and 'R' indicates Riken. They are all to the same specifications and rings of different makes can be interchanged, *providing* it is done in sets.

To remove rings, put the piston firmly on the bench with the ring gap facing you. Start with the top ring. Put a thumb on each end and press gently outwards to expand the ring. As soon as it will clear its groove, lift it – still keeping up your thumb pressure – and slide it off the top of the piston.

The top ring is relatively easy, but lower rings have to pass over other ring grooves and care must be taken

A peg locates two-stroke piston rings to prevent rotation

not to let them snag. Two-stroke pistons have a peg set across each groove, whose purpose is to prevent the ring rotating and fouling its ends in the exhaust port. These pegs can be helpful when changing rings. Having expanded a ring, turn it so that the next peg will come to the halfway point as the ring is lifted over it. This then gives some protection against trapping the ring during removal. With lower rings, some mechanics prefer to remove them downwards, across the solid skirt of the piston. If you adopt this method, be careful not to score the piston.

Not universal, but fairly common, is the use of spring-steel expanders under rings. Simply ease out any that are fitted. Special piston ring removing tools are available, but these basically do only what your fingers do, albeit with a little more control.

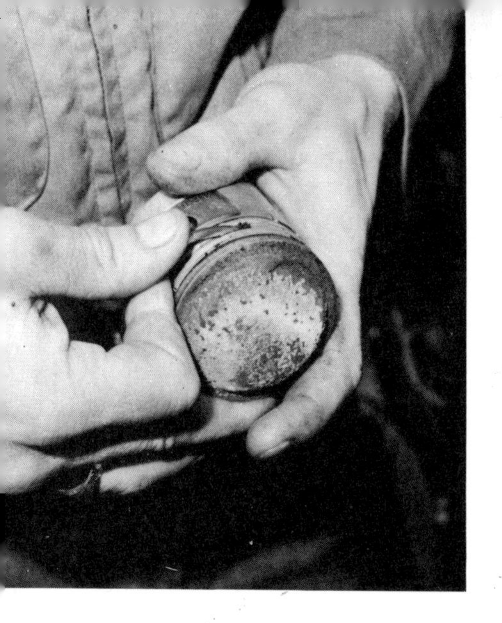

Use a piece of broken piston ring to clean out the grooves

Fit the ring squarely to the bore and measure the gap left between its ends

Decarbonise the piston crown, the ports and the combustion chamber, as already described. In addition, use a piece of broken piston ring (or a small strip of hardwood bevelled to form a miniature scraper) to remove carbon from the ring grooves. Check, also, the underside of the piston crown. It is possible for light deposits to form, over a period, where oil mist in the crankcase has impinged on the hot metal of the piston. Scrape the upper, lower and inner ring surfaces.

Check the rings for serviceability by inserting them, one at a time, into the bore. Slip the piston in from the other end, and use it to align the ring so that is absolutely square, about a quarter of an inch from the bottom of the cylinder. Then measure the ring gap with feeler gauges. Permissible gaps vary from bike to bike, but typically a gap would be 0.006–0.008in (0.15–0.20mm) and the ring would be scrap once the gap reached 0.040in (1.00mm).

Next check the ring for fit in its groove. Insert the end of the ring, face outward, into the piston groove. Viewed from the top, the piston and ring should look like a figure '8'. Now roll the ring completely round the piston. It should slip along freely. If it binds at any point, note the position and then open up the groove very gently with a fine file. A points file or, at a pinch, an ordinary nail file will do the job.

Before refitting the rings, make absolutely certain that you have the right ring for the groove and that it is being refitted the correct way round. Look for those manufacturer's marks stamped on the upper ring face. The locating peg, too, is usually made in such a shape that the cutaway in the end of the ring will fit only one way

A badly scored piston must be discarded

round. Sometimes, the upper and lower rings are finished in different colours, so that one is light and the other dark.

Check the sides of the piston for damage. Even a slight seizure can mark the working surfaces and leave material standing proud. If uncorrected, this makes that cylinder permanently prone to 'picking up'. Smoothing-out damaged areas on a piston is a job that needs care and a light touch, but otherwise it is straightforward enough. Use 400-grade wet-or-dry paper to rub away – very lightly – any deposited metal. When the area is smooth, wash the piston thoroughly with paraffin to remove all traces of abrasive material. Some purist mechanics maintain that even a gentle use of abrasive on light alloy is bound to drive grit into the pores of the material. They prefer to dress the area with a fine file, very lightly applied. While it is permissible to smooth out damage in either way, there is no possibility of restoring a piston that has been deeply scored, or one on which the lands between the grooves have been damaged. In either case, it is better to scrap the piston and fit a new one.

Where piston damage is found, the bore must be examined too. Material from the piston may have welded itself to the bore, and there may also be scoring. This is particularly likely if a ring has broken, since the ends of a fractured ring can be highly efficient cutting tools.

Light alloy deposited on the bore surface can be removed by use of a bearing scraper. Also – providing the bore is subsequently swilled out with paraffin – it is permissible to use 400 grade wet-or-dry paper, well wetted with paraffin, to polish off the last remnants.

Refit the rings to each piston, once you are satisfied that all components are serviceable, and make a final check by using feelers to measure the ring side clearance in the groove. Typical standard clearances would be around 0.004in (0.09mm) for a top ring and 0.003in (0.05mm) for a lower one. Usually, the service limit is about 0.006in (0.16mm) for all rings.

Before refitting the piston, check the gudgeon pin and small-end bearing. Take the pin out of the piston and insert it into the bearing. Clearances in this heavily loaded area are microscopic – radial play of more than 0.002in (0.05mm) makes the bearing unserviceable. The standard clearance is likely to be no higher than 0.0009in (0.02mm), so accurate measurement demands the use of a micrometer. Your tactile senses are a good guide, however. Clearances that small cannot be measured by touch, but if you can feel even the slightest movement up or down when you alternately pull and press the pin the likelihood is that the bearing is worn.

Caged needle roller bearings can be removed from the con-rod eye by gentle pressure. Plain bearings – less common in modern practice – need to be pressed out. The time-honoured way of doing this is to butt the new bush against the face of the old. On the other side, place a piece of tube just a little bigger than the diameter of the bush. Use a G-clamp to hold the parts together; gently tightening the screw on the clamp then presses the new bush in and the old bush out in one operation. Usually, the new bush will need to be reamed, once it is in place, and any oil holes or slots drilled or cut.

The last stage of the top overhaul is to decarbonise the exhaust system. Deal with the tailpipe as already described, but for a full overhaul also check the exhaust pipe itself. Carbon can easily build up in the pipe bends. One way to remove it is to soak the pipe in a strong solution of caustic soda. This eats away carbon, but be warned – it also eats away light alloys and human tissues. No light-alloy component should be placed in a caustic soda bath; it will instantly corrode. Wear protective gloves to handle the soda bath and the parts and use a pair of eyeshields to guard your eyes against splashes. On occasion, when nothing else has been to hand, a full-face helmet, visor down, has provided adequate eye protection.

An alternative to soaking the carbon out is to acquire a length of used chain – preferably bicycle chain or the chain off an old moped – and simply thread it through the pipe. See-saw the chain from end to end and the links will steadily scrape away all those deposits that otherwise cannot be reached.

One final way of dealing with heavy carbon in exhausts is to burn it out, using a blow-torch. This can be highly effective *providing* the system is removed from the bike first and the job is done well away from any possible fire risk area. A gas torch is the best tool for the job, although a blow-lamp will serve. Once the carbon is incandescent, it will continue to burn given just the occasional lick of flame.

For rebuilding the motor, you will need a little oil to smear on the bores and bearings, new gaskets as applicable and, in the case of multi-cylinder engines, a few strips of wood of equal depth and ring clamps for each piston.

With single-cylinder strokers it's easy enough to compress each ring in turn as the barrel is slid over the piston – providing, of course, you take care to compress the ring so that its ends are against the peg. Start with the piston at about half-stroke, to give yourself a bit of room for manoeuvre, and simply lower the barrel until the top of the piston enters it. Squeeze the top ring gently, and ease the barrel down just enough to trap it. Even with a stud-located barrel, it's usually possible to twist it a little each way to ease entry by 'screwing' the first ring home.

Now hold the barrel steady, compress the second ring, and ease the barrel down again. As soon as the ring has entered, support the piston at its lower face and push the barrel right down to it. Then seat the barrel.

Hold it in place and gently turn the engine to check that the piston slides smoothly up and down the bore. Then refit the head; tighten the head nuts a little at a time using the maker's recommended sequence if possible or diagonally if this is unknown. Lastly, use a torque wrench to tighten the nuts to the specified setting.

Refit the ancillaries – the reed valve unit, if removed, the exhaust, the cleaned and regapped sparking plug (a new one at each decoke makes better sense). Run the engine, and recheck the torque of all nuts and bolts after the first ten miles.

Do not force the barrel down if it will not slide easily

Rebuilding a multi is different in detail rather than in principle. The problem is to insert two or three pistons into their bores. Luckily, many multi-cylinder two-strokes have individual cylinder barrels and these can be treated as three separate single-cylinder engines. Where there is a single block containing multiple bores, however, the procedure has to be modified.

Set all pistons to about half-stroke. Install ring clamps on each to hold the rings compressed. A ring clamp is basically only a sheet-steel sheath, marginally larger in diameter than the piston, with a bolt and nut which can be tightened so that it will hold the rings in compression. Since it is not a clamp fit, it slides down the piston as the barrel is lowered on to its upper edge, feeding the compressed rings in as it moves. It is then undone and removed before seating the barrel.

Ring clamps can be improvised from any sheet metal, providing care is taken to remove any sharp edges that could gouge the light-alloy working surfaces. Even a discarded tin makes suitable raw material. A ready-made alternative is to use a

Jubilee screw-drive clip tightened around a shim-steel 'apron' just sufficiently to hold the rings in compression.

With the pistons set, and the clamps in place, position the wood blocks – one on each side, and one in the middle, will be adequate. They must be of such a height that the barrel can be lowered down to stop just short of the pistons.

With the assembly resting on the wood blocks, feed in the first piston. When the rings have entered, remove the clamps, and then support the next piston while the engine is turned just sufficiently to bring it, too, up to the mouth of the barrel. Don't get too enthusiastic when turning the motor, or the piston that has already been inserted may come out again. If needs be, reduce the working height of the blocks before attempting to fit the second piston. With a twin, one piston will rise as the other falls.

Depending on the particular motor, it may be possible to insert all pistons at the same time at around the mid-stroke position, when both are at the same distance from the crankcase mouth. It's all a matter of how much working clearance you have below the barrel. Where all pistons will enter, the depth of the blocks used as barrel supports must be such that the barrel can be lowered on to the pistons, rather than each piston in turn being eased up into the bore. One thin block on top of a thick one helps here. With the two blocks installed, the barrel should come just short of the pistons so that it is supported while you line them up. Sliding the top block away then allows the barrel to come down sufficiently for the pistons to enter.

Top overhaul methods, four-strokes

So far as the actual decarbonising routine is concerned, the procedure for four-strokes is similar in principle to that for two-strokes. So, the first job for a four-stroke owner is to read the foregoing two-stroke section.

Like the two-stroke, the four-stroke has piston, rings, combustion chamber, ports, exhaust pipe and tail-pipe. It has a barrel or block that has to be removed for access to the rings and small-end bearing. It is possible to carry out a short decoke simply by removing the head, leaving the piston and barrel undisturbed. This can save much dismantling in the case of motors such as the Honda CX500 or the 'Gold Wing', in which the bottom half of the engine needs to be stripped – at least partially – to enable the pistons to be removed. With a short decoke of this type, the piston crown alone is cleaned, as already described in the two-stroke section, while the rings are left undisturbed.

At first sight, it is a technique that omits an important part of the top overhaul. However, four-stroke rings are far less vulnerable than those on a two-stroke and, being free to revolve in their grooves, also tend to be self-cleaning. With car engines, piston removal is only carried out at long intervals, when the bores and rings are judged to have worn. This is usually after the engine has run for a minimum of 40,000–50,000 miles and is having its second or third top overhaul. Allowing that a bike engine is usually a higher-performance unit requiring a sharper state of tune, there should still be no need to lift the barrels in the first 30,000 miles.

When the time comes, the procedure is – again – almost identical to that already described. There is no complication with ring pegging, but four-stroke motors usually have an extra ring – a deep, slotted one, whose purpose is to scrape excess oil off the bores. This is known as an oil control ring, or a scraper.

One point to watch is that rings for different positions have different profiles in many cases. The top ring may have rounded shoulders, as on the Suzuki GS400/425 range, or its shoulders may be bevelled and the working face angled inwards, as on the small Honda 'step-throughs'. The second compression ring can have an entirely different profile, with perhaps a bevelled working face, or a notch on the underside. The oil control ring can even be built up out of a central spring-steel spacer, using two thin 'side rail' rings.

It is vitally important, therefore, to ensure that any ring that has been removed is reinstalled in its correct groove and the right way round. Differing methods of identifying the rings are used, but as with two-strokes it is usually safe to assume that the ring identification marks will be on the upper surface. The top ring also frequently has a hard chrome finish and appears bright whereas the second ring, lacking it, looks greyish.

Where the barrel has been lifted for a full top overhaul, it is essential to ensure that all sealing rings for oilways between the barrel and the crankcase are renewed. A new cylinder base gasket should be installed as a matter of course, and before this is done all traces of the old one must be removed. This often means scraping the remnants away with a sharpened piece of hardwood, or the rounded end of an old hacksaw blade, using paraffin as a lubricant. Care has to be taken not to let the scrapings fall into the crankcase, or enter any of the oilways.

It is now common practice for gaskets to be treated at the factory with a heat-actuated sealant which bonds to the adjacent metal surfaces as the engine warms up. Gaskets of this type have to be fitted dry – no oil, no grease, and most certainly no jointing compound. They also tend to have a tenacious grip and to make removal of components rather difficult. It's worth remembering that if the barrel appears to be solidly held when you try to remove it the cause may be a concealed bolt or nut that you have missed, and to double-check the point. When you are certain that all fastenings are off, it's probably the gasket that is bonding the barrel to the crankcase. Examine the finning, and you'll find that there are sections that are much shallower than others, where a strengthening rib has been cast in or an oilway passes through. Those are the spots to hit – hard – with a rubber mallet to jar the block free. It's crude but usually effective, although even professional mechanics have been known to break a cooling fin in the process. On a very few engines, the point is catered for by indentations being cast into the bottom of the block where a lever can be inserted. Use the facility if it's there, but never try to lever off a block by driving a tool into the crankcase/barrel joint. All sticking barrels will eventually yield to a combination of scientifically applied brute force with the rubber mallet and periodic application of local heat round the recalcitrant joint.

Head removal, four-strokes

Start the top overhaul by cleaning the outside of the engine. This not only prevents dirt entering the 'works' but also ensures that the parts themselves are more pleasant to handle.

According to model, remove the tank and then carry out whatever preliminary stripping is necessary. With multi-carburettor bikes it saves a lot of work and heart-burning if the 'nest' of carbs is left undisturbed. It is usually possibly to undo the inlet stubs, leaving the carbs and their complicated balanced linkage still in place on the air hoses. At worst, the whole carburettor/linkage assembly should be removed as a unit. Rebalancing multiple carburettors is *not* fun.

Also to be removed as a unit, wherever possible, is the exhaust system. Although this can be dismantled, it is always better to leave the pipe/silencer joints

Multiple carbs cannot always be removed in sets but do so wherever possible

A C-spanner may be required to remove the exhaust pipe

The silencer is usually held to the sub-frame by a bracket

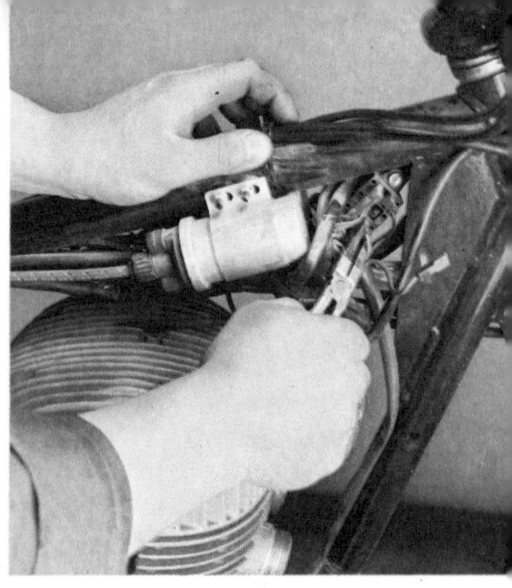

Various engine/frame electrical leads may have to be removed

undisturbed and so reduce the possibility of introducing an oil or gas leak into a previously sound assembly.

Where the head can be removed with the engine still in the frame the preliminary dismantling is virtually complete at this stage. Only the HT leads and, possibly, the LT leads need to be disconnected, and the tachometer drive freed where this terminates on the head. For an engine-out job, extra dismantling usually involves parting the chain and sometimes detaching the footrest hangers, foot controls, air filter box and so forth to give access room. The clutch cable needs to be freed – it is often better to leave it attached at the engine end and simply disconnect it at the lever, unthreading the cable as the motor is lifted. There is normally a junction box for the alternator leads, too.

It pays to drain the oil – up to half a gallon of lubricant adds to the weight you have to lift – and where the oil filter is mounted in an external housing taking it off at this stage makes for a less awkward shape to be manoeuvred out of the frame.

Double-check that all engine cables and leads are free and then remove the engine mounting bolts and, where applicable, the engine plates. The unit should now be reasonably easy to lift out. Up to a 250, this could be a single-handed job. Larger motors really demand two pairs of hands, especially to ensure that nothing snags on the frame tubes to cause damage to the finish.

Before removing the cylinder head, make sure that all preparations have been made. The valves, for example, need to be kept in their proper order. So, too, do pushrods. The best way to do this is to have ready a piece of stiff cardboard punched through with the appropriate number of holes. These

A drift may be required to remove the mounting bolts

There are mounting bolts at front and rear of the engine

should be labelled in groups – 'No 1 cyl: ex pushrod; in pushrod; ex valve; in valve', for example. There is no need to make provision for the valve springs, however, since these should be discarded and new springs fitted at each top overhaul. Given the work involved in renewing springs, it is simply not worthwhile to miss the chance of changing them.

Similarly, items such as inlet guide oil seals and all oilway O-rings should be discarded and new parts fitted on rebuilding. Decoke sets will usually include them, but to avoid being caught with no parts and no bike on the road, check when you buy the decoke set that it is in fact complete.

Single-overhead-cam motors

A typical head removal sequence for a single-overhead-cam (sohc) twin such as that of Yamaha's XS250 would be first to remove the contact-breaker cover and then centre-punch matching marks on the head and the contact-breaker backplate so that the timing will not be 'lost'. The complete breaker assembly can then be removed. Usually this involves undoing the cam centre bolt and a couple of plate locking screws – *not* the fixed point mounting plate screw – so that the cam and backplate can be slipped off. The centrifugal advance/retard unit is then pulled off the shaft. Designs differ, but there will normally be a mounting peg or dowel to detach as well.

Some motors have a single cambox held by screws or bolts; others have an additional breather cover bolted on. Remove the cambox cover first. It is common practice, with sohc engines, for the rockers to come away with it.

Chain-driven camshafts normally require the tensioner to be released at this point. The slippers may simply slide out, or they may be held by a single bolt on the cam-chain tunnel.

The cam cover must be removed for any cylinder head work

The upper jockey sprocket must be unbolted on double-overhead-cam power units

Clamp the camshafts until the bearing caps are off

Shims are used to make adjustments to the valve clearances

Remove them, and there will be sufficient slack in the chain to permit the camshaft removal to proceed.

The best way to deal with the chain is to twist a piece of stiff wire round it, so that it can be dropped down into the tunnel and then recovered easily when rebuilding starts. With the wire attached, undo the camshaft sprocket securing bolts – these are usually specially shaped fastenings which *must* go back in their original places – and then pull the sprocket and chain together away from the shaft. The shaft can then be slipped out of the head, the sprocket removed, and the chain dropped into the tunnel.

Double-overhead-cam motors

With a double-overhead-cam (dohc) motor such as that of the Suzuki GS750 'four' or GS425 twin the procedure is complicated by the use of bucket tappets and a long single chain driving two camshafts. On this type of motor, the cam-chain tensioner first has to be locked – a matter of undoing its adjuster screw locknut slightly, then tightening the screw – and then removed. With the tension off the chain, the upper jockey sprocket can be detached.

To prevent the pressure of the valve springs canting the camshafts as their bearing caps are released, and so damaging the journals, each shaft has to be clamped for this operation. The clamp stays in place until the bearing caps are off, when it is released to free the camshaft. Then the bucket tappets and the shims are slipped out – a bar magnet is the best tool for this tricky job, although it can be done in some cases using a pair of tweezers or even a piece of dowelling with a dab of grease on the end.

Bucket-tappet motors have their valve clearances adjusted by means of shims and the thickness of each shim can vary from cylinder to cylinder. It is essential that when the shims are removed they should be kept in their proper order, or rebuilding will be hindered.

The rocker assembly is usually bolted on

The head should come off with a sharp tug

Pushrod motors

Pushrod engines – the Honda CX500 Vee-twin unit, for example – are easier to work on since they have no head-mounted contact-breaker system and no bucket tappets. Here, one is almost back to basics. Remove the rocker cover. Undo the bolts holding the rocker assembly, working criss-cross so that spring pressure is evenly relieved, then lift the assembly off. Spin each pushrod smartly to break the oil film in the cam follower – neglect this, and the follower may be pulled out of position – and lift out the rod. This is all that is involved, although on all water-cooled motors the cooling system must also be drained.

Head removal, general

Now the procedure is similar for all engines. Following the head bolt sequence set out in the workshop manual, release all head bolts a few turns at a time.

Where the sequence is not known, use the 'rule of thumb' method of working from the centre outwards, loosening to left and right alternately.

Check for those 'hidden' head fastenings. Some of the ohc models have a small bolt inserted from below on the cam-chain tunnel, and there may also be a small bolt coyly concealed in the finning in the general area of the sparking plug hole. Such fixings should be removed first.

Give the head a sharp tug. If this fails to free it – and we've noted that current gaskets do tend to have a tenacious hold – use internal pressure. If you have left the plugs in place, you will be rewarded here. A quick dab on the kickstarter – or on the starter button if you're all-electric – will send the pistons up the cylinders, generating a pressure which is usually enough to break the joint. If not, then it's a question of jarring the head off. Before picking up the rubber mallet, however, make a second very careful check that no fastenings have been left in place. Jarring a freed-off head with the right tools and the right amount of force will usually do no damage – though accidents will and do happen – but welting a head that is still securely bolted to the block is almost certain to end in damaged fins.

When you are absolutely sure that nothing but the gasket is holding the head firmly – the studs are not usually a tight enough fit to do so, but may be contributing if there is corrosion on the adjacent surfaces – give the head a hard sharp blow with a rubber mallet. As with all hammering, one good blow is more effective and less likely to damage the workpiece than a series of taps.

Repeat the jarring at each corner of the head until the joint 'gives'.

If you have no rubber mallet, use a block of softwood bedded end-grain on against the head to form a pad, and strike the other end of the block with a heavy ordinary hammer.

Where jarring fails, local heating may work. Playing the flame of a gas torch round the joint – keep the torch moving all the time so that the heating is even – and then jarring again will eventually do the job. Where you suspect that stud corrosion is a contributory factor, however, it may be necessary to exercise patience and constantly dribble penetrating oil down the studs, leaving it to soak through overnight.

Removing the valves

Apart from a couple of oddities – the Honda CB450/CB500T range, with torsion bar springs, and 'desmo' Ducatis with no springs at all – all current bikes have similar valve arrangements.

All use the poppet valve, held to its seat by single or double coil springs pressing upwards on to a valve cap. The cap is retained by split collets which engage in a recess in the valve stem and in a taper in the cap. To free the valves, a valve

A valve spring compressor is required to remove the valves

spring compressor is used. This is basically a screw clamp, one end of which seats against the valve head while the prongs engage on the cap. Wind up the screw, and the spring is compressed until the cap is clear of the collets. These can then be eased out with a screwdriver and the compressor released to free the cap and spring. The valve itself slides out of its guide, though on some machines a small valve stem oil seal may have to be removed first. It is more usual for this to be accommodated in a cap pressed over the top of the guide.

With the Honda torsion bar system, the removal procedure is to loosen the torsion bar securing bolt, and then to tension the bar. An arrow is stamped on the end of it to show the direction in which force should be applied. Keeping up the tension, the bolt is then removed and the bar pulled sideways out of the head, with one hand, while the other holds the valve return rocker. This is splined to the bar, and comes free as the bar is withdrawn. Take care with the torsion bar, since this type of spring is very sensitive to surface damage. Torsion bars must also invariably be refitted in their original positions. The valve is held by a miniature cap with collets, freed by pressing the cap down the stem.

On the desmodromic Ducatis the arrangement is somewhat similar, but while the Honda uses a torsion bar spring to actuate the lower rocker, the Ducati has a mechanical operation.

Split collets usually hold the valve in place

With the springs off, the valve is withdrawn

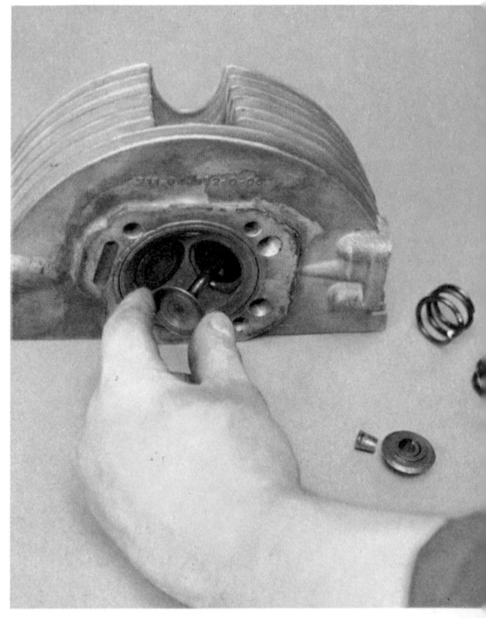

Above: in the desmodromic Ducatis, miniature collets hold the valve cap in place
Below: the Ducati desmodromic layout

Spring check

With all bikes other than these, it's best to make it a rule always to renew the valve springs when the head is lifted. Springs shorten in use, and it makes sense to take this chance of changing them. If you want to economise, however, you *can* check the springs for serviceability. You'll need one new spring for the job, a G-clamp or vice and three small pieces of steel sheet. Place the new spring and the old one end to end – separated by one of the steel pieces – in the clamp. Put a steel piece at each end to act as a bearer. Tighten the clamp – carefully, to avoid the springs flying out of the vice's grip – until both springs are lightly compressed. Now measure them. There should be no significant difference in their length if the old spring is still serviceable.

Ports can be cleaned out with a rotary wire brush

This test is more reliable than that of simply measuring the free length, which is a figure that alters for each bike. As a rule, however, take it that a spring that has shortened by 2.5% on a free length test has passed its service limit. So, if you measure a spring that should be 50mm long and you find that it is slightly less than 49mm in free length, it is unfit for further use.

Valve stem oil seals

Here again, it is best to regard these small and relatively cheap parts as expendable. The seals prevent oil escaping from the valve chest into the combustion chambers – and you don't need to burn much oil to lose the cost of a new seal!

Simply lift off the old seal and discard it. When you refit the valves, remember to lubricate the seals with oil before inserting the stems, to prevent any chance of scuffing the seal faces.

Decarbonising the head and piston

In general, follow the procedure already described under the two-stroke section. However, when using a wire brush in a power drill to clean the combustion chambers, protect the valve seats by dropping the valves back into place.

Checking the valves

Use wet-or-dry paper torn into strips about an inch wide to polish the exposed areas of the valve stems, after first scraping away the worst of the carbon. Scrape and polish the valve head. Examine the valve seat; some pitting is normal, but this should be only superficial. Heavy pitting means the valve is useless or that it and the head seats must be recut by a workshop.

Some makers, such as Suzuki, specify a valve service limit based on the thickness of the valve head up to

A badly pitted valve must be discarded

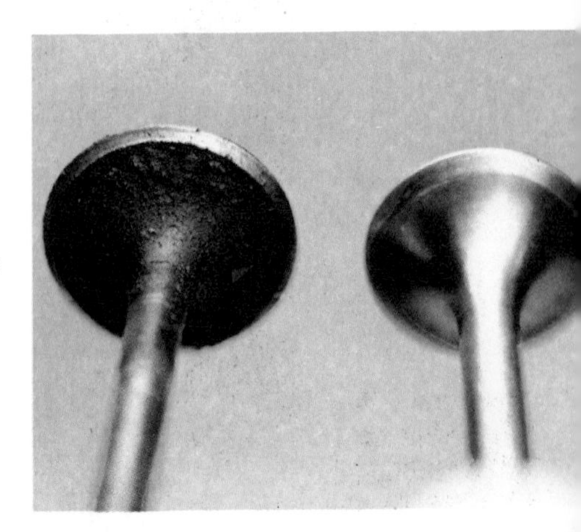

Engineer's blue provides a good guide to valve seating

Don't recut a valve seat without knowing the correct angles

the conical seating. Typically, this should be around 1mm, the valve being discarded when it falls to half that thickness. A second check is on the thickness of the seating area itself. This is established by using engineer's blue or red lead on the seats and rotating the valve in the head. The valve is then lifted, and the thickness of the resulting marks measured. Typically, the seating area on the valve head should be a millimetre wide. If it has increased by half as much again, the valve is unserviceable.

Checking the head seats

The same test will have shown up any deficiency in the head seats. Here too the standard seating area will be around a millimetre, and the permissible increase in width half as much again. It is possible to recut the valve seats, using hand-operated cutters, providing the correct angles are known. These are usually given in the workshop manual. On the GS425, for example, the seats have a 15-degree inner bevel; a 45-degree middle bevel; and a 75-degree outer bevel. The 15-degree and 75-degree cuts are made first, taking off as little metal as possible. Then the 45-degree cut is made and is continued until the correct seat width is obtained.

On the CB 200, valve seat grinders are used for bevels of 60, 90 and 120 degrees, again finishing with a valve seat width of 1/1.4mm.

Lapping-in valves

This process used to be known as 'grinding' the valves and it was a brutal operation, using coarse paste to rip away metal until the valve was sunk into its seat. It worked with the old engines that some seem to

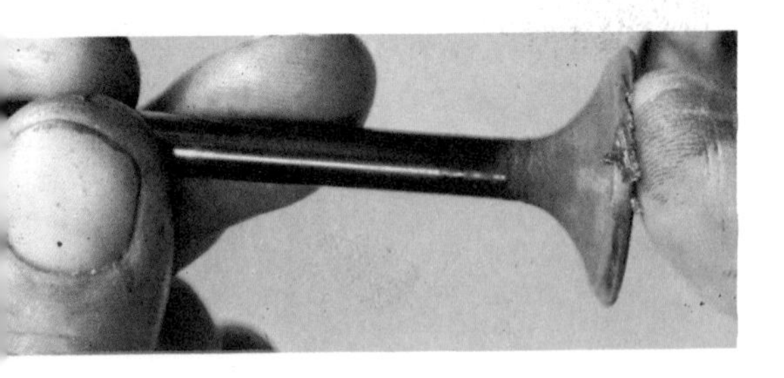

Smear grinding paste evenly round the seat

regard as classics, but with modern high-performance motors such tactics are out. Valve lapping is intended to give the final touch to carefully recut seats, or to seats that were within the specified limits and that needed no recutting.

After cleaning and polishing the combustion chamber, ports, valve stems and valve head, the final operation is to reseal the valve by lapping away any minor surface inconsistencies.

Use only fine grinding paste. Attach the valve grinding tool to the valve head – or use a large-bladed screwdriver where the head is slotted to take it. Smear grinding paste round the valve head seat, and drop the valve into place. To ease lifting and turning, some mechanics interpose a light coil spring between the valve head and the guide. Pressing lightly to hold the valve to its seat, rub the stem of the tool between your palms to oscillate the valve on its seat. After a dozen or so cuts, lift the valve and turn it through 90 degrees. Press it on to its seat again, and repeat the lapping-in until the valve has made one complete turn. Then lift it, and swill away all the paste with paraffin.

Examine the seats in the head and on the valve. You should see just one continuous thin grey line of contact round each. If the line is broken, add more paste and lap again. Purist mechanics impart a final polish by giving one extra lap with fine paste diluted with paraffin after line contact has been established.

Once lapping is finished, thoroughly wash all components in a paraffin bath to make certain that all traces of abrasive have been removed. It's the very last thing you want inside your engine, so be meticulous about this. Dab the parts to remove most of the paraffin, then leave them to dry off.

Checking guides

The only really accurate method of assessing valve/guide wear is to rig a dial gauge horizontally, its foot just touching the stem with the valve lifted partly out of the guide. The total side play in that direction having been measured, the gauge is repositioned so that a second reading can be taken at right angles to it. On average, play should be no more than 0.04mm, with a service limit of around 0.1mm.

Not many of us have dial gauges, of course, so we have to settle for cruder means. Taking a feeler gauge of service limit thickness, shave off a sliver about a millimetre wide to form a tiny feeler. Press the valve hard to one side, and try to slip this miniature limit gauge into the guide/valve gap. If it fits, you've passed the service limit and need new guides. If it doesn't, and you cannot *feel* excessive play when working the valve from side to side, then your guides have life in them yet.

Renewing guides

Most guides are an interference fit in the head, and are located vertically by either a circlip or by a machined-in shoulder. One can drive them out from the port end, upwards, using a shouldered drift and a heavy hammer.

First, heat the head to around 100°C. The quickest way is with a gas torch, but you could roast the head in the oven or even dunk it in a bath of boiling water. Insert the drift into the guide and butt the shoulder against the end. A sharp hammer blow should drive it out. Fit the circlip to the new guide, if it is the type that requires one, and insert it from above. Insert the drift, this time in the top of the guide, and drive the guide home. When the head has cooled, ream the bore of the guide to the correct dimensions.

Valve stems

There is no point in fitting new guides if the valve stems are worn. Make wear checks in both directions, as with the guide, preferably using a micrometer. However, a vernier calliper will give reasonably accurate results. If the valve is within limits, place a straight-edge along the stem and check visually that there is no distortion. Alternatively, roll the stem along the edge of a flat surface. Discard any valve that has a worn or bent stem.

Rocker gear

Slide the rockers off their spindles – with some motors this must be done before the camshaft can be removed – and check the contact surfaces for wear. There must be no pitting. With screw-type adjusters, an indentation forms where the tappet contacts the valve stem. When this becomes pronounced, it is impossible to

Slide the rockers off their spindles in order to check wear

Wear such as this indicates a lack of lubrication

obtain accurate tappet clearances, since the feeler gauge measures the unworn sections only, while the valve stem meets the worn part. Discard the indented adjusters and fit new ones.

Check the rocker-to-spindle clearance. This is usually very fine and there should be no perceptible play. A clearance of 0.1mm is a typical service limit, beyond which both parts should be renewed.

Pushrods

Bent pushrods usually indicate a bout of over-revving, perhaps due to a missed gearchange. A fall-off in performance and an increase in valve gear noise after such a mishap suggests that the rods should be checked for truth.

Place the rods horizontally on a plate glass face-plate and check that they roll easily. A straight rod will do so; a bent one won't. Renew any rod that does not pass this test.

Head faces

To check the truth of the cylinder head face, set a straight-edge at a slight angle across the inverted cylinder head, and run it across the head's entire width. If you can see gaps between the head and the straight-edge, stop moving it and measure the extent of the warp with feeler gauges.

Permissible warp varies from motor to motor, but Kawasaki recommend that the entire head of the Z1000 'four' should be replaced if as much as 0.25mm is found. A new Kawasaki head, incidentally, has a maximum distortion of 0.05mm.

Less severe wear can be rectified by having the head surface ground by an engineering shop. Minimal wear can be dealt with at home by lapping the joint on a face-plate.

Camshaft journals

Common practice is for overhead camshafts to run unbushed in the head, but Kawasaki use split plain bearings. The wear in the camshaft journals can be checked using Plastigage – a useful but professional material for which you will probably have to go to a motor factor. Do the job when the head is refitted.

Install the camshaft lower bearings and lay a strip of Plastigage so that it will run along the axis of the shaft. Add the shaft itself, complete with drive chain. Fit the upper camshaft bearing caps, and torque the assembly down. The effect is to squash the Plastigage strips.

Now undo the caps, remove the camshaft, and use the special gauge supplied with the strips to measure them. The reading tells you what the internal clearance between shaft and bearings is. On the big Kawasaki, the clearance can be no more than 0.16mm on any bearing before *all* bearings have to be renewed.

Honda, who do not use bearings in their silicon-rich alloy heads, simply recommend on 'fours' such as the CB400F and CB550F that the bearing surfaces should be inspected visually and that the head should be renewed if they are worn or damaged.

Camshaft check

Purists may wish to check the camshaft to ensure that it is running true. This is done by mounting the shaft between V-block centres, rigging a dial gauge and noting the readings. A variation of around 0.1mm usually means that the shaft is hopelessly bent. Most of us have to be content with a visual examination, however. Look for any signs of surface damage on the journals and the cams. These shafts are case-hardened and once the skin is breached they can wear with catastrophic speed. The result is ever-changing tappet clearances and a very noisy engine, together with swarf dropping into the sump. Renew the camshaft if there is significant surface pitting. Check the cam followers, too, for similar damage.

This camshaft has suffered overheating and excessive wear

Barrels and pistons

Proceed with checking barrels and pistons as for two-stroke engines. Extra points to watch on four-strokes are that there will be oilway seals between the barrel and the crankcase, that in some designs the gudgeon pins can be removed only with the aid of a hydraulic press and that there may be cam followers in the base of the block in pushrod motors.

Before rebuilding, it is permissible to remove oil glaze from the cylinders, where these are of cast iron or steel. They should be rubbed, criss-cross, with very fine wet-or-dry paper cloth, well wetted with paraffin, until a matt working surface is obtained. This procedure is normally carried out only when new rings are to be fitted, as an aid to bedding-down.

Rebuilding

The rebuilding procedure is common to four-stroke and two-stroke motors. With the four-stroke, however, there is the added complication of installing the valve gear.

Refit the valves to the cylinder head first. After seating the valve caps, give each valve a sharp tap on the stem with a plastic-faced mallet to ensure that it moves and that the collets are securely home. Then invert the head, and fill each combustion chamber with paraffin. Leave it a while, and check that there has been no leakage past the valves that may call for extra lapping. This is the stage at which tuners like to measure the capacity of each combustion chamber by using a graduated beaker to pour in the paraffin. They then rout out the chambers with the smallest capacities until each is even. This results in a minimal improvement in engine smoothness.

Refit the cylinder head, and offer up the camshaft(s) in ohc motors. Where more than one shaft is to be installed, it is usual for the different shafts to be marked for position and handing. Exhaust camshafts are stamped 'Ex', inlet camshafts 'In'. Where the shaft will fit either way round, it will also be marked 'L' or 'R' at the appropriate point. Before dropping the shaft into place, smear a little molybdenum grease evenly over its journals and lubricate the various bearing surfaces in the cylinder head with engine oil.

For timing the valves, it is essential to have the workshop manual for the particular bike, since marking systems vary from make to make and from model to model.

With pushrod motors the problem does not arise, since the camshaft will have remained undisturbed in the crankcase. However, here it is essential to lubricate the cam followers and to dribble a little engine oil down the pushrod tubes and over the rocker mechanism.

Before refitting the valve cover on ohc motors, give their valve gear, too, a squirt of engine oil so that they do not start up dry. Then fit the cover and torque down its fastenings to complete the rebuild.

Bottom-End Overhauls

Stripping and rebuilding the bottom end is a bench job, but since even a light engine tends to be a rather heavy object to handle as much of the dismantling as possible should be carried out with the motor still in the frame.

Lighter work

It is not always possible to lift the head and barrels before dropping the engine out. Where it can be done, though, it should be done. Besides reducing the weight that has to be handled, it also makes for a much less clumsy object to manoeuvre out of the rather confined space available.

If that option isn't open to you, there are still useful jobs that can be done. With the side covers off, the clutch can be removed and so can the generator unit. It is usually possible to remove the starter as well and the carbs can come off the head.

With the motor lightened as much as possible, place a support underneath it – the heavier engines sometimes demand the use of a small car jack – and release the mountings. Then either lift the motor out of the frame or, in the case of spine-frame bikes, perhaps lift the front wheel and swivel the rest of the bike clear of the engine.

Cleaning up

The first job to do on the bench is to clean away the dirt that is almost certain to be adhering to the underside of the crankcase. It will be ninety per cent road filth, which will be very gritty, and which must not be allowed to find its way inside the engine. A stiff brush and some paraffin will quickly deal with it.

Preliminary strip

With all ancillaries removed, you will have on the bench just the

A small hydraulic bottle jack in use

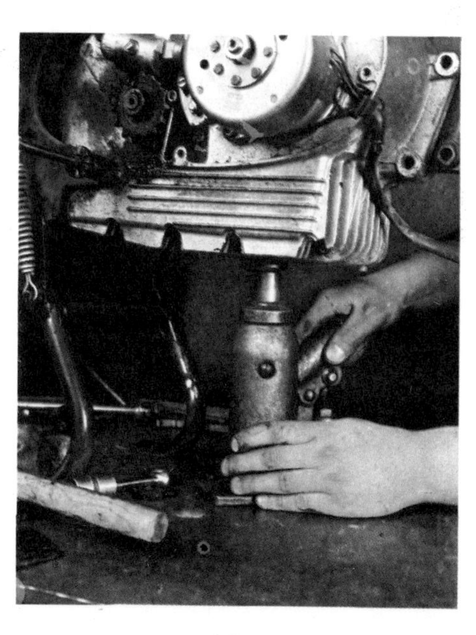

crankcase/gearcase assembly, with the crankshaft, rods, gearshafts, selector mechanism, kickstart mechanism and internal drives still in place. A bottom-end strip is for attention to the engine parts only, but unfortunately with unit-construction machines quite a bit of the transmission also has to be removed.

With the clutch already off, and on most bikes the primary drive dismantled, the next step is to remove just those parts of the transmission that must come off before the cases can be split. Obviously, this varies from bike to bike. On the Honda CB250N motor, for example, it's the selector arm that comes away first – just spring it out of engagement with the selector drum and pull it off. On the Yamaha XS250, the kickstarter mechanism comes off before the selectors.

An exception is a bike on which the cases split vertically, not horizontally. On the 50cc Suzuki, for example, all the selector mechanism can be left in position in the right-hand case, while the lefthand case is lifted off – an option not open to a mechanic working on the Suzuki's bigger brother, the GT500 two-stroke twin that has horizontally split cases. With the selector arm out, however, the rest of the transmission will not normally need to be disturbed, providing you're reasonably careful.

Splitting the cases

Check, very carefully, the position of all crankcase fastenings. It is usual for these to be bolts or screws inserted

Opposite page: bottom end of the engine, without ancillaries but with the crankshaft, connecting rods, gears etc still in place
Left: crankcase fastenings can differ in length. Take careful note of their positions on dismantling
Below: after all the fasteners are removed a little tapping should soon split the crankcase

from the underside, but there are instances where there are also a few that enter from the upper case into the lower. A further complication is that not all the fastenings are of equal length, and when – as with the XS250 – you are subsequently faced with a mixed bag of 21 screws to sort out, the wisdom of making up a rough sketchplan to show which goes where, *as they are removed*, really strikes home!

Even the types of screw used can differ quite widely. At one time, the Japanese factories had an obsessive devotion to cross-headed screws, which could usually be removed only after placing a drift against each head and jarring the threads with a sharp hammer blow (or by using an impact screwdriver).

Some makers then moved towards socket-headed screws – fine, so long as you made up your own adaptor to enable a hexagon key to be used with a socket set. Now, hexagon-headed bolts with integral washers appear to be in favour, and life is easier for all.

When releasing the crankcase fastenings, follow the rule of starting as centrally as possible and working diagonally side to side, freeing each fastener off a little to relieve tension, and then spinning them out when they are all loose. When you are certain that all fastenings between the crankcase halves have been removed, tap around the joint with a rubber mallet and the lower case should come away, leaving all the internals in the inverted upper case on the bench.

Removing the crankshaft

With most bikes, the rest of the job so far as the engine is concerned is little more than a formality. Just lift the crankshaft out of the case, complete with rods and perhaps the cam chain, and proceed with the bearing checks. The process is not invariable, however, since some motors are more complicated. The Honda CB250N/CB400N parallel twins, for example, have a massive oil chamber/main bearing holder still retaining the crankshaft, and there are also counterbalance shafts and their drives to remove. These also have to be considered on the Suzuki GS400/425 range, among others.

The 'fours' also tend to have an extra stage before crankshaft removal, although this is quite a simple one. It is common practice for the primary drive on this type of motor to be taken by an endless Morse chain from a chainwheel in the centre of the crank to a chainwheel/shock absorber unit mounted on a countershaft. The gear train is then driven, through the clutch, by a second reduction from this shaft.

Since the chain is endless – and massive – the countershaft has to be released and the chain lifted off it

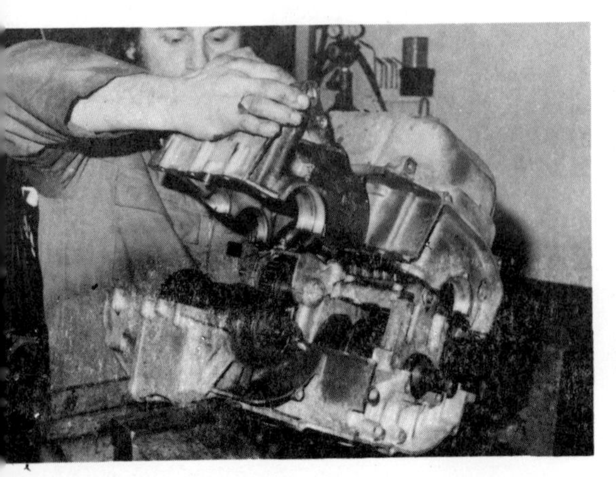

Here the crankcase is split and all the internals are revealed in the lower half

The Honda CB250N's oil chamber and main bearing holder being lifted out

before the crankshaft can be removed. This is usually easy enough – on the Honda CB400F, for example, the shaft just slides out, leaving the chainwheel unit loose in the case. On the Kawasaki Z650, it can be tapped out with a suitable drift, while on the Honda CB550F it pulls out with the help of an extractor, just like the alternator rotor. As a point of interest, an old C90 spindle makes an excellent puller for both units.

Splitting two-stroke crankcases

This is one area in which the simplicity of the two-stroke sometimes disappears. Two-stroke crankcases have to be gastight, and it is not always an easy job to open them up. Worse still, the motors that *should* be the most straightforward are often the trickiest.

There's no substitute for a look at the workshop manual when deciding whether a two-stroke case can be easily split or not. East European bikes, for instance, have a reputation for being easy to service. Yet, both the 350cc Jawa twin and the 250cc MZ single really demand the use of some pretty sophisticated pullers to part the cases. With the MZ, you *can* manage by judiciously jarring the projecting shafts with a rubber mallet, while suspending the motor by the opposite case just clear of the bench but it is not a procedure which is really to be recommended.

Similarly, there is no consistency even within makes. While on a Suzuki GT185, for example, this is a perfectly straightforward job – just split the upper case from the lower – the TS125 from the same stable needs a jig-cum-puller of remarkable complexity.

Crankshaft check

Once the shaft is on the bench, the checking procedure varies according to the type. All two-strokes, and some four-strokes like the Honda CB175, have built-up cranks. There is very little indeed that can be done with any built-up crankshaft. Built-up cranks invariably have anti-friction bearings (ball, roller, or needle-roller) at the big ends and the mains. The crankshafts are built up from cheeks and pins, assembled under a hydraulic press with a capacity of around 10,000kg (11 tons), and then accurately aligned. There is no way the average home mechanic can strip one of these. Sometimes, not even the main bearings can be removed without press tools. Although careful leverage might work in a few cases, it could also result in distortion or damage and it's better regarded as an emergency measure only.

One is therefore back to assessing wear and deciding whether a service-exchange crank is warranted. Nowadays, main bearings tend to be large and lubrication good. There is no reason why the original mains should not last the life of the bike, and you'll be very unlucky indeed if the time-honoured test of spinning the cleaned and oiled race and listening for roughness in fact produces a negative result.

The big end is a different matter, since it leads a hard life and cannot be made as bulky as the mains. Set

Above: a built-up crankshaft in final and component form
Right: a main bearing race being spun; wear will manifest itself as excessive noise

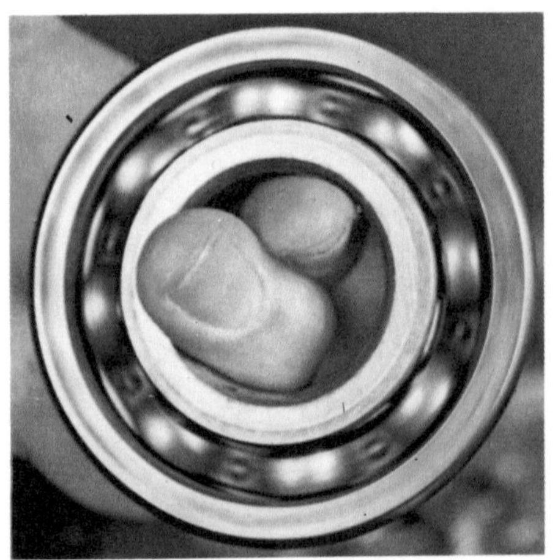

the crank at tdc, grasp the small end and alternately pull and push on the rod. There should be no play at all. Then check the amount by which the rod can move sideways. This is a matter of measurement, not judgement. Press the rod to one side, as far as it will go, and use a set of feelers to measure the gap between the side of the rod and the inner crank cheek. A workshop manual will give the exact figure, but as a generalisation you can take 0.015/0.020mm as a representative standard clearance, and anything over 0.1mm as past the service limit.

Crankshaft runout should be checked by setting the shaft up in V-blocks or between centres and using a dial gauge. Mount the shaft in the blocks, so that it can rotate

Crankshaft run-out being checked by means of a dial gauge

freely, and then take readings to determine the truth of the shaft. With a simple two-stroke 'single' assembly built up from a pair of flywheels linked by a crankpin, all that's needed is a reading on each mainshaft. A small parallel twin, like the CB200, needs readings taken at half a dozen points – both mainshafts, atop both inner main bearings and on both inner crank cheeks. With this particular motor, the readings on the mainshaft and bearings should show a standard run-out of 0.02mm, and on the cheeks 0.05mm. Service limits are 0.15mm at any point except the cheeks. On the mainshafts of a simple two-stroke, like the Kawasaki KE175, run-out would be 0.03mm standard, with a service limit of 0.10mm.

One-piece shafts

Very similar measurements need to be made on one-piece shafts, but with the one-piece crankshaft using plain bearings the guesswork can be taken out of assessing the wear. The main bearing shells are split and can be removed from the cases – if necessary – by hand. The big-end bearings are also split and to part the rods from the crank involves nothing more complicated than undoing a couple of nuts so that the bearing cap can be taken off. The rest of the rod, complete with its upper bearing shell, can then be pulled off the shaft.

Plastigage can be used to measure bearing wear accurately. It is used as described earlier: insert a Plastigage strip; refit the shaft or cap; torque down its fastenings; remove it again; measure the flattened Plastigage with the special gauge provided.

The next step is to use a micrometer, or even a vernier gauge, to take cross-measurements on all journals. You then have a complete picture of the state of your bearings and – once you have also checked it on V-blocks or between centres – of the crank as well.

The Plastigage check tells you how much clearance there is between the bearing shell and the journal. Typically, on medium-sized 'fours' like the CB400F or CB550F Hondas, a maximum permissible clearance would be 0.08mm. A twin such as the Kawasaki Z400 is similar, with a service limit of 0.1mm.

Tell-tale evidence of badly worn bearings

Split shell-type bearing (left) and needle-roller bearing (right)

Worn bearing shells should be discarded and new ones fitted in their place. Generally, a service life of around 50,000 miles can be expected from a set of shells, although plain-bearing motors have covered upwards of 100,000 miles without being stripped. The best course is to practice preventive replacement if the motor has to be dismantled for some other reason, thus saving a major job later on. Otherwise, noisy operation and loss of oil pressure tell of the need for new shells. Where heavy bearing wear has occurred you can usually see signs of it when the shells and journals are examined (scoring on the journals and the white metal gone from the shells) and the crank journals will almost certainly be oval.

This is where the cross-measurements come in. Journals must be round, not oval, and if the dimension in one axis is significantly greater than that taken at right angles to it, the journal must be reground and oversize bearing shells fitted. An engineering shop will do the entire job for you, regrinding all the journals and supplying the appropriate shells. As a guide to the degree of ovality that can be tolerated, the 850cc Norton 'Commando' must have its journals reground if the difference between dimensions is greater than 0.038mm. Four different bearing oversizes are used to fit various crankshaft regrinds.

It's as well to leave the selection of Honda shells and rods to the experts, since the 'fours' have a complicated coding system that needs to be observed if the engine balance is to remain unaltered. The rods are coded for weight in seven categories, ranging from 281 to 315 grams, and the big ends are also coded in three categories. Three crankpin outside diameter groups are specified for the 400; two for the 500/550 range. Finally, the shells themselves are colour-coded to match various combinations of con-rod and crankpin.

Crankshaft end float

One further dimension has to be considered. The crankshaft has to have a lateral clearance, but this must not be excessive. This clearance – end float – enables the shaft to turn freely, without binding as the metal expands under heat. Around 0.50mm is a fair average, and this is often built in by the natural play in the assembly. Some motors, however, have thrust washers to limit end float; others may be shimmed.

Balance shafts

Some engines with imperfect balance – notably parallel twins in the motor cycle sphere and V4s in cars – need balance shafts to counteract vibration which could otherwise reach unacceptably high levels at the engine speeds that are now common. These shafts may be gear-driven, as on the Suzuki GS400/425 series; or chain-driven like those on the Kawasaki Z400 and the Honda CB250/400N 'Dream' and 'Super Dream'. When rebuilding one of these engines, it is essential to phase the balancers properly. The Suzuki is probably the easiest, since to time it to the correct position, 180 degrees out of phase with the crankshaft, merely involves meshing the two pinions so that punch marks on both mate.

A counter-balance weight from the Honda CB250N twin

On the Hondas, the balancers each carry two marks – TC and TH. The front balancer is offered up so that the line scribed above the TC mark is aligned with the face of the upper crankcase half. The front balancer is then used as a datum for the rear, whose TH mark is set so that it is parallel to the TC mark on the front unit, both being positioned with the crankshaft set to tdc.

The Kawasaki system is more complicated to install, since each balance weight, sprocket, spindle and bearer assembly must be offered up as one. The balance weight and sprocket have to be mated first, with the punch mark on the sprocket facing outwards, central on the balancer. Then, before the assembly is installed, the crankshaft is rotated until its oil holes align with the upper crankcase face. One balancer assembly is then installed, with the arrows on the bearer blocks pointing away from the crankshaft and the chrome-plated link on the chain centralised against a line marked on the bearer block. The second balancer is then added, aligning the mark on the bearer block, the second chromium-plated chain link and the punch mark on the sprocket.

Crankshaft installation

By and large, crankshaft installation is just a matter of inserting the shaft and its rods into the crankcase. Watch out, however, for odd traps like the dowel pins used on most Honda engines to locate the bearings. If the pin fails to engage in its hole, the assembly

On most Honda engines a dowel pin is used to locate the bearings

won't fit. If the hole contains any sort of liquid – oil, solvent, or even water – the peg may seal against it and split the metal. Remember, also, that chains cannot be fitted once the shaft is in place unless they are of split-link type. These are rarely used internally. Therefore, primary-drive and cam-drive chains must be looped on to their sprockets before the shaft is offered up.

With split bearings, install the caps and then torque the bolts or nuts to the recommended settings, taking each up a little at a time and working to the pattern set out in the workshop manual. If none is given, work from the centre outwards, one step each side.

All bearings should be given a generous squirt of oil before installation, so that they do not run dry for the first few moments after start-up, before the sump oil begins to circulate.

Four-stroke plunger oil pumps

Few large-capacity machines nowadays use any form of pump other than a gear pump or a trochoid rotor type. Plunger pumps and rotary/reciprocating pumps may be met on classic and vintage bikes, but only Triumph still fit a plunger pump to four-strokes. Both types, however, are used on two-strokes.

The Triumph pump is basically two pumps in one – a feed pump and a scavenge pump mounted side by side in a common casting. The plungers are actuated through a drive block which engages with a peg, mounted eccentrically on the induction camshaft nut. It is a simple pump to service. Having unbolted it from the crankcase, you can pull out the two plungers and slip the drive block out of place. A squared cap screwed into the base of each pump cylinder holds the spring and ball that forms the valve for the scavenge return port (on the rear pump) or the pressure feed port (on the front). Wash all parts in a solvent, measure the springs, check the balls for roundness and pitting and use a micrometer to check the plunger diameters. Insert the drive block into the plungers, and check the working clearance, which should be not less than 0.0381 to 0.1143mm.

Reassemble by first oiling the balls, springs and plungers generously. Fit the valves, and pour 1cc of engine oil into the cylinder of each pump. Then install the plungers, and press them in until oil can be seen at the outlet ports. Slightly relieve the pressure, watching the outlet ports, and check that the level remains the same. If oil is drawn back into the pump, the valve on that side is not operating properly. With brass-bodied pumps, the trick is to remove the cap and spring and lightly tap the ball against its seating to reseal it. Obviously, this method won't work with a cast-iron type, but here a machine shop may be able to rework the seat satisfactorily.

For many years, Honda used a single-plunger pump driven by a connecting rod from an eccentric on the rear of the clutch body. This type of pump can be removed only after stripping the clutch, when the clutch body, the pump and the drive are detached as a unit.

The plunger can then be drawn out of the pump, leaving it still attached to its connecting rod on the clutch, to which it is held by a snap rod and interposed washer. Early versions of this pump had spring-loaded ball valves that could be dismantled for checking and cleaning, but later versions are sealed units on which only the plunger and the wire-mesh base filter can be detached.

After cleaning, there are two measurements to be taken. The first is to establish the plunger/body clearance – in the case of the CB200, for example, 0.025/0.036mm, with a service limit of 0.17mm – and the clearance between the big end of the pump drive rod and the eccentric. Standard CB200 values are 0.025/0.075mm; the service limit is 0.15mm.

Four-stroke gear-type oil pumps

Used, for example, on the Z1, Z900 and Z1000 Kawasaki range of 'fours', the gear type of pump relies upon the pressurising effect of a pair of meshing gears within a close-fitting bodywork. In Kawasaki's application, the pump is immersed in the sump, drawing in oil through a relatively coarse mesh filter and forcing it through oilways to an adjacent fine filter. Should the filter element become blocked, a valve opens to enable the oil to bypass the element, maintaining lubrication with unfiltered oil.

To remove the oil pump, the sump pan has to be dropped. The pump is bolted into position and comes away complete with its large drive gear. This is located on the pump spindle by a circlip and a pin and it is also shimmed.

The body is split by undoing a ring of six screws, and the cover can be jarred free – once these are out – by tapping gently on the end of each gear spindle, using a rubber or plastic mallet.

Since gear pumps rely on the gear teeth for generating pressure, any damage to the teeth means that the pump must be scrapped. It is not a repairable item. Look, therefore, for chipping or pitting of the teeth – each gear can be lifted out for examination. If the gears pass muster, refit them. Then use feeler gauges to measure the gear teeth/pump body clearances. These measurements must be made at the points at which the teeth run closest to the body. If, on measurement, the gear/pump body clearance exceeds 0.10mm the entire pump must be renewed.

If the reading is anywhere between 0.003 and 0.0036mm, the pump is in

An example of the trochoid-rotor type of oil pump

perfect condition. Fit a new gasket to the body, refit the cover and drive, and install it. It is essential, before fitting the new gasket, to clean up the mating surfaces of the body and cover using solvent and a blunt scraper. Be very careful not to allow any frass to enter the pump itself. Use Loctite on the cover screws and on the pump bolts. This is essential. A bolt or screw that worked loose could fall into the 'works' and wreck the motor.

Four-stroke trochoid-rotor pumps

Probably the most widely used pump on current bikes, the trochoid-rotor type is of a high-efficiency design in which a four-lobed inner male rotor

The trochoid-rotor pump exploded

revolves in a five-lobed outer female rotor, which itself is driven by the inner rotor to turn in its housing in the body. The outer rotor is eccentrically mounted.

Honda, on bikes as diverse as the CX500, the CB250/400N and the C50, Suzuki, on their 'fours' and dohc twins, and Kawasaki, on their Z400 twin, employ this type of pump. It is usually gear-driven, although Honda fit chain drive on the CX500 and CB250/400N. This drive, of course, has to be tensioned. On the CX500, it is done by swinging the oil pump around a pivot bolt, and then locking it down when the top run of the chain has 2.0/3.5mm play in the centre.

Suzuki's check-out procedure is typical. The two halves of the pump body are split, then the inner rotor is turned until the peak of one lobe of the outer rotor is at its closest point to a lobe of the inner rotor. The clearance between them is then measured with feelers. On the GS400/425 series, the clearance should be 0.2mm. It is 0.25mm on the GS750 and 0.35mm on the Honda CX500. Renew the rotors if the measurement exceeds the service-limit figure.

Next, the clearance between the inner rotor and the body must be checked – again using feelers. On the Suzukis, the limit is 0.25mm; on the CX500 it is 0.35mm; on the Kawasaki it is 0.25mm.

Lastly, the rotor side clearance should be checked by placing a straight-edge across the body and the rotors and inserting a feeler into the gap. Suzuki and Kawasaki both quote service limits of 0.15mm. Honda specify no clearances for this test on the bigger pumps, but on the much smaller pump, on the 50cc and 70cc step-throughs, a normal reading is 0.02–0.07mm – the same as the rotor-to-rotor clearance. Rotor tip clearance on this smallest pump is normally 0.15mm, with a service limit of 0.2mm.

When measuring these very fine clearances, it is essential to use metric feelers for absolute accuracy. The imperial equivalents are, at best, approximations and they can be sufficiently inaccurate to be misleading.

Breathers and relief valves

Engine breathing – not the induction/exhaust aspect, but the breathing that inevitably takes place at the crankcase end of the motor – was at one time invariably controlled by a timed valve or a pressure-operated valve. These rarely worked satisfactorily, which is perhaps one reason why bikes used to have an evil reputation for oil leakage. A build-up of pressure in the crankcase is quite sufficient to open a joint slightly, and then to pump oil out.

Current practice is to use either a 'maze', in which air is expelled through a labyrinth of complex passages, or to take the gas by tubes to a separator in the air filter housing and condense out the oily liquid content, which is then drained, and return the rest to be filtered, and burned in the combustion chambers.

An oil pressure relief valve is designed to 'blow off' once the oil pressure reaches the region of 5 or 6 bars. It consists, normally, of a spring-loaded piston in a heavy body. It may be mounted on the pump itself – as on the CX500 – or in the crankcase, as on the Triumph twins. Normally, it requires no maintenance. It can be checked by pressing in the plunger to ensure that it moves freely – quite a heavy push is needed, of course – and it can be cleaned by dismantling it and washing the components in meths. The Triumph valve has a cap nut securing the spring and plunger, the Honda valve an internal circlip and washer. As with all components containing heavy springs, take great care not to let the springs fly out into your face.

After cleaning the unit, and making certain that the relief holes through which the oil will be bled once the valve operates are clear, lubricate all the components before reassembly.

Two-stroke oil pumps

Normally, two-stroke oil pumps are sealed units which cannot be serviced. They are simply unbolted, and replaced if they are faulty. Unlike four-stroke pumps, however, they do require adjustment, since it is modern practice to link them to the throttle. Apart from setting-up, the only requirement may be renewal of the control cables. This is done in the normal way, by freeing the nipples and undoing the adjusters. One slightly unusual system, however, is used on the Jawa range, where the pump cable runs to the throttle slide itself. Here, the cable has to be reset

Below: oil pumps on two-strokes are usually linked to the throttle

Above: when removing the oil pump, be careful not to lose any of the 'O' rings or seals

– using the adjuster on the mixing chamber top – until the slide can be heard to tap against the body of the carb when the throttle is opened and then released. Careful adjustment is essential with this system, since it is the oil pump cable drum that is controlled directly by the throttle, its movement being relayed to the carburettor by the second cable. The first stage is, therefore, always to check the oil pump drum setting, then to establish that there is the proper drum/throttle slide relationship.

Transmission

Apart from a handful of moped-type automatics, usually working on the expanding-pulley system, the vast majority of current two-wheelers have purely mechanical transmission systems with anything from two to six gear ratios. The general layout is for the engine to drive the gearbox through a reduction gearing, either by chain or by pinions. In the case of centre-driving multis, this reduction may be split by use of a countershaft. This type of two-stage primary drive is usually by Morse chain from the crankshaft to the countershaft and then by pinion from the countershaft to the clutch. A very few machines – the BMW range, for example – have a direct primary drive through an engine-speed clutch.

The reduction gears are torque multipliers. They reduce the engine speed, but increase the torque proportionately. Very occasionally, there is a top gear ratio which *appears* to be an overdrive – the gearshaft turns more quickly than the crankshaft in a true overdrive – but when the total primary drive ratio is taken into account there is, in fact, still a reduction gearing.

From the gearbox, the secondary drive – except on a scooter such as the Vespa, where pinions are employed – is either by chain and sprockets or by shaft. A shaft, if used, drives the rear wheel in turn through helical gears, turning the drive through 90 degrees.

In effect, all bikes are friction-drivers, since all power is transmitted through the clutch. This consists of friction plates linked to one side of the drive and plain plates linked to the other. Heavy springs hold the plates hard together so that the drive is transmitted, but it can be freed at any time by operating the clutch control. The lever is coupled to the release mechanism, which relieves the spring pressure and allows the driving set of plates to continue turning, while the driven plates stand still or turn at a different speed, governed by the rear wheel.

Completing the transmission system are the various shock absorbers, either rubber cushions or an arrangement of spring-loaded face cams. These take the jerkiness out of the system and protect it against sudden shocks.

Primary drives

As far as diy techniques are concerned, all but a very few rather antiquated machines have non-adjustable primary drives. There are no day-to-day tasks to carry out, and since the components are both stout in construction and invariably well lubricated a modern primary drive system will usually last for the life of the machine.

With gear-type primary drives, examine the pinions whenever the engine is overhauled. Look for the usual damage that would mean replacement for any pinion set – pitting or deformation of the teeth, cracked or broken teeth – and if any damage is found renew all the meshing pinions, since the breakdown of one will have damaged the rest.

Chain primary drives, where the chain is of the endless Morse type, should be inspected for signs of damage to the rivets. Otherwise, it is unlikely that any problems will be encountered.

Ordinary chain drives can suffer from the usual chain defects of stretch, cracked rollers and hooked sprockets. Again, it is mainly a matter of inspection. If the chain is worn, the sprockets will be worn too and all must be renewed.

Chain secondary drives

Wear, sometimes through maladjustment, is quite likely to have taken its toll of a chain secondary drive, which is the most vulnerable system on most bikes. The chain has to operate with the minimum of lubrication, while exposed to water and road filth for most of its life. It is hardly surprising that wear can be so rapid that, on some bikes, chain renewals are necessary within 5000 miles. This lamentable record is partly due to poor design, often aggravated by sheer neglect. Open chains are vulnerable, but careful cleaning, lubrication and adjustment can go a long way towards rectifying their deficiencies.

Curiously, a motor cycle chain is a rather impressive piece of precision

This type of endless primary drive chain is unlikely to give trouble

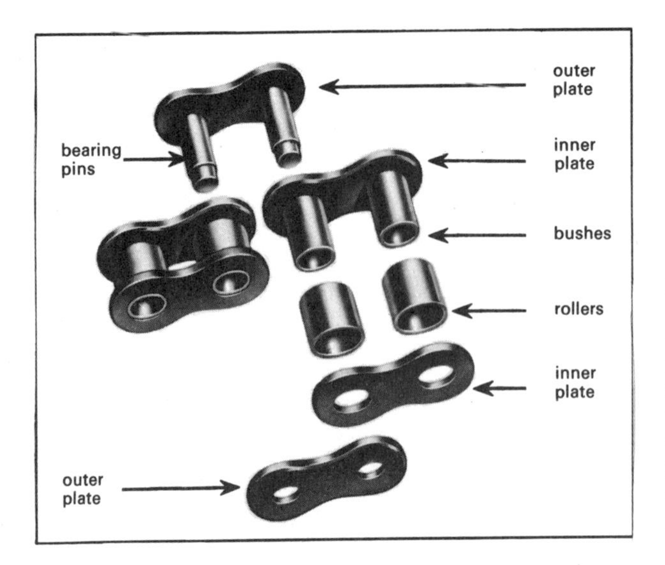

Left: the various components which make up one link of a chain
Right: pliers, and *not* a screwdriver, should be used to separate the connecting link
Below right: sealed chains need little but a periodic spray with chain lubricant

engineering. Every link comprises rollers with hardened steel bearing surfaces, located between link plates which are closed rivetted. There are built-in clearances for lubrication, and when used with properly matched sprockets the chain will transmit power with an efficiency of something like eighty per cent, which is about twice as good as the best shaft/helical-gear system. On top of that the chain is lighter, and to some extent self shock-absorbing.

Where a chain can operate under ideal conditions – constantly lubricated and between fixed centres – it is probably the best way yet devised for transmitting the type of power produced by a bike engine. Unfortunately, few of its requirements are ever met. Full enclosure in a chaincase goes some way towards it, but these items are commercially very rare and even so the action of the rear suspension causes the chain to wrap round the sprockets and so accelerate wear. Without enclosure, the best that can be done is constantly to clean and lubricate the chain, but there is another snag – you must be certain what type of chain you're dealing with. Most of the chains in current use benefit from removal and immersion in a paraffin bath. However, superbikes like the Honda CBX and the big Suzukis are increasingly being equipped with sealed chains. In these, the pins carry neoprene O-rings at each end of the roller, sealing in lubricant that was applied during manufacture. These chains need nothing more than an external refresher from a spray-can of chain lubricant to keep them in good working order. Immersing them in a solvent may actually harm them by causing the seals to perish and release the lubricant.

For the majority of bikers, however, it is the old-fashioned chain that has to be lived with.

Caring for it really demands that it should be removed at intervals of about 2000 miles, washed clean by use of a stiff brush and a bath of paraffin, and then hung up to dry.

Actually detaching it from the bike is sometimes not so simple, as makers went through a stage of rivetting chains up instead of using a spring link to secure them. Now, the spring link is easy to deal with. Just set one jaw of a pair of pliers on the open end of the link and the other

A proper chain tool has to be used when splitting a rivetted chain

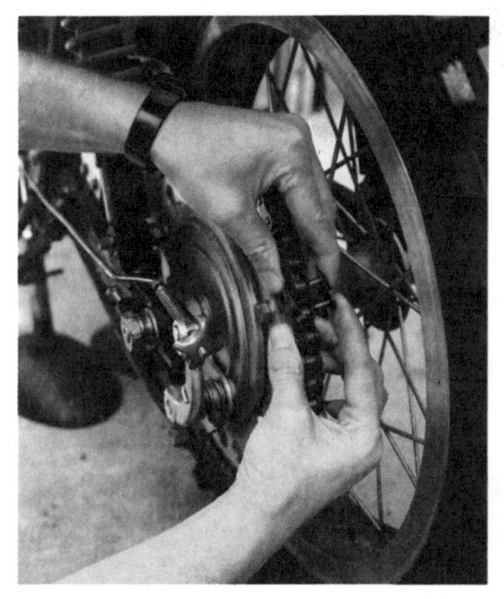

A replacement spring clip being fitted. This is done with the ends on the sprocket

behind the pin on which the link is clipped and press. The pliers will force the clip out of place. The crude way is to lever it up with a screwdriver, but this distorts the clip and if it *has* been taken off like that it really ought to be discarded and a new one fitted. With the clip off, the outer link can be eased away and the chain 'broken' by sliding the now-open link out of the rollers.

Rivetted chains have to be broken by use of a chain tool. This has spring-loaded claws which enable it to be positioned over one of the rivets; the tool's centre punch is then screwed up to drive the rivet out. The tool is then placed over the second rivet and the operation repeated. On assembly, the new link may be re-rivetted into place, though most people fit a spring link.

When breaking a rivetted chain, don't just select a link at random. It is usual practice for a 'soft' link to be fitted and this is usually identified by being polished, by the use of a light colour or by a dab of yellow paint. The average chain splitter won't even dent a hardened rivet, so it's essential to locate the right link first.

If you have an old chain, it is useful to join it to the end of the present one, so that as you withdraw one for cleaning, the other takes its place. This makes refitting easier if the gearbox sprocket cover is not removed. A piece of string may suffice, but the front chain cover *ought* to come off if the job's being done properly in any case. The secondary drive isn't just a chain. It's a chain and two sprockets. If either sprocket is worn, then the whole system ought to be renewed; there is no point in fitting one new part on its own.

Wash the sprockets with paraffin – you can't examine them properly if they're covered with grease – and then check their teeth, one by one. All the teeth must be regular. If the ends are hooked in one direction, the sprocket's worn out. There must be no elongation of the areas between the teeth, since the chain has to be a close rolling fit, and the ends of the teeth must be blunt, with the original chamfer still plain. If the teeth are sharp and jagged, wear is far advanced and – again – the sprocket must be scrapped, together with the rest of the system.

If the sprockets stand up to inspection, check the chain. Once it has been washed, hang it up to dry. Then put it on its side, pick it up, and hold it out in front of you. It will take up a curve, since there is a little clearance at each pin, and a couple of hundred pins add up to a fair movement at the end of a metre and a half of chain. It should be, at worst, a shallow curve giving a drop of no more than 130/150mm. If it drops into something that looks more like a quarter-circle, then the chain is worn beyond recovery. If the chain passes this rough first test, it can go on to the second, which is to measure the chain stretch; this is quite easy to do. Just tap a headless nail into the top of the workbench, or into a length of planking, and hook the chain over it by inserting the nail through the first pinhole.

You now need a foot ruler – continental and Japanese factories

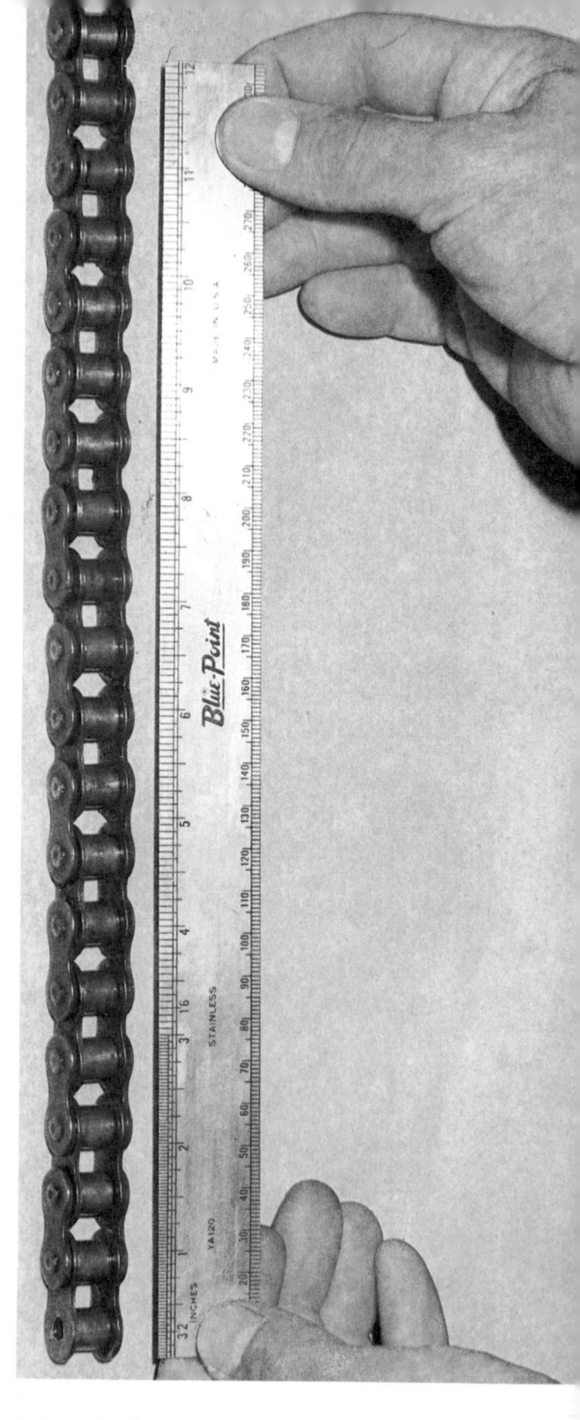

A foot ruler is required for checking that chain stretch is within correct limits

specify their chains in imperial measurements – with which to measure the length of the first run of chain when it is compressed. With $^5/_8$in chain, 16 pitches should measure 10in. With $^1/_2$in chain, $11^1/_2$in covers 23 pitches and with $^3/_8$in chain 24 pitches measure 9in. A pitch is the distance between pin centres.

Now pull the chain taut on its nail and again measure the appropriate number of pitches. With $^5/_8$in chain, it can have 'grown' to $10^7/_{32}$in before the chain must be renewed. For $^1/_2$in chain, the outside limit is $11^3/_4$in, for $^3/_8$in chain, it's $9^3/_{16}$in.

There's a third check to be made. This is on suppleness and is simple. Just hold the chain at one end and run it into a pile on the bench. It should bend around quite easily. Any stiff areas should be eased with solvent, then oiled. If it still suffers from stiff joints, discard it.

By now, you know precisely whether or not your final drive is fit for further service and the rest of the operation is the same for both used and new chains.

Have a tin of chain grease heating on a ring. Tie a loop of wire at one end of the chain and lower the chain gently into the molten grease, winding it round so that it lies neatly coiled and fully immersed. Take the grease tin carefully off the heat and leave it to cool. Before it solidifies, lift out the chain and hang it up over the tin to drip dry. All the bearing surfaces in the chain will be well filled with grease.

If new sprockets are to be used, fit them now. The gearbox sprocket

is usually bolted into place, with tab washers to lock the bolt heads. If so, a new washer will be needed for each bolt. A few bikes have circlips to retain the sprocket instead.

The rear wheel must be removed from the bike to allow the sprocket to be changed. This normally involves removing the rear wheel spindle, and this invariably has a split pin or a spring ring as added security. If it's a split pin, a new one will be needed on assembly. The same applies, in many cases, to the bolt holding the rear brake torque rod, which must be detached to allow the wheel to be withdrawn. The brake rod nut, too, must come off.

With disc rear brakes, it is often essential to unbolt the brake calliper and tie it to the frame. Don't free the hydraulic pipe unless it is absolutely necessary and once the

Opposite page: with the sprocket removed, the cush-drive can be dismantled to reveal the rubbers
Left: the rubber bushes should be distortion-free and unperished

calliper is off don't touch the brake pedal or the pistons will be pushed out of their housings and you'll have brake fluid – a very efficient paint remover – all over the paintwork.

Pull out the rear wheel and unbolt the sprocket. It may need to be tapped off with a softwood block.

When it is off, take the chance of inspecting the cush-drive rubbers, where a rear-hub shock absorber is used. They may be cushions on which bear vanes formed in the sprocket carrier, or they may simply be rubber bushes in which pegs engage. They should be free from distortion and there should be no sign of perishing. Fit the new sprocket and replace the wheel, but at this stage leave the spindle nut fingertight.

Now install the chain, refit the spring link and press on the spring clip with its closed end facing the normal direction of travel. Adjust the chain in the usual way, taking up on the adjusters until there is the correct up and down play on the lower run. Then verify the front/rear wheel alignment, unless you have a bike like the Ducati, with pivot-point adjusters which keep the wheel automatically in line. Given a good eye, it can be done within reason by setting the front wheel dead ahead, and looking down the centre line of the bike from a point well behind it. The two wheels should appear as one. It's better, however, to make up a special alignment board. Use a piece of planking that's as long as the bike and nail to it a strip of wood whose length is the same as the diameter of the front wheel and whose width is half the difference between the width of the front and rear tyres. If this gauge is then placed so that it touches the front wheel at two points, it should also touch the rear wheel at two points as well. If not, reset the drawbolts till it does.

Subsequent chain care

Every 1000 miles, wipe the chain with rag and then spray it with chain lubricant, spinning the wheel slowly so that it is well distributed. Check the play in the chain at four points. Chain stretch is not even. It is caused by wear in the pins, and this can happen more on one part of the chain than on others. The 'tight' section of a chain is the unworn bit. Always make any adjustment at this tightest point and, to keep the wheel aligned, count the number of flats through which each adjuster is turned, taking up one flat at a time on each side.

Clutches

Clutches rarely go wrong on their own account, but they can be damaged by lack of attention to other parts of the bike. A sticky clutch, for example, is far more likely to result from a pinched or rusted cable than from an internal fault. Even something that looks minor, and seems quite unconnected with the clutch, can have its effect. For instance, on certain Hondas a screw missing from the chain cover may stop the clutch from functioning correctly, as that is where the clutch release is situated and when the lever is pulled most of the thrust will be lost pushing the chain cover outwards, instead of operating the clutch pushrod.

When adjusting the chain tension, count the number of flats the adjuster moves

To overhaul a clutch on most chain-drive bikes is simplicity itself. Drain the oil, detach the kickstarter pedal and undo the screws holding the cover, underneath which is the clutch. To change the plates – one of the few overhaul jobs ever needed – just undo the bolts or nuts that compress the clutch springs, let the clutch centre come away, and draw out the plates. You'll need to keep a careful note of plate sequence, since it is not unknown for the inner and outer plates to be of a design different from that of the others. Otherwise, it's just a case of plain plates alternated with friction plates.

One strange unit is the clutch, used on some Suzukis, in which the springs are held to the outer cover by pegs inserted through spring eyes. For this, you need to make up a special tool with which to lift the springs

while the pegs are pulled out. You can use an old-fashioned buttonhook; otherwise, bend a cycle spoke into a hook shape and form a ring-type handle at the other end.

Clutch centres and bodies generally do not need to be detached unless you need to reach some other component – the gear selector mechanisms, for example, or the pump drive on some Hondas – and they can present difficulties. Normally, a clutch centre is retained on the shaft by a single nut. This will usually be locked by a tab washer, which has to be flattened. Then it is necessary to lock the drive to prevent the shaft turning. There are several ways round this. Sometimes, the easiest method is to slip the bike into gear, roll it off its stand, and undo the nut while a helper sits aboard with a foot jammed hard down on the brake pedal.

Another method, where the motor has had a top-end strip, is to refit a

Above left: here the bolts holding the clutch springs are being undone
Above: remove the clutch springs for checking. Where necessary, they should be replaced with new springs
Below: plain and friction plates alternate in the clutch. They will need to be checked for wear and warping

piston to one of the small ends and insert a couple of blocks between the piston skirt and the crankcase mouth. Turn the motor gently until the piston locks on the blocks, then undo the nut.

Yet canother trick that can be used – with gear primary drives – is to make up a thick pad of rag and jam it between the teeth of the primary gear train.

Locking the clutch centre so that the nut can be removed is one thing; getting at the nut is another. Honda, in particular, tend to use castle nuts in this application and unless you have the right spanner there's no way of shifting one of these. Lacking the proper tool, there's little for it but to take the unit to a Honda dealer for attention, or buy the tool, although you could file an old socket until it has the 'dogs' necessary to engage in the nut.

Some Honda clutches are much easier than this. On the CB400F a snap ring secures the clutch centre. A huge snap ring is also used to hold one of the special plates to the clutch centre on this model. With the centre removed, the body, which rides on a plain bearing, lifts off.

Suzuki have a different system on their GS750 clutch, where the bearing is a caged needle roller. To reach this bearing, a spacer has to be removed from the centre of the clutch body – a job done, after detaching the clutch centre, by screwing a couple of 6mm screws into the spacer and pulling it. The bearing then slips out, and the clutch body can be eased out of engagement with the drive.

Clutch plates

Examine all plates for signs of scoring, blueing, or distortion. A plain plate is checked by placing it face downwards on a face-plate, and measuring any gap between the two with a feeler gauge. Typically, a 0.2/0.3mm warp is enough to warrant scrapping the plate.

The amount of 'meat' on the friction plates is checked with a vernier gauge. The exact thickness varies from make to make and model to model, but around 2.5mm can be taken as fairly representative of a plate that needs relining.

Clutch springs

The best method of checking clutch springs is that already described for valve springs, although here again a free-length measurement is still a useful guide. To use it, you really need to know the standard free length of the springs, or to have the maker's own service limits. Usually, a maximum shortening of around three or four per cent is the most that

A vernier gauge can be used to measure the free length of the clutch springs

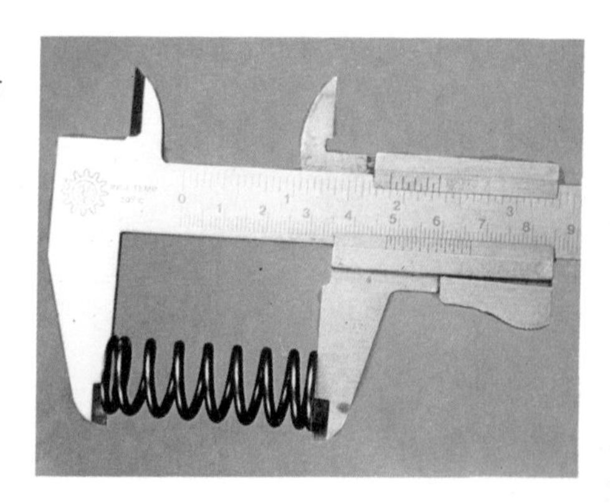

can be accepted, so the 34.5mm springs on a Kawasaki KH250 would need to be renewed when their free length was down to 32.5mm, the 40.4mm springs from the GS750 when they reached 39mm or the 43.5mm springs from a Tiger when they measured 41mm. Owners of Norton 'Commandos' with diaphragm spring clutches can look smug – except that this type of spring needs a very elusive special tool to compress it until its securing snap ring can be released. Never, incidentally, try to remove a diaphragm spring without the tool. You'll be lucky if the only result is a wrecked clutch body.

Diaphragm-type clutches need a special tool for dismantling

Clutch release mechanisms

Apart from the car-type clutch releases on some bikes with engine-speed clutches and centrifugal clutches on commuter models, most release mechanisms are variations on the 'clutch-rod and mushroom' theme. A metal 'mushroom' with a hardened head bears on the inner face of the clutch thrust plate. A rod, usually with a bearing ball interposed, presses on the mushroom at one end and on a quickthread carrying the clutch arm at the other. When the release is operated, the clutch lifter runs down the quickthread, pressing the rod outwards. This, in turn, lifts the mushroom, which pushes the thrust plate outwards against the resistance of the springs. This relieves the spring pressure on the clutch plates so that the friction plates are no longer driven by the plain plates.

Clutch adjustment basically involves varying the effective length of the lifter/rod/mushroom assembly by screwing the quickthread in or out. Overhaul is confined to removing the lifter assembly from the cover – usually, just one securing bolt holds it – and washing it in paraffin. It is then dried, the quickthread checked and the whole assembly well greased and refitted.

Transmission shafts

Apart from a very few bikes on which the gearbox end cover is detachable on its own, reaching the internals usually involves splitting the complete engine/transmission unit. The basic work involved was described in an earlier chapter (p. 113ff) and it should be followed as a guide up to the point at which the cases have been split. This normally leaves the transmission shafts and the kickstarter shaft in place, although on the Yamaha XS250, for example, the kickstarter assembly simply lifts away when the clutch cover has been detached.

Removing the transmission shafts for examination is another lift-out job. Take care to check whether the bearings are dowelled into place and, if so, whether the dowels have a taper that demands their installation in just one particular position on reassembly.

The mainshaft cluster usually offers little choice in the matter of repair. Some are machined from a single billet, although it is more usual these days for separate pinions to be pressed on to the shaft, except for the first-gear pinion, that is, which is usually integral. In theory, any damaged pinion apart from that one can be removed and renewed. In practice, it takes a well equipped workshop to undertake the job. It is also quite common for the bearings to require the use of a heavy hydraulic press for removal and renewal.

Examine the mainshaft pinions for signs of damage to the teeth. Then wash the bearings in paraffin, lightly oil them, and spin them. They should revolve smoothly and with just a light whirring sound. If they are stiff,

Mainshaft gear clusters give little scope for diy repair

or noisy, they almost certainly need to be renewed.

On the layshaft, it is certainly feasible to remove and renew all the pinions. They are usually located laterally by locking washers or by circlips. When stripping a layshaft, however, have a notepad and pencil handy to jot down the exact position of every component as it comes off.

It is impossible to give an exact pattern that would apply to all bikes. However, the Suzuki GS400/425 is fairly typical. A needle roller bearing is separated from the first pinion by a washer. After that comes a pinion-and-dog, with lateral location by circlip, then a splined washer, then a further pinion. Now come a large splined washer, followed by a small one, another pinion, another circlip, a pinion-and-dog, a circlip, a plain washer, a pinion and a bearing pressed on to the shaft.

Actually, given careful inspection, there is usually no need to strip the gear trains. Check condition of the teeth and the dogs, and ensure that there is no damage to any of them. Rounded-off dogs can cause the bike to jump out of gear, while a broken-off gear tooth swilling around inside a gearbox can be lethal.

To take an engineer's view, if a layshaft pinion is renewed, then the mainshaft pinion with which it meshes should also be replaced. This is a counsel of perfection that is probably not normally put into practice, however.

Kickstarter mechanism

Kickstarters normally work either on a quickthread or on a ratchet system. The quickthread type, as exemplified on the Kawasaki triples, is a very simple device on which the kickstarter gear – guided by a hairpin-type spring locator – moves along the rotating quickthread on the kickstarter spindle and into mesh with the first-gear pinion. When this pinion overruns, it throws the starter pinion out of engagement. The pinion also disengages when the starter pedal is released, and the return spring turns the shaft back in the opposite direction.

This type of unit is dismantled by lifting it from the casing and removing the spring guide, the spring and the circlip on the spring holder. Removing a further circlip allows the pinion to be taken off. Check for damaged teeth or for wear on the quickthreads before reassembling. Note that the gear holder *must* engage in the guide in the crankcase, or the pinion will simply revolve, without sliding into engagement.

With a ratchet type, the usual method of operation is that the ratchet slides down the quickthread to engage with a side ratchet on the kickstarter pinion. It then revolves the pinion, which is in mesh with a gear on the layshaft. Otherwise, the two systems are similar and the same checks should be carried out.

On some Triumph models, an internal ratchet operating inside the pinion was used instead.

Gear selectors

If the selector mechanism is going to give trouble, the likeliest sources are the vulnerable springs on the

Above: the springs in the gear selector mechanism are often a weak point and should be checked once the gearbox is dismantled
Above right: the gear selector drum showing the cam tracks
Right: the gear selector mechanism

arms in the clutch housing. These should always be checked first. On some bikes, the spring on the selector arm, or the hairpin spring on the stopper arm, are prone to breakage. This can leave you with gear selection in only one direction, or with a hit-and-miss selection that tends to jump out.

Internally, the usual selector mechanism comprises a drum in which cam tracks are cut, with selector forks whose pegs engage in the tracks. As the drum is moved, the cam tracks cause the selector forks to slide to a preset pattern – a sort of mechanical computer.

Representative of current design practice, the selector mechanism used on the Honda CB250/400N range is also employed on the CX500. The selector drum is held by a plate secured by staked screws. The selector forks are carried on a pull-out spindle and after the forks have been detached the selector drum simply lifts out.

Checks on the forks should include a close examination to ensure that they have not become twisted –

renewal is the only cure here – and the fork thickness should be measured, or the clearance of the fork in the sliding gear groove ascertained. The workshop manual for the bike will tell you which is appropriate.

Fork clearance measurements on the three-cylinder Kawasaki two-strokes, for example, should be within the 0.05–0.25mm range, with new selector forks specified once this rises to 0.6mm. The clearance is measured by inserting the fork into the groove and checking the side clearance with a feeler gauge.

On the CX500 it is the width of the fork 'finger' that is specified. Normal dimensions are 5.93/6.00mm. When the finger has worn down to 5.50mm, it must be changed.

Look for any arc-shaped wear on the sides of selector forks – clear evidence that they have been abraded by a rotating pinion – and run a finger-tip along the sides of the fork to seek out any burrs. Slight burring can be corrected by lapping on a face-plate, but major damage calls for new forks.

Forks can also wear internally, as they slide on their shafts. Up to 0.03mm is all that Honda permit in the way of wear at this point – a quite typical service limit.

Shaft final drives

It is no job for an amateur to strip the final drive unit on any of the shaft-driven machines. Resetting the mesh of helical gears is a tricky job, and there has to be a preloading operation carried out too. It would be easy to do more harm than good.

The gear selector forks should be checked for any signs of bending or twisting

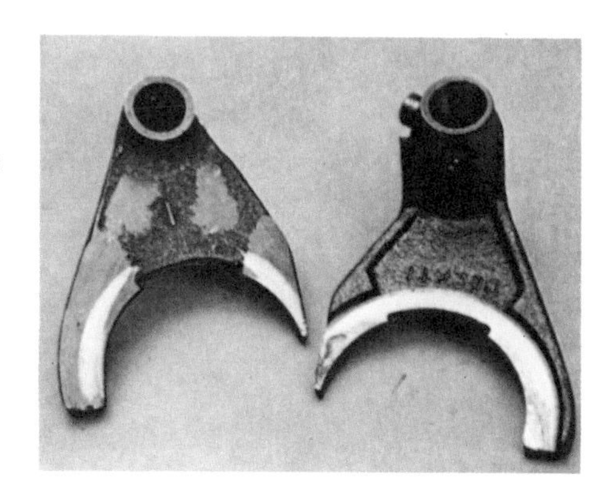

Replacement is the only cure for worn selector forks

Carburation

Bike carburettors come in two main categories – slide type, or constant-vacuum type (sometimes called 'constant velocity' or CV). Like most carbs, they are easy to work on provided that one simple rule is followed: when servicing a carb, you must take out only one item at a time. In that way, you won't end up with a handful of assorted jets, all looking alike and all seemingly interchangeable.

Also, with carb work, you need a delicate touch. Adjusting the float chamber fuel height by bending the needle arm through 45 degrees will certainly achieve *something*, but not what you were aiming for. Gentle handling is essential, for these are finely calibrated instruments. Even a piece of wire used to rod out a blocked jet is capable of enlarging the orifice and upsetting the whole balance of the mixture. That is why you should use air pressure to clear jets, with a natural bristle as a poor second best if the obstruction can't be shifted in any other way.

Slide carburettors

With a slide-type carburettor, a slide set in the mixing chamber is linked to the throttle control to vary the amount of mixture taken into the cylinder. This mixture has to be in the ratio of just under fourteen parts of air to one part of petrol by weight. That means that, by volume, something like 99.9cc out of every 100 induced is air. It's up to the carburettor to mix in the tiny remaining 0.1cc of fuel.

In the slide carburettor, the ratio is maintained by air control though a

A selection of motor cycle carburettors

cutaway in the slide and by the variable position of the slide, by a tapered needle fixed to the slide which varies the amount of fuel that can pass through the needle jet, by the capacity of the main jet and by the level of fuel in the float chamber in which the jet is immersed. In addition, there are special arrangements made for supplying a richer mixture for starting, and the 'whiff of gas' needed for idling.

Constant-vacuum carburettors
In appearance, a CV carburettor looks like the slide carb's grandfather. It is not dissimilar, but it is certainly bulkier. Most of the bulk results from the use of a piston or a diaphragm and slide to carry the needle. Here, the slide serves only to produce the correct mixture. The throttle control is a butterfly valve set in the rear of the unit.

The CV carburettor is still a basically simple instrument. The key to its operation is that the upper side of the piston or the diaphragm is surmounted by a chamber linked to the carburettor venturi, but not to the outside air. Its underside is open to a second chamber, linked to the surrounding atmosphere but not to the venturi. As the difference between the two pressures changes, so the piston, slide and needle lift

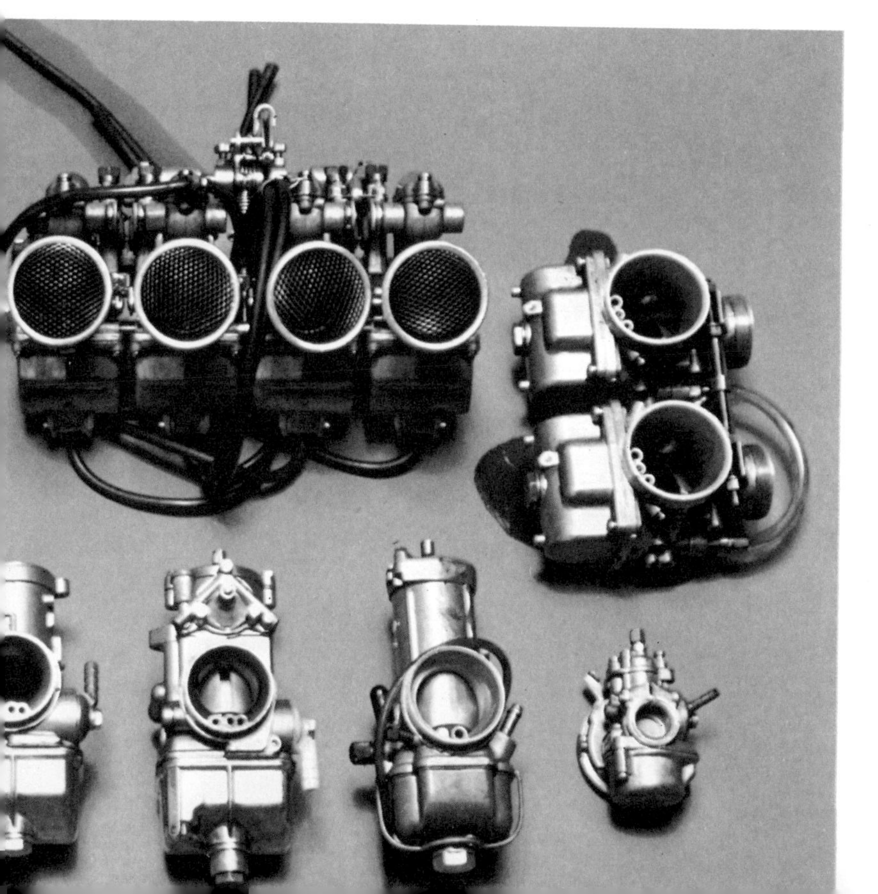

or lower. In theory air always passes below the piston at a constant speed, although in a changing volume. The result is automatic variation of the fuel/air mix, to suit the engine operating conditions, and almost perfect vaporisation.

Multiple carburettors

One carb to each cylinder sounds a great idea – until you have to work on them. Balancing a nest of up to six carburettors is a job that demands the use of instruments – either one vacuum gauge per carb, or a manometer. Luckily, the mechanical linkages are sturdy and multiple carbs tend to hold their adjustment well, so rebalancing is not an everyday job.

When working on a multi-carb motor, the carburettors should be removed as a single bolted-up unit

The components of a Dell'Orto carburettor
1 throttle spring
2 cover
3 accelerator pump diaphragm
4 accelerator pump spring
5 accelerator pump cover
6 throttle slide
7 float chamber screw
8 carburettor body
9 & 10 fuel union and filter
11 clip for needle
12 needle
13 float pivot
14 float needle valve
15 float
16 starting jet
17 atomiser
18 accelerator pump jet
19 needle jet
20 slow running jet
21 main jet
22 float chamber

12

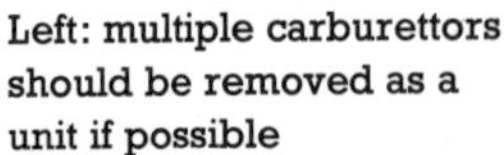

Left: multiple carburettors should be removed as a unit if possible

and the actual linkage should not be disturbed unless it is absolutely essential. Once it has been freed off, the full balancing procedure will have to be employed on the rebuild.

Slide carb strip

The actual makes of slide carburettors include Keihin, Mikuni, Amal, Bing, Dell'Orto and Jikov, but the basic layout is sufficiently similar to be generally recognisable.

First, the mixing chamber top must be removed. Normally, it has a knurled ring which is unscrewed by hand. The throttle slide, complete with throttle needle, then pulls out on its cable.

To free the slide usually involves nothing more complicated than holding the cable still and pushing the slide upwards, against the pressure of its spring until the cable nipple can be disengaged.

The return spring lifts out, and underneath is the circlip that carries the needle. This may, in some instruments, be held by a U-spring. Take out the needle, and make an immediate note of the needle notch in which the circlip was placed. Raising the needle allows more fuel to pass through the needle jet; lowering the needle reduces the flow.

Examine the needle. The commonest damage is bending, often caused by some previous owner jamming it against the body bridge when reassembling the carb. With some of the earlier Amals, in particular, it was almost fatally easy to get the needle into the wrong hole.

Take no chances with a suspect needle. It's cheap, so renew it. Check the slide for any surface damage; on an old bike, it could possibly be worn as well. It should be a smooth sliding fit in the body, but it should not be free to rattle around. If in doubt, renew it – the saving in fuel alone will pay for the new bits in a few months.

It is essential, incidentally, to fit a slide with the right cutaway. It's not there because its decorative, but to meter the air. It's the cutaway that has the main influence on mixture strength between one-eighth and one-quarter throttle. An over-rich mixture in this range indicates too small a cutaway; a lean one means that it's too large. Check your workshop manual to find which

The throttle cable is quite easily freed

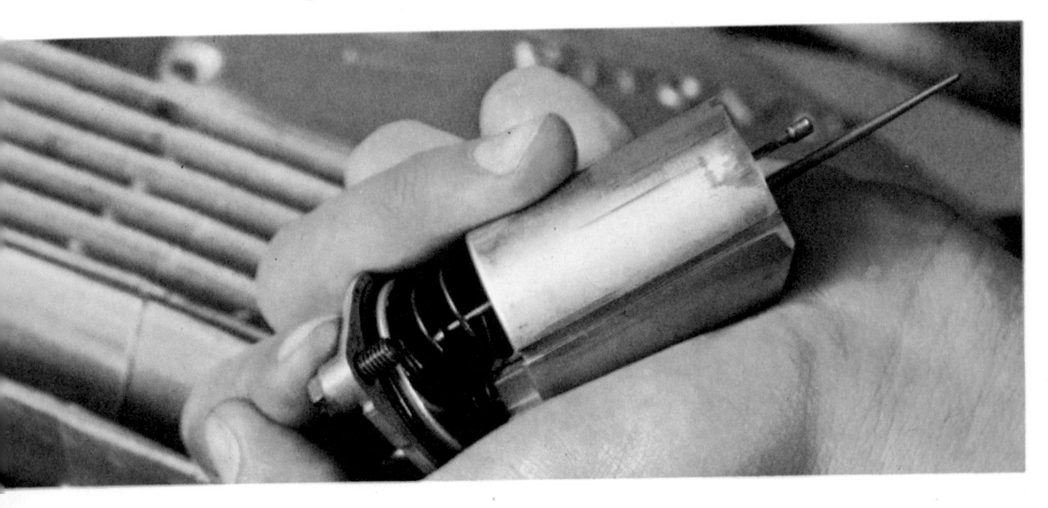

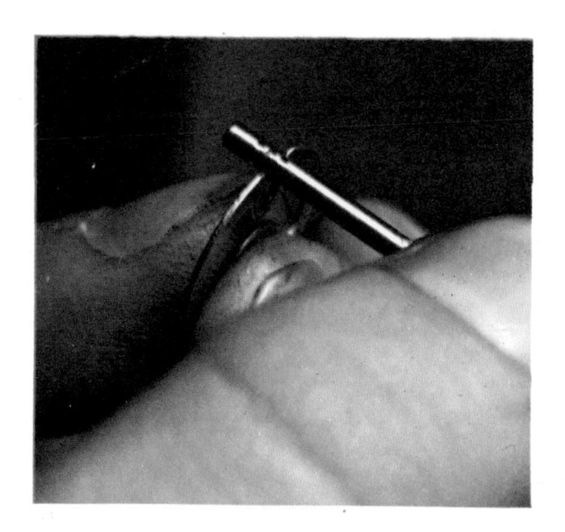

There are several notches in which the needle clip can fit

If the slide is badly scored, it must be replaced

slides are recommended for your bike.

Now remove the carburettor from the motor – two nuts on a pair of studs usually hold it. The fuel pipe is almost certainly a push fit on the float chamber intake stub, perhaps with a spring clip to be expanded before the pipe will pull off. You may also find a drain pipe trailing from the float chamber and this may need to be unravelled from clips that could also hold the battery vent pipe and a couple of drain pipes from the air filter.

The carburettor should then slip easily enough out of the hose linking it to the filter. Although some machines have a screw-clamp on the hose that must be released first, others have a hose with a spring clip that allows the carb to be pulled away.

Drain the contents of the float chamber. On the latest instruments, that just means undoing the float chamber drain screw – a taper valve – to allow the fuel to pour out of the drain tube. Earlier types are messier: what looks like a drain screw, set low on the chamber, is actually a drain plug. Remove that and a chamberful of petrol will cascade over your hand.

Those with a steady grasp can undo the float chamber – usually, four small crossheads hold it – and ease it gently downwards still with its fuel. This is preferable in more than one way, since it gives a chance to look at a sample fuel content. A little fine dirt in the well of the chamber is to be expected – what doesn't flush out can be wiped away when the fuel is drained – but globules of water are a danger sign that the tank itself needs flushing. All petrol contains a little water, but it shouldn't normally reach the carburettor.

Next, the float and the needle valve can be detached and checked.

Methods of securing the float vary, from a single crosshead holding a clamp plate to secure the float pivot to a push-fit pin in cast abutments on the cover. This type of pin is sometimes lightly tapered, but is more usually parallel. If it doesn't respond to a gentle push from one side, don't start tapping it with a punch. Just try it from the opposite direction, and it will probably respond. If so, note which way round to install it. The float assembly is delicate and extreme care must be taken not to bend the arm or tab which controls the height of the fuel in the chamber (it may be slotted to engage with a shoulder on the needle).

Check the float for leaks – shaking it from side to side close to your ear and listening for any sound of fuel slopping inside is a good guide. If a leak is suspected, a further test is to 'boil' the float in water; as the air inside heats up, it will emerge as a line of bubbles from the hole.

Leaks can be repaired – use solder on a brass float or epoxy resin on a plastic one – but *only* if extreme care is taken not to add so much weight that the float no longer does its job properly. On balance, it is better to fit a new float rather than try to reclaim a damaged one.

Check the needle valve. This is sometimes a sealed assembly, which just screws out of the float chamber cover. Normally, a copper seating washer is used under it and this must be in good condition. With the sealed type of valve, check its operation by holding the pin in the closed position while you try to blow through the fuel inlet; you can easily feel whether or not the valve is completely closing the passageway. Then release your finger, and the valve should open at once, with no stickiness. Oscillate it, while still puffing away. There should be instant shut-off and instant release.

If there is a ridge on the needle valve, replace it

Where the needle is demountable, lift it out of the housing for close examination. The taper should be regular and the needle straight and there should be no ridging around the nose. That is a sure sign of a badly worn needle and if you can even *feel* a ridge by running your fingernail down the needle then the needle is past its best and should be renewed. It is probable that the housing, too, has become damaged and it is better to replace both parts of the valve at the same time. You can

The jets are screwed into the carburettor body

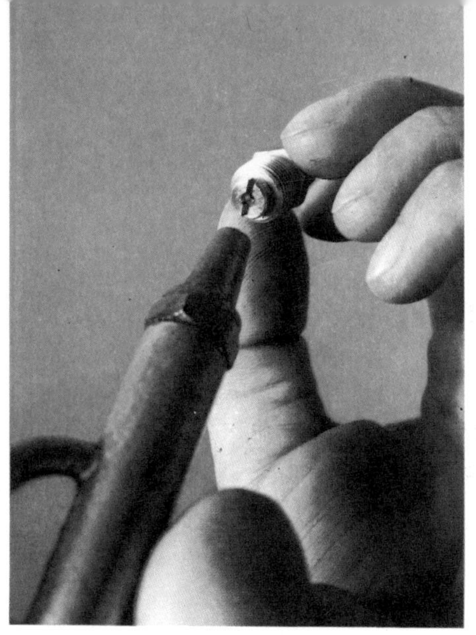

All the jets should be blown through with compressed air

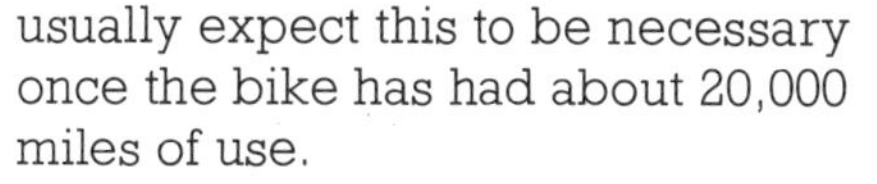

usually expect this to be necessary once the bike has had about 20,000 miles of use.

By this time, all the removable jets will also stand renewal, because although only liquid flows through them this liquid contains microscopic particles which have a scouring action and create wear. Jets are removed for renewal, or for checking and cleaning, merely by unscrewing them, and if you remember to restrict yourself to taking out one at a time, and then refitting it before you take out the next, you won't go too far wrong.

However, there is a snag: not all jets are intended to be removable and no general instruction can cover all possibilities. You can, however, safely assume that where any screw-type fitting on your carburettor is either staked into position, or is marked with paint, then it is not to be touched. An example is the small recessed jet just behind the main jet on the Mikunis fitted to the GS750. This is preset at the factory, then sealed with yellow paint, and it must not be disturbed.

Blow through each jet as it is removed, and then hold it up to the light to double-check that it is clear. Put a blast of air through all body fuelways and airways. The easiest method is to use a spray can of air – actually, they are made to 'power' portable foghorns or small paintsprayers – but as an alternative it's easy to make up a taper-tube adaptor that can be fitted to a tyre pump. It is worth renewing any gaskets used to seal the bowl – nowadays, usually an O-ring let into a groove. Winkle out the old one, and press the new one into place.

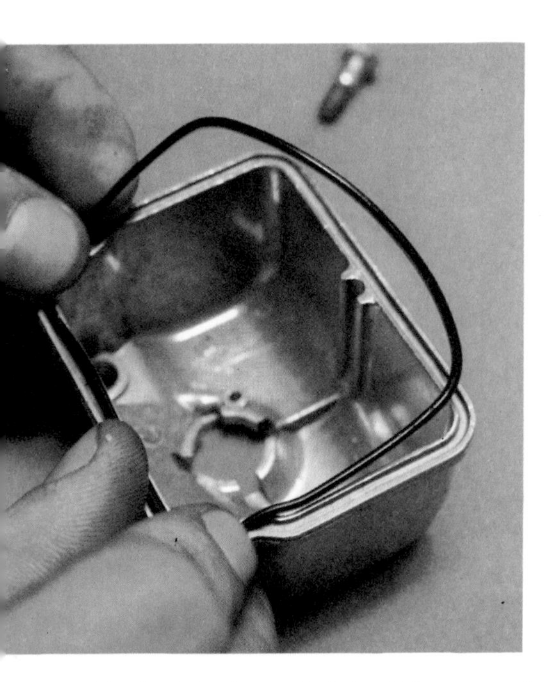

The float chamber gasket should be renewed

Install the needle valve and float, and check the fuel level, where recommended. This is usually measured with the float arm just in contact with the needle, but not actually compressing it. On the Keihin carbs fitted to the CB400F the correct level is 21mm; on those for the CB500F and CB550F it is 22mm, measured from the carburettor body to the bottom of the float. Adjustment is made by bending the float arm gently until the correct measurement is obtained. The same method is followed with the Mikunis on the GS400/425 series, although here the height is 26.3mm (± 1mm). By contrast, the Amal carbs on the Triumph Bonneville and Tiger twins have no provision at all for fuel-level adjustment.

When rebuilding, take care to insert the slide so that the slot in its side engages with the peg fixed in the carburettor body. If the slide will not enter the body, twist it gently from side to side until the peg engages, but never try to force it down. If it won't slip in easily, something is wrong. Remove it again, and check what it is.

Chokes

Mixture-enriching devices are usually one of two types. The first is a supplementary air slide, which simply cuts the amount of air being induced into the engine while the amount of petrol supplied remains the same. With slide-type carburettors, the air slide is usually set ahead of the throttle slide, in its own guides. It is lifted by a direct-acting linkage, and where multiple carburettors are used there is normally an interconnecting rod between the chokes so that all operate together. On CV carburettors, a butterfly choke valve is employed. This usually has a small supplementary spring-loaded plate which allows air to be drawn in with the choke butterfly fully closed – a necessity if the engine is to run at all.

The alternative type of enriching device, used on the Mikuni carbs, is a starter plunger. This is basically a small spring-loaded piston that can be drawn clear of an extra feedway, so that more fuel can be injected into the airstream.

Constant-vacuum carburettor strip

For most practical purposes, a CV carburettor is much like a larger version of the slide carb, and much of the preceding general section has equal relevance here.

A typical CV carburettor is the Mikuni, using a diaphragm and slide rather than the piston employed on the Keihin. The German Bing is another diaphragm-type carb. When stripping a Mikuni, start by detaching the float chamber, inverting the carb, and measuring the float height with the reverse end (depth gauge) of a vernier calliper. There must be no gasket on the carburettor body during this check, and the float arm must be in contact with the needle, but not compressing it. An alternative way to ensure this – applicable to any carb that has a float hinged on one side – is to hold the carburettor with the float pivot uppermost, and let the float hang down against the needle. On the Mikuni fitted to the GS400, the float height should be 23.6mm under this test. Adjustment, again, is made by bending the float tongue, very gingerly, until the right setting is obtained.

Continuing the stripdown, the float pin can be removed, the float assembly lifted off and the needle removed for examination. Next, unscrew the emulsion tube from the centre of the body face, followed by the rich-mixture plunger system. Check all the orifices for blockage.

The suction chamber cover is held by four cross-headed screws. Underneath is the spring and the diaphragm. Check the diaphragm carefully – while it is in position – for any tears or punctures. If it is sound, the best bet is to leave it in place, unless it is essential that the slide and needle should be examined. If the diaphragm is faulty, the piston slide must also be renewed, since the two are serviced as a unit. When refitting a Mikuni diaphragm, note that there is a cutaway in each side of the top of the chamber which must be engaged with tabs on the diaphragm.

Jet checking is carried out as for slide carburettors.

Multiple carburettor linkages

As has already been noted, there is usually no need to uncouple a 'nest' of carburettors, since virtually all modern multiple arrangements use a single interlinked control and a common mounting. If you do plan to remove one or more of the units for individual attention, it is essential to have the appropriate workshop manual to give detailed instructions for uncoupling and resetting the linkage.

Setting up a single carburettor

Strictly speaking, with emission regulations to comply with, the setting-up of carbs should only be done with the aid of a tachometer and a CO meter – an exhaust gas analyser. In practice, it can be done by resetting the pilot air screw so that is about 1½ turns open from its fully-closed position and then, with the motor warm, adjusting the throttle stop screw to give an idling speed of, usually, 1000rpm. With this done turn the pilot air screw first one way, then the other, by about half a turn at a time until you find the fastest idling speed. That done, reset the throttle stop until the tickover is

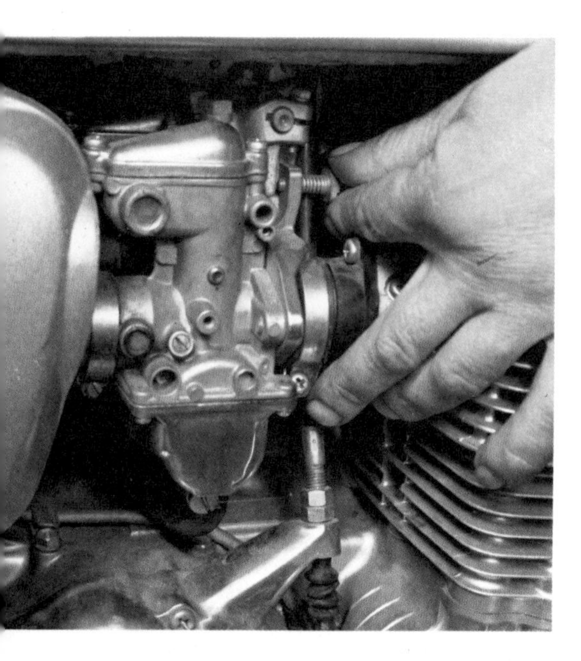

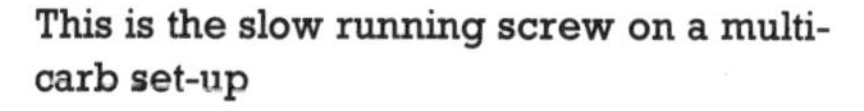

This is the slow running screw on a multi-carb set-up

The mixture can be adjusted with this screw, but synchronisation requires instruments

again in the recommended range. Blip the throttle to check that the pick-up is immediate, with no stalling. If the engine hesitates before accelerating, slightly alter the pilot screw setting to enrich the mixture, then re-adjust the throttle stop to maintain the correct tickover.

Setting up multiple carburettors

Usually, multiple carbs have a linked throttle-stop adjuster. To set them up, you'll also need to have a nest of vacuum gauges – one for each carb – or a manometer nest.

With the engine warmed up, set it to the lowest reliable tickover you can obtain. Then reset each pilot air screw in turn, moving it by no more than 45 degrees at a time in either direction, to obtain the fastest possible idling speed. This must be right on all the carbs, whether you are dealing with a twin, triple, quadruple or sextuple layout. This is where the vacuum gauges come into play. You'll find a screw plug on each induction pipe. Remove it and screw in the appropriate adapter to take the vacuum gauge pipe. Short adaptors go on outer pipes, long ones on inner pipes. You'll find that on some bikes there just isn't room under the tank to get the take-offs into place. There, you need to remove the tank and fix it to the seat or to a carrier with aero-elastics. Use a longer pipe to connect the tank tap to the carbs.

Your vacuum gauges will have damping valves. Close these, start the motor, and then loosen each of the damping valves until the needle on that gauge just begins to flutter. It should *not* be swinging wildly: just trembling. The object is to obtain an identical reading on each gauge. A normal vacuum reading would be between 16 and 24cm of mercury (cm Hg) and steady. Adjustments are made by loosening the clamp bolts on the throttle linkages and lifting or depressing each individual throttle arm until all gauges read the same – in practice, that means within 3cm Hg throughout the 'normal' vacuum range.

With twin carburettors, it's possible to do the job without special equipment by judging the intake noise on each unit. Detach the air filter hoses, and start up the engine. Set the pilot air screw as described, and then adjust the throttle stop on one carb only to obtain the right tickover.

Use a length of hose to enable you to listen to the hiss of air in its intake. Then transfer the hose to the second carb and adjust that too until the same sound is obtained. You can switch your hose from carb to carb to check that you are getting the same sound each time.

Air filters

Apart from the normal servicing, air filters do not normally need attention. Constant misfiring during or after wet weather, however, can be due to water entering the filter housing and soaking the element. The engine must not be run with the element removed. The obstruction to the airflow offered by the element is

The air filter element is usually held by a single screw

An air line can be effective in cleaning the filter

taken into account when the carburettors are jetted. With the increased airflow obtained without an element, the effect is drastically to weaken the mixture.

Petrol tank

The petrol tank contains several mechanical parts which may require attention. The petrol tap filter may need cleaning from time to time, and it is best to do this at the end of the winter, when the dregs of fuel may also contain water. This will normally be trapped in the tank well, since the tap pickup is raised above the floor of the tank itself. Let the tank run almost dry first, then remove it – the the usual arrangement is for the nose to slide on to pegs carrying rubber buffers, while the rear of the tank is secured by a rubber strap or a single bolt. Open the filler cap, and pour all the petrol that remains into a bowl. Then remove the fuel tap. If the filter is badly clogged, it should be washed in a solvent such as meths.

Where there are signs of rust in the tank, block off the petrol tap orifice with a cork or with tape, and drop a handful of bearing balls into the tank through the filler. If you cannot find any of these, have a word with your garage foreman, or the man who runs your local cycle shop. Thoroughly shake the tank, so that the balls hammer against the walls and chip away any rust. Then pour them out and flush the tank again with methylated spirits. Internal rust is difficult to kill, but there are compounds marketed which, it is claimed, will do the job.

Check the fuel tap by blowing through from the fuel pipe end. With the tap to 'Off', your cheeks should simply puff out. Set it to 'On' – and then to 'Res' – and there should be a healthy hiss through the filter mesh. Many taps can have the action stiffened up simply by tightening the screws on the tap centre securing plate.

Also check the filler cap. The vent hole must be clear – if no air can enter, no fuel can leave – and the washer must be sound to prevent fuel slopping out when the tank is full.

Fuel lines

Remove these periodically, and examine them for cuts. If the outside appears to be sound, pull each pipe straight and hold it up to the light. Look through it, and make sure there are no loose flaps of rubber.

Ignition System

Apart from the routine jobs already dealt with on the system, there is only one major diy task possible – checking and adjusting the timing. This can range from little more than a rule-of-thumb adjustment up to a scientific exercise, depending upon the bike and the equipment at your disposal.

At one end of the scale, all you need are your eyes, a good sense of feel and a cigarette paper. At the other, you can have a set of dial gauges or an electronic tuner complete with sensitive tachometer and stroboscopic lamp.

At its most rudimentary, on a few mopeds, the timing operation comprises setting a mark on the rim of the flywheel against a mark on the crankcase, and then checking that the contact-breaker points gap is within a specified range – usually 0.3 to 0.4mm. In all cases, the points gap should be correctly set before the timing is checked or adjusted.

Mostly the operation is more complicated than on a moped. While the best method is certainly to time with the use of a stroboscopic lamp – available, these days, for the price of two or three gallons of petrol – it is still possible to do an accurate job with simpler equipment.

The timing adjustment itself is made by causing the points to open earlier or later, relative to the rotation of the crankshaft, since the spark occurs almost simultaneously with this. A stroboscopic lamp does

A transistor radio, or a special device like this, will give an audible indication that the points have opened

The points for cylinders 1 & 4 and 2 & 3 are often paired in four-cylinder engines

the job of checking the timing for you accurately and at various engine speeds, while a simple test lamp or buzzer will announce the moment at which the points break when the engine is not running. The points are also just opening when a transistor radio, set to a null position between broadcasting stations and placed close to the engine, emits a highly audible click as the crankshaft is slowly turned.

Single-cylinder timing

Taking a simple example, timing adjustment on the Honda C50/C70 range is typical. There is a mark 'F' (for 'Firing') on the flywheel and a static mark on the crankcase. The contact-breaker points are reached through a slot in the flywheel, so more rudimentary methods are suitable here. The transistor radio is perhaps the best variety. Switch on the ignition, set up the transistor, and slowly turn the flywheel. As the two marks align, the transistor should click. If it does so before the marks align, the timing is too far advanced. It it does so afterwards, the timing is retarded. To adjust, loosen the screw that locks the contact breaker to the backplate. Move the contact breaker to the right to advance the ignition, to the left to retard it. Lock the screw, and check the result. Make further slight alterations until the setting is correct, reset the points gap in the usual way and then recheck the setting.

Multi-cylinder four-stroke timing
It's quite common for each cylinder on a twin to have its own contact breaker, while on fours two breakers share the cylinders between them. Nos 1 and 4 are paired, as are Nos 2 and 3. Each set is timed independently. As an example, here's how it works on the Suzuki GS750.

To time by use of a test lamp, check the points gap and then connect one lead of the lamp to earth and the other to the live terminal on the 1/4 set of points. It will light up, with the ignition on, and stay alight until the points break. Rotate the engine by hand, and watch the timing marks and the lamp. As the F1/4 mark aligns with the datum line on the crankcase, the lamp should go out. Check by rocking the crankshaft back and forth across the F1/4 position. The lamp should light up each side of it, and go out as the marks pass each other. If not, reset the timing of Nos 1 and 4 cylinders by loosening the three screws that hold the entire backplate. Set the F1/4 mark accurately in line; move the plate until the lamp goes out. Nip down the screws, and recheck the setting.

A stroboscope will 'freeze' these timing marks while the engine is rotating

Then connect the lamp to the live terminal of the second set of points, and carry out the same check using the F2/3 marks. If adjustment is needed, however, you should *not* loosen the backplate screws this time. Instead, free the three screws that lock the half-plate carrying this one set of points, and adjust it independently in the same way.

With a stroboscopic lamp, the job is simpler still. First emphasise timing marks with paint or nail varnish. Then connect the lamp, according to its makers' instructions, to No 1 cylinder. Normally, this just involves disconnecting the plug lead, inserting one lamp lead into the plug cap, and taking the other to the plug terminal. The lamp will now flash every time a pulse of HT current passes down the lead. With more sensitive professional equipment, a clip-on sensor is incorporated.

Start the engine, and run it at 1000–1500rpm. Point the strobe at the timing marks. They will appear to 'freeze'. If they coincide, the timing is right. If not, loosen the screws holding the backplate just sufficiently to enable you to move it and – with the engine still running – turn the baseplate to align the marks. If the rotating 'F' mark is being frozen before it reaches the static mark the timing is over-advanced, and the baseplate needs to be turned slowly in the direction of rotation of the crank to correct it. If the 'F' mark is frozen after it has passed the static mark, the timing is retarded and the baseplate must be moved against the direction of crankshaft rotation instead. When the marks coincide, lock the baseplate screws.

Next, the action of the auto-advance mechanism can be checked by speeding up the motor to around 2500rpm. At around this speed, the 'T' mark should align with the static mark and a second adjustment of the baseplate can be made to achieve this setting if necessary.

Now stop the motor, disconnect the strobe, and refit No 1 plug lead. Couple the strobe to No 2 plug, and repeat the operation with the 'F2/3' marks, but in this case moving only the halfplate carrying the contact-breaker unit for the second pair of cylinders.

Multi-cylinder two-strokes

With two-strokes, the procedure for ignition timing usually requires use of a dial gauge to determine piston position, combined with a test-lamp, transistor or buzzer to indicate the breaking of the points.

The method adopted on the Suzuki triples is a typical example. The dial gauge is screwed into the No 1 cylinder plug hole and all the other plugs are removed. With top dead centre accurately located on No 1 cylinder, the gauge is zeroed. Then the motor must be turned, slowly, in its normal direction of rotation until the gauge shows that No 1 piston is at the specified point in its travel. With the GT380M, for example, this is 2.30mm before tdc. On the Yamaha twins, where the same method is used, the RD200 has to be set with the piston 1.81mm btdc, and these settings are critical to within plus or minus 0.10mm. This is why the job cannot be done without

Some electronic ignition systems have an adjustable backplate such as this

the dial gauge, and why it is vital to take care over checking the settings to ensure that everything is spot-on before the timing is altered.

You *must* refer to the specific manual to ascertain the correct settings; there may even be different settings for different cylinders on one bike. Don't forget to carry out the contact-breaker resetting procedure cylinder by cylinder, before the timing is altered, using the procedure described for four-strokes. Watch out for motors that have centrifugal advance mechanisms. These may require the unit to be set in the fully advanced position, usually by slipping a peg into holes drilled in the two plates. Also, don't automatically assume that the contact-breaker cam will revolve in the same direction as the crankshaft. On the Suzuki 380, for example, it is geared and turns in the opposite direction.

Contactless ignition systems

Electronic capacitor discharge ignition systems remove one source of bother from the bike, since there are no points to adjust; in fact in some cases – as on the Honda CX500 – they really remove *all* servicing problems from the ignition system, since you cannot even reset the timing. This latter is not common to all CDI arrangements, however. For instance, the Kawasaki two-stroke triples have an adjustable backplate. Typical of this layout is the KH400 series, on which the ignition settings can be adjusted by first checking that the marks on the stator plate and crankcase align, and then – after adjusting them if necessary – by finishing off with a strobe check. In this, the strobe is linked to the lead to the left-hand plug, and it is then pointed at the timing marks with the engine turning at 4000rpm. The marks should still appear in alignment. If not, the three screws holding the stator plate should be loosened just sufficiently for the plate to be moved. It should then be turned until the marks align and the screws are then retightened to hold the timing. Yamaha's CDI system can be similarly timed by moving the pulse coil relative to the stator.

Lighting

Today, given reasonable care, a motor cycle's electrical system is very reliable. The worst that can befall it is for the master fuse to blow, which will kill both lights and engine. This is one good reason for keeping a check on the system.

Battery care

The system's heart is the battery. This demands little more than a visual examination every week to ensure that the electrolyte level is correct. Most bikes now have batteries with see-through cases marked with maximum and minimum level lines to make this easy. There are some awkward examples, but never let the battery become 'out of sight, out of mind'.

Batteries must be topped up only with distilled water. During charging, it is the water content of the electrolyte that boils off, not the acid. Therefore, it is the water content alone that must be made good. Only distilled water is pure enough for the job. Tap water contains all manner of foreign bodies, which may not harm humans, but which can form deposits in a battery that will short out the plates. It is acceptable to use the water that is obtained by defrosting the freezer compartment of a domestic refrigerator, which is, in effect distilled.

Batteries also need to be kept in a fair state of charge. A flat battery is a dying battery, since the vulnerable plates will rapidly become sulphated (a coating of unremovable lead sulphate). At least once a month, the specific gravity should be checked by means of a hydrometer. This is basically a transparent tube, containing a float, into which a sample of electrolyte can be drawn by operating a bulb at one end while a tube at the other is immersed in the liquid.

Draw off a sample and hold the hydrometer at eye level to check where the float is riding. A reading

A typical wiring system

1 tachometer
2 speedometer
3 headlamp connectors
4 indicator
5 charge warning light
6 horn
7 headlamp
8 engine earth
9 light switch
10 terminal block
11 generator coils
12 electric fuel tap
13 coil – cylinder 1
14 coil – cylinder 2
15 spark plug cylinder 1
16 spark plug cylinder 2
17 electronic ignition 'box'
18 magnetic flywheel
19 ignition switch
20 fuse box
21 regulator
22 battery
23 stop light switch
24 rear light unit
25 flasher unit
26 earth
27 earth
28, 29, 30, 31 flashers
32 small connector
33 large connector

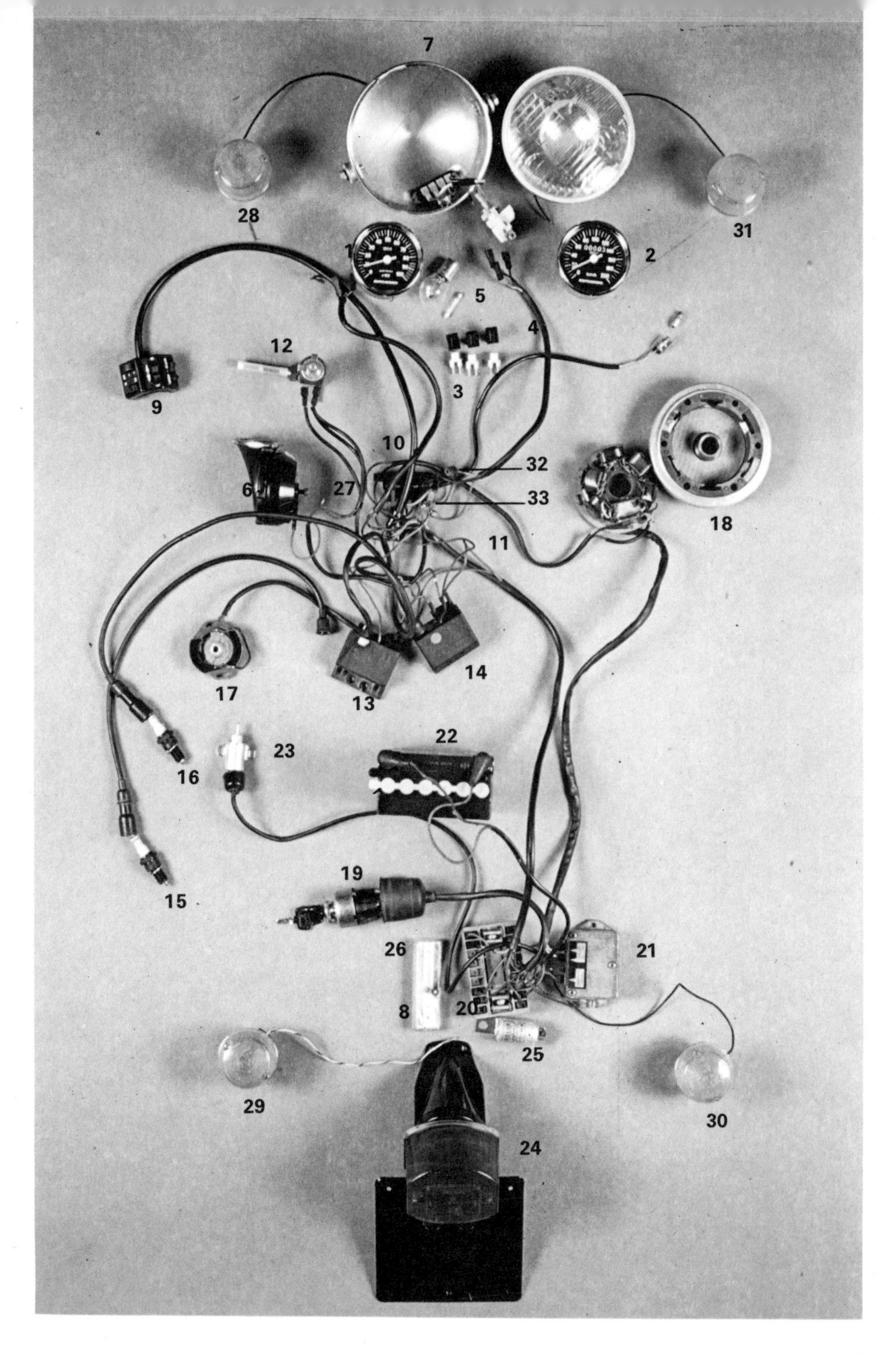
7
28
31
1
2
5
4
12
3
9
10
32
6
27
33
18
11
17
13
14
22
23
16
19
15
26
21
8
20
25
29
30
24

Above: most batteries have translucent cases with marked maximum/minimum fluid levels

of 1.130 or less indicates a completely flat battery, while 1.140–1.160 shows that it is almost flat. From 1.170 to 1.190 you have a quarter-charge, at best, and from 1.200 to 1.220, half-charge. Three-quarters charge is indicated by a reading of 1.230 to 1.250 and full charge from 1.260 to 1.280.

A battery that is slightly down on charge can be given a trickle charge overnight. It's advisable to disconnect the battery terminals, otherwise the transistorised voltage control unit will be damaged by the input. Also check the battery vent tube. If it's kinked, gassing can blow the casing open. Have no naked lights – or any electrical equipment that can spark – near a charging battery. It gives off highly inflammable hydrogen that, if ignited, can blow the battery apart and scatter acid.

Charging or not, the terminals should be disconnected periodically so that they can be cleaned back to bright metal and then smeared with an anti-corrosion jelly – Vaseline is an acceptable substitute – to ward off any future accretion. The same treatment should be given to the contact area between the earth lead and the frame. Any build-up of corrosion on any of the battery connections will cause voltage drop, and reduce the efficiency of the electrics.

Below: apply vaseline or purpose-made jelly to battery terminals to prevent corrosion

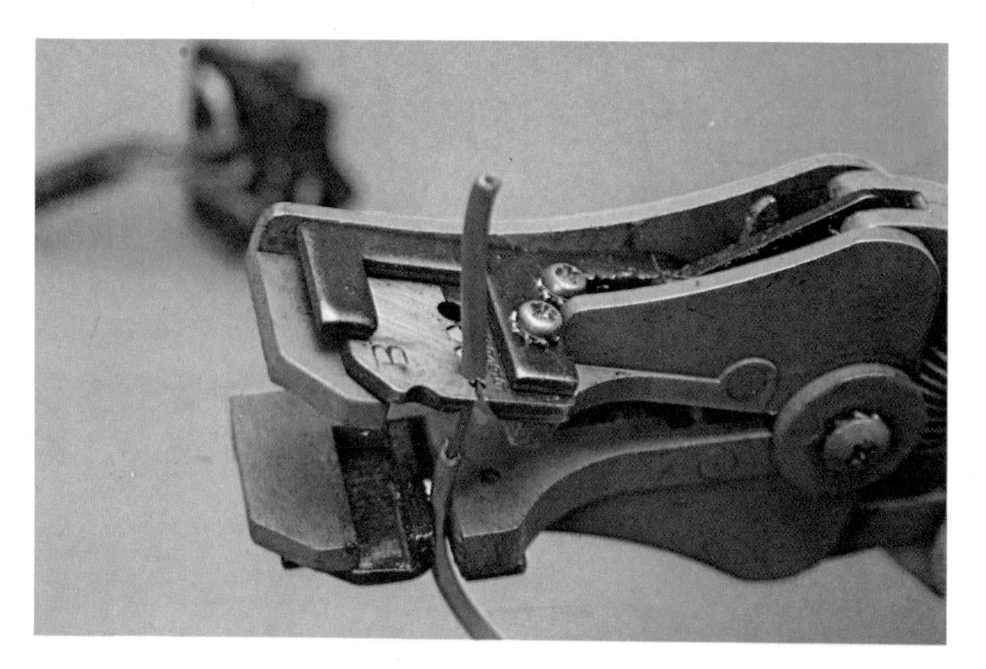

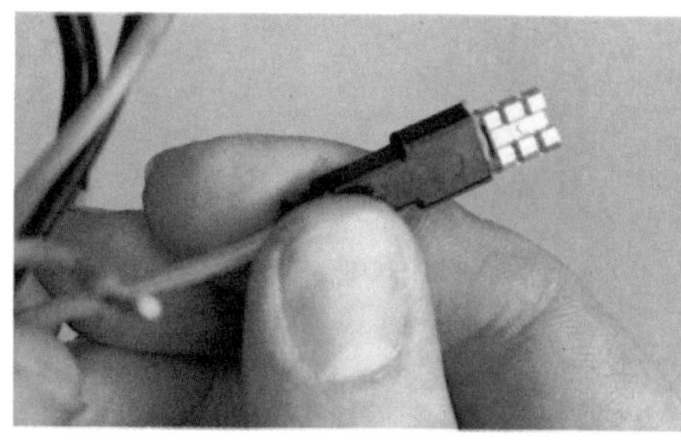

Above: it is best to use a proper wire-stripping tool to bare wires
Left: insulating sleeves should be fitted to connectors

Connector care

Bear this need to avoid high resistances in mind when working your way through the electrical system. Check each terminal and each connector in turn and ensure that it has a bright metal-to-metal contact. Matters are restored easily enough by scraping or polishing both surfaces.

The best way to deal with a loose or faulty terminal is to renew it. Use the wire-cutting jaws of a pair of pliers to snip away the old terminal, then bare the inner conductor by stripping off the outer insulator and fit a new terminal. This may be crimped in place, using a crimping tool. Alternatively, sweat it on with solder, and then lock the tangs on the terminal over the insulator, using a pair of pliers.

Always fit an insulating sleeve when remaking a connection. Bare connectors carry with them the risk of short circuits, and a possible burn-out of the wiring. Any auto-electrician will sell you new insulating sleeves, but if necessary it's acceptable just to wind a turn or two of insulating tape around the connector instead.

The same procedure should be followed when joining wires – perhaps because a break has to be repaired. Strip the insulation away for about 10mm on each side. Clean the inner conductors in meths, dry them, and then twist them securely together. Run solder over the joint to secure it, and then wrap it with insulating tape. Never rely on joints that are just twisted. Eventually, corrosion sets in and the result is yet another area of high resistance to reduce the efficiency of the wiring. It is even better to use a soldered snap connector to restore a break.

Bulb condition

Modern headlamps have quartz-halogen bulbs, giving brilliant lighting. They are, however, very prone to overheating. If you need to remove a halogen bulb, take great care not to handle it by the quartz 'envelope'. You may think your fingers are absolutely clean, but in fact by just touching the bulb you deposit a fingerprint that, although invisible, is greasy. Once the bulb heats up, this grease forms a hot-spot and the envelope rapidly and irrevocably discolours. You then have to fit a new, expensive bulb.

Should you inadvertently touch the glass of a halogen bulb, wash it thoroughly with methylated spirits and then allow it to drip dry. If you wish, you can wipe it carefully with clean soft cloth instead – but the wash in meths is essential.

Reflectors

Another area which should not be touched is the lamp reflector. Nowadays, these are usually sealed with the lens to form a single unit, but on the older-style lamps with removable lens units it is still possible to deposit fingermarks on the silvering. These, again, set up a rapid deterioration. Wash with meths and polish *very* lightly with a soft cloth. Where a reflector has been attacked by weathering, there is no real cure other than resilvering, although a temporary improvement is possible by the use of jeweller's rouge and the type of cloth used on delicate silvered surfaces. This is nothing but a palliative, but it may extend the life of a damaged reflector by a few weeks while you obtain a new one.

Bulbholders

Almost invariably, except in the case of push-on headlamp bulb connectors, bulbholders have a spring-loaded plunger or a spring contact which bears on the contacts of the bulb. In addition, the metal of the connector and the metal of the bulb cap are part of the earth-return system. When checking bulbs, always ensure that the contact surfaces of bulb and connector are polished back to bright metal. Check, also, that the spring in the holder is capable of keeping the plunger hard against the bulb. It can be lubricated with a fluid such as Rocket WD-40.

To test the life left in a conventional bulb, check the envelope visually and discard any bulb on which it has darkened, because this is a sure sign that the bulb is about to blow a filament. Next hold the bulb in one hand and flick the envelope with your fingernail. This *may* snap the filament, but if so, it was due to fail anyway and it's better that it should do so when tested in the garage, rather than on the road.

Lens check

Scratched lenses cannot transmit light efficiently. Each surface of each scratch dissipates light at an angle, instead of allowing the lens to concentrate it. Examine all lenses very closely for this type of surface damage, and discard any that is extensively cut.

Also renew any lens that is cracked – it will allow moisture to enter the lamp, and attack the reflector – or any that has discoloured. This is a particular fault with tail lamps, the red tending to fade after a few years' exposure to light. This check should be made in the dark, with the lamp on. If, at a distance of a few metres, the light has a whitish tint then the lens is due for renewal. It's not just illegal to show a white light to the rear, it's also highly dangerous.

Whenever the lens units are removed for inspection of the lamp and reflector, examine the sealing gasket. Since it is partially exposed to light, it can tend to perish. Once it does so, and distorts, it allows water to enter the lamp. It's not uncommon to find that a bike that spends its lifetime standing outside has lamps partly filled with water. Eventually, this will cause failure of the lights.

Switches

With few exceptions, modern switches are sealed units on which nothing can be done. The only cure for a faulty switch is to detach it and fit a new one. Use of a water-displacing fluid – Rocket WD-40 or its equivalent, again – once or twice each winter will help keep switches in good working order.

With ignition switches, run a little light oil in on the key periodically to keep the tumblers lubricated. In winter, when the switch may tend to freeze up, one of the special lock lubricants should be used. Failing this, lightly moistening the lock with car-type antifreeze applied on the key will prevent the switch freezing up. Be very careful not to get antifreeze on your paintwork, however, or it will damage it severely. Also be careful after applying any liquid to the lock not to put the dirty key in your pocket without wiping it.

Rolling Chassis

Chassis repair open to a diy mechanic is limited to the brakes, the steering head bearings, the front forks, the rear fork pivot, wheel bearings, damper renewal and minor ancillary parts. Major repairs such as frame trueing or wheel building must be left to the professionals.

Disc brake overhaul

Although the majority of disc brakes currently fitted to bikes on the British market are made in Japan, virtually all of them originated from Girling and are produced under Girling licence. The main types in use today – apart from those on European machines – are all single-piston calliper units, in which one pad is pressed against the disc by the direct action of the piston, while the other is brought into contact by the calliper sliding or swinging as a reaction to piston movement. A few lightweights have cable-operated disc brakes instead.

Unless the piston is to be removed for new seals to be fitted there is no need to drain the hydraulic system before working on the brakes. If the piston is to be removed, however, the fluid will have to be pumped out by following the procedure described earlier for draining the system before renewing the fluid.

For all practical purposes, brake servicing usually means no more than pad renewal. This is accomplished by unbolting the calliper from the bike – in the case of sliding units – and dropping the wheel where a swinging-calliper is used. The calliper body is then split, allowing the fixed pad to be withdrawn.

With the sliding-calliper unit used on Suzukis, for example, the fixed pad is held by a single cross-headed screw inserted through a cap on the inner side of the unit. Freeing this screw allows the fixed pad to be withdrawn. The slider is then slipped towards the now-empty fixed-pad housing, giving room for the piston pad to be eased out.

Where piston removal is necessary the system is first drained, and the union on the flexible brake hose is disconnected so that the entire brake can be removed from the bike. Then the pads are removed. The two bolts on which the slider is mounted are next undone, and the slider moved to give room in which to reach the piston dust seal. The piston is grooved, and a pair of screwdrivers can be inserted to lever it out of place. Lastly, the slider is detached. If a piston proves stubborn, the hydraulics can be reconnected and the unit pumped out.

Yamaha four-strokes generally use a brake with wedge-shaped pads

Removing a pad securing pin. Arrowed, the bleed valve

The hydraulic brake master cylinder reservoir. Take care no dirt enters it

rather than the round ones used on the Suzuki. On this brake, too, the fixed pad is held by a cross-headed screw, but to remove the pads the bolt securing the cover to the calliper body also has to be undone. The cover then pulls off, leaving the pads free for removal. Here again, this is as far as you can go without draining the fluid and detaching the complete calliper. If this is done, you can also remove the piston. Take off the dust cover, which is held by a wire circlip – and lever out the piston.

On the latest Hondas, a somewhat similar brake is employed. Here, the cover is held by two bolts, and the base slides on pins that are protected by rubber bellows. The pads slot into the base and are wedge-shaped.

The earlier Honda swinging-calliper brake used circular pads. In these, the fixed pad is held in its housing by a split pin. To renew this pad, the two bolts holding the outer (piston) housing to the brake arm are undone and the inner housing taken off. The pad can be pulled out once its split pin has been removed. The outer pad can be detached either with the wheel dropped out and the inner housing unbolted or with the brake arm detached from the forks by removal of its pivot and adjuster bolts. Further stripping is similar to that of the other brakes described in this section.

When a piston is removed, it must be thoroughly washed in methylated spirit or fresh hydraulic fluid. So, too, must the bore in which it operates. When refitting a piston, and seals, they must also be lubricated with clean hydraulic fluid. No other form of lubricant must be used.

To determine whether or not the parts are fit for further service they should be checked with micrometers. Tolerances are very fine. The Suzuki brake bore, for example, has a nominal diameter of 42.85mm, and a service limit of 42.89mm. The piston has a standard diameter of 42.82mm and a service limit of 42.77mm.

Where the piston is not to be disturbed, but new pads have to be fitted, the piston must be pressed back into its bore to give clearance for the new pads. This will force fluid back into the reservoir, which could overflow if care is not taken. The trick is to push the piston part-way home and then syphon out some of the fluid. The easiest way is to insert a short length of plastic tube so that its end is immersed in the fluid. Place a thumb over the other end, and the suction will hold a column of fluid in the tube for disposal. Repeat this as necessary until the piston is pressed fully home in its bore. With a twin-disc layout, the other piston must be locked in place by inserting a wedge into the disc gap, or it will be expelled instead.

When fitting the new pads, it is usual to smear a little white brake grease on to the pad mounting plates, at the points at which they will bear on the face of the housing and the piston, in an effort to prevent 'squeal'. Be sparing with this grease, and make absolutely sure that it does not contaminate the friction surfaces. On Suzukis, only the fixed pad must be greased.

Bleed the brakes and with the Honda swinging calliper carry out the adjustment procedure so that there is 0.15mm clearance between the disc and the inner pad.

Master cylinder

Normally, diy stripping of the master cylinder is not to be recommended. It usually means having a special pair of long-nosed, right-angled circlip pliers, and the clearances involved between the parts are even finer than those of the piston/bore in the calliper.

The procedure is similar on most master cylinders. An internal circlip, just accessible after the front brake lever has been removed, has to be released first. Then the piston, check valve, coil spring and primary cup can be slipped out or – if they stick – gently expelled by inserting a smooth wooden dowel from the opposite end.

The bore can be checked – standard bore on the Suzuki GS400 unit is 14mm and the part is worn out if the bore is 14.05mm. Piston tolerances are even closer – 13.96mm standard, 13.94mm the limit. Figures like these explain why it is essential to guard the working surfaces of hydraulics from so much as a scratch. One needs something more akin to laboratory conditions, rather than those of a workshop,

The front wheel has to be removed before drum brakes can be overhauled

when dealing with hydraulic systems.

For rebuilding, the parts must be thoroughly lubricated with fresh fluid, and the piston unit must be pre-assembled for insertion into the bore, using a new primary cup as a matter of course. Once the assembly is home, fit the circlip and then make certain that it is properly seated by oscillating it in its groove. As with all other spring rings, a new circlip has to be used here.

Drum brake overhaul

Mechanically operated drum brakes are simple to overhaul compared with hydraulic discs. Removal is easy – take out the wheel and the backplate usually draws off unimpeded, although some are held to a false spindle by retaining nuts.

To change the shoes, simply pull them apart – against the resistance of their springs – until they can be eased away from the cam at one end and the pivot at the other.

If the shoes are off, there's no good reason why the chance shouldn't be taken to grease the cam spindle. Just

To remove the brake shoes from the hub they must first be pulled apart

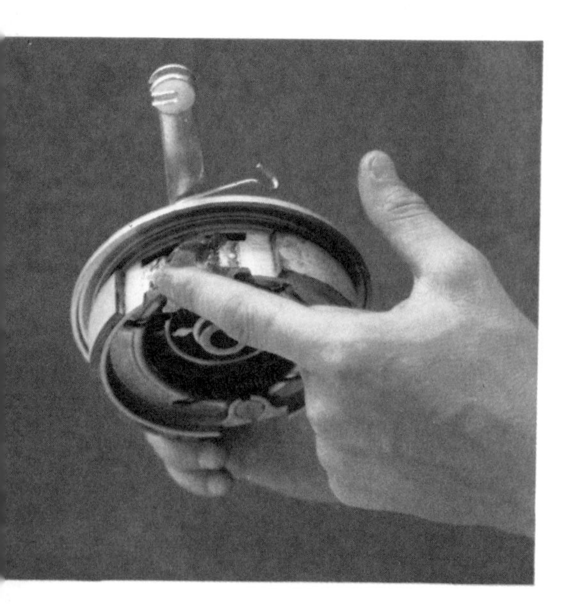

The spring locating holes should be smeared with brake grease on reassembly

detach the brake arm – split, usually, and locked by a pinch-bolt – and press it out. It may well be shimmed and if so, make certain that you keep all the washers and know which side to place them. Clean the spindle and its bushing; apply brake grease (or lithium-based grease, if the makers recommend it) and refit the spindle and arm.

New shoes should be linked by the springs removed from the old ones, making certain that they go into the original positions. Then, with the pivot and cams lightly smeared with brake grease, expand the shoes until they engage with first the pivot and then the cams. Ease them home, and work the cam by operating the brake arm to ensure that they take up their proper position. Smear the engagement holes for the springs with brake grease; clean all dust out of the drum; and refit the backplate.

Wheel bearings

Current wheel bearings are, almost without exception, non-adjustable: when they wear, they have to be renewed. To do so, remove the wheel and take off the dust caps, (there may also be screwed rings). Insert a drift from one side, slightly angled so that it rests against the inside face of the far bearing. Hit the drift smartly with a hammer, and the bearing should be driven out, which should leave you a clear space in which to insert the drift to drive out the second bearing.

Wash the bearings in paraffin and then very lightly oil them before

Here a bearing housing is being removed with a drift and hammer

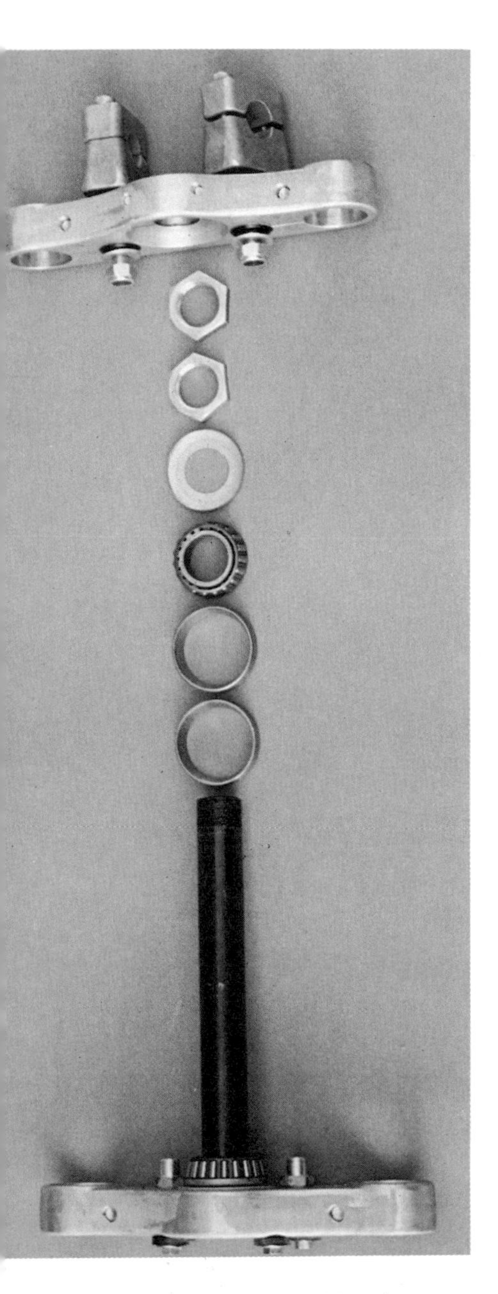

Above: a typical steering-head bearing assembly in exploded form. It utilises caged taper rollers

spinning them as a test. If they are noisy, discard them and fit new ones. Otherwise, assess the amount of wear. If the bearings are within limits, and the tracks are not pitted, they can be refitted.

Pack the bearings – new or old – with grease. Clean out the hub, and pack that too with fresh grease. Don't fill it; too much grease will melt as the brakes heat up and burst past the seals. Instead, just line the hub all round to a depth of about 6mm. Drive in the bearings, using a block of softwood as a 'cushion' between the bearings and the hammer.

Head bearings

Head bearing tracks are renewed in much the same way as are wheel

Below: undoing a clamp and the nut above before removing a steering assembly

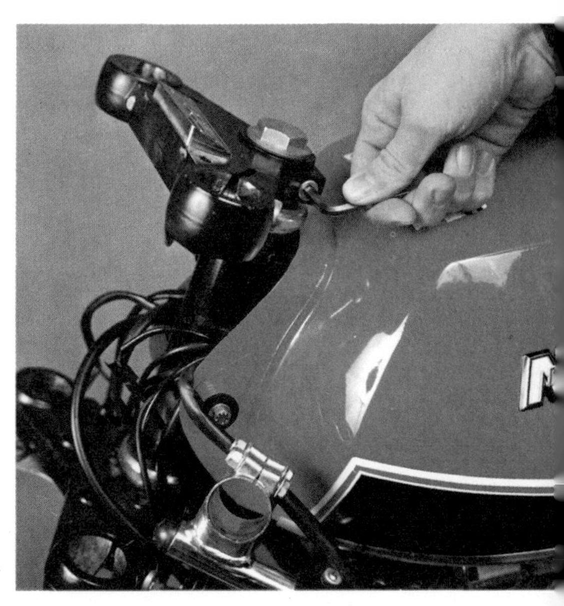

Right: on models which feature ball races, care must be taken not to lose any of the bearing balls during disassembly
Below: the upper bearing track has to be drifted out of its housing
Below right: when reassembling the bearings, the bearing balls should be pressed into a bed of grease to hold them in position

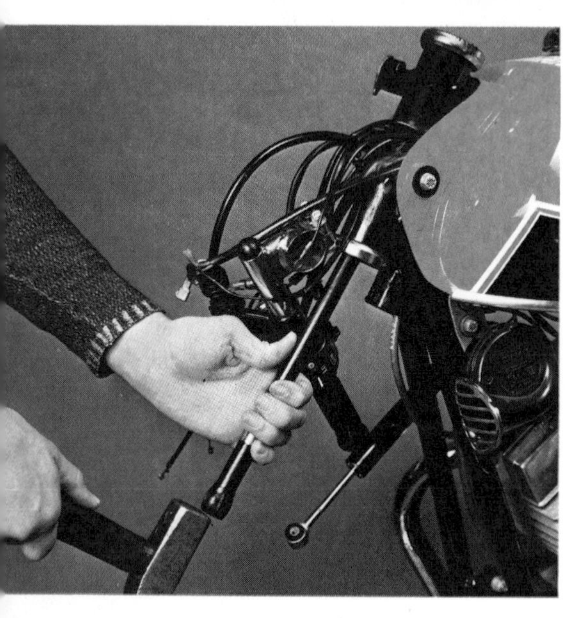

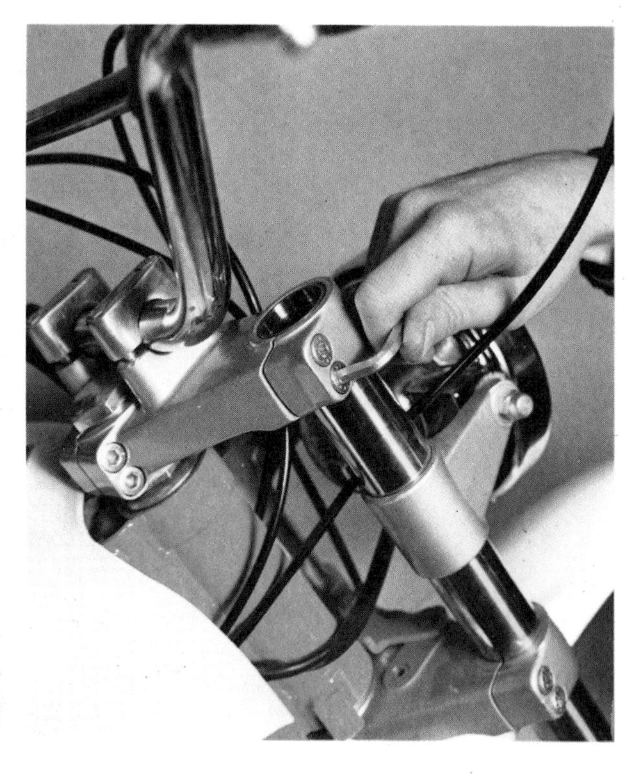

The fork legs will slide out once the yoke clamps are released

bearings. Once the front forks have been removed, the upper bearing track can be driven out from below and the lower track by inserting a drift from the top of the head. With ball races, a lower track is carried on the front fork yoke. Where taper-roller races are used, the yoke carries the caged rollers instead. In either case, this part of the bearing can usually be levered free of its seating and slipped up the stem. A pair of tyre levers makes the best extractor.

To assemble a ball race, coat the tracks thickly with grease and lay the balls into this 'nest' of lubricant. It will hold them securely in place while the forks are offered up. The races can then be adjusted in the normal way.

Fork legs

Rather than removing the entire fork assembly for attention, it is more usual to treat telescopic forks as two units, either of which can be detached individually. Suzuki practice is typical. The spindle clamps and speedo drive should be undone so that the wheel can be dropped out and, very importantly, wooden strips must be inserted into the spaces between the brake pads vacated by the discs. That stops the pistons from being summarily ejected if you should happen to press the brake lever.

The callipers should next be removed from the legs – two bolts each, in this case – and tied securely out of the way. Don't just leave them hanging on the pipes – it'll cause damage.

With the mudguard off the fork legs will be ready to be dropped. The clamp bolt at the top yoke is freed off first, followed by the clamp bolt at the lower bridge. A steady pull on the leg then draws it clear, leaving the headlamp supported on its bracket. On bikes with upper fork leg shrouds, the leg still pulls out to leave the shroud nipped into position between yoke and bridge.

Where a leg is to be stripped, it must be drained. Suzuki have a drain hole just above the spindle, closed

Above: it may be necessary to lever the clamp open slightly to free the leg
Right: the forks on this model are drained via the drain hole above the spindle

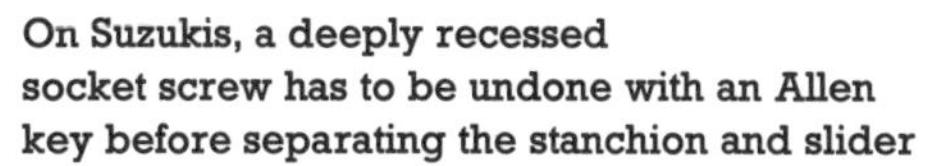

On Suzukis, a deeply recessed socket screw has to be undone with an Allen key before separating the stanchion and slider

Seals which are to be replaced can be levered out with a screwdriver, though care must be taken

by a screw. Honda usually omit a separate drain in favour of pouring the fluid out through the filler orifice at the top of the leg, although it is possible to drain the oil by undoing the socket-headed bolt that is deeply recessed into the leg above the spindle. Take care – it also retains the complete slider. For draining purposes, it's quite sufficient to loosen the bolt.

Fork leg strip

Again, Suzuki practice is typical – although, like those of Kawasaki, their fork legs demand special tools for the job. With the leg removed and drained, the spring is slipped out and then an Allen key is used to remove the socket screw set in the base of the slider. This is deeply recessed, demanding use of a long extension and a special tool. Once the socket has been loosened, the gaiter at the top of the slider can be eased from its slot and the stanchion and slider parted.

On some of the Kawasaki forks the operation is almost identical; on others, the slider is secured to the leg by the upper collar nut. These forks are dismantled by securing the lower end of the slider into a vice – well padded, to prevent damage – and then applying a chain wrench to the collar nut to unscrew it.

Forks will normally be stripped only for renewal of the slider bushes

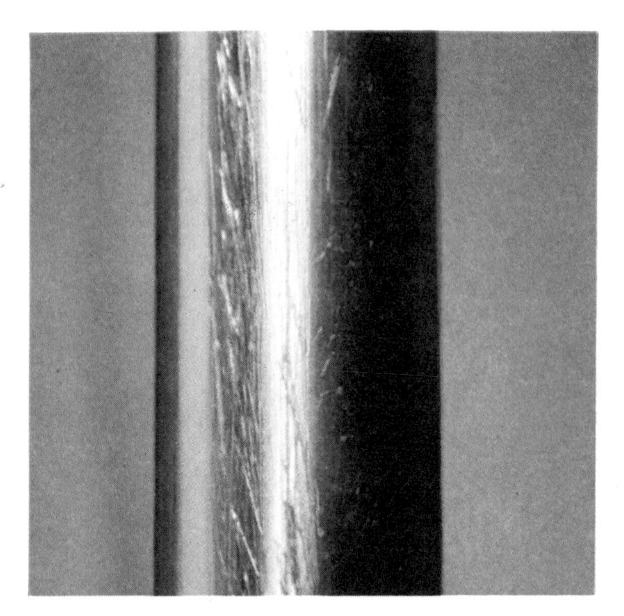

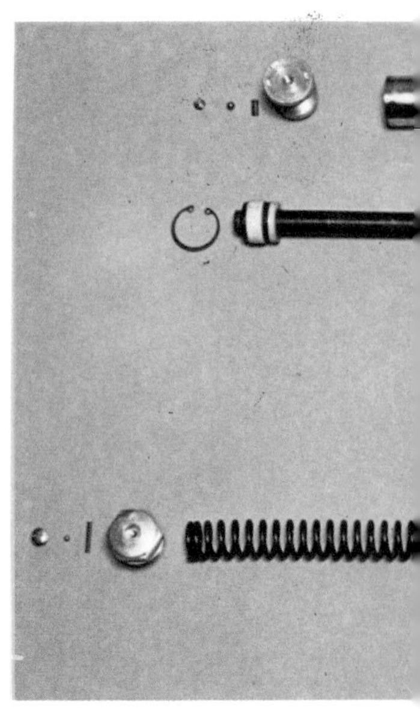

This stanchion is too badly scored to be rescued simply by polishing

or the vulnerable oil seals. It is common practice for the seal to be located by a wire circlip, which can be eased out with a screwdriver. Then the seal can be lifted out. Professional mechanics use a tool designed to do the job, but since the seal is to be renewed it is permissible to lever this, too, out of place by use of a screwdriver, providing due care is taken not to gouge the light-alloy slider. With the seal out, the fork bush can usually be removed without difficulty, although a little local heat to expand the slider will do the trick in stubborn cases. Fit the new bush and the new oil seal, lubricating it with oil so that it presses home easily. Providing the seal is offered up square to the slider it will be easy enough to tap it home with a block of softwood.

Check the section of the stanchion that operates within the seal. If the original seal has failed for any reason other than sheer old age, the likeliest answer is surface imperfections on the stanchion. It may be possible to polish-out the damage, but if not the stanchion must be renewed, or it will simply cut the new seal and re-open the leak.

Fork springs

When removing the springs, make a note of which way round they are intended to be refitted. Some springs are multi-rate, the action stiffening with the severity of the bump. These have widely spaced coils at the lower end and more closely-spaced coils at the top. On some bikes the spring is tapered instead. Here, the smaller-diameter end is the lower one. Still others use a pair of springs

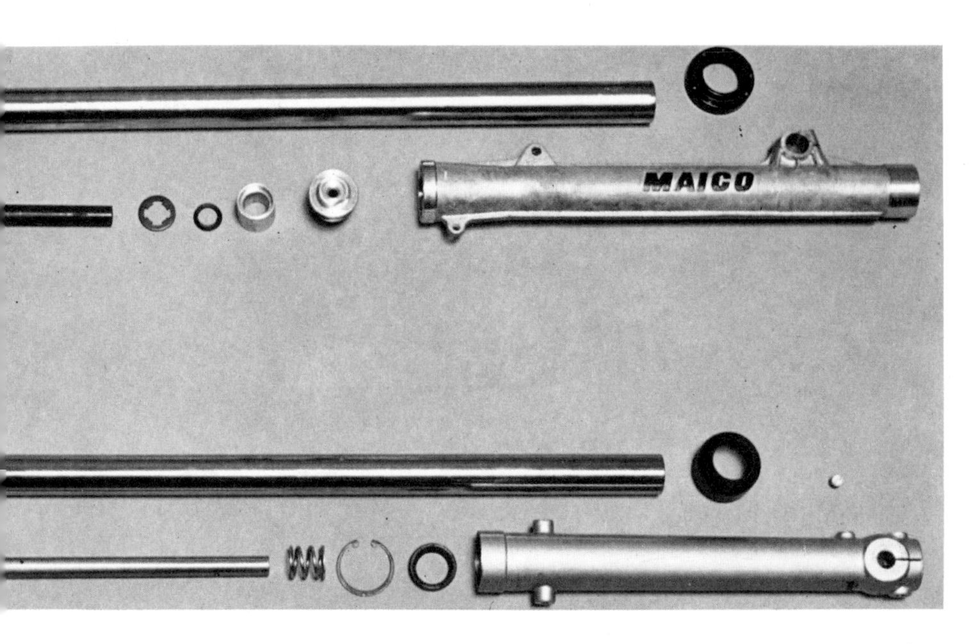

The fork leg in exploded form

separated by a collar. This gives a multi-rate action. The smaller spring is usually the upper one.

Fork springs can weaken with use, the coils compressing so that the free length alters. Check the measurement of the spring against the standards set out in the appropriate workshop manual. Usually, a spring needs to be renewed when its free length is around three per cent less than that of a new one.

Rear damper units

Apart from removal of the springs and renewal of the pivot bushes, rear spring/damper units offer no scope for diy work. To remove the springs, they should be locked with spring compressors – tools rather like huge valve spring compressors. The collets retaining the upper collar can then be removed, and the compressor gradually freed to release the spring. Some springs are heavily compressed, and if not released properly can shoot out with a lethal force.

Simply inspect the rear dampers for signs of fluid leakage. If they are letting oil escape they must be scrapped – and the dealer who supplies the new dampers might just as well have the chore of fitting the springs as well.

Rear fork pivot

In the past and even on some shaft-drive bikes of today, the rear fork pivot was a giant taper-roller bearing. Nowadays, it is usually little more than a spindle and some plain bushes. They all have a major job to do, however; if there is play in the rear fork pivot the rear wheel will

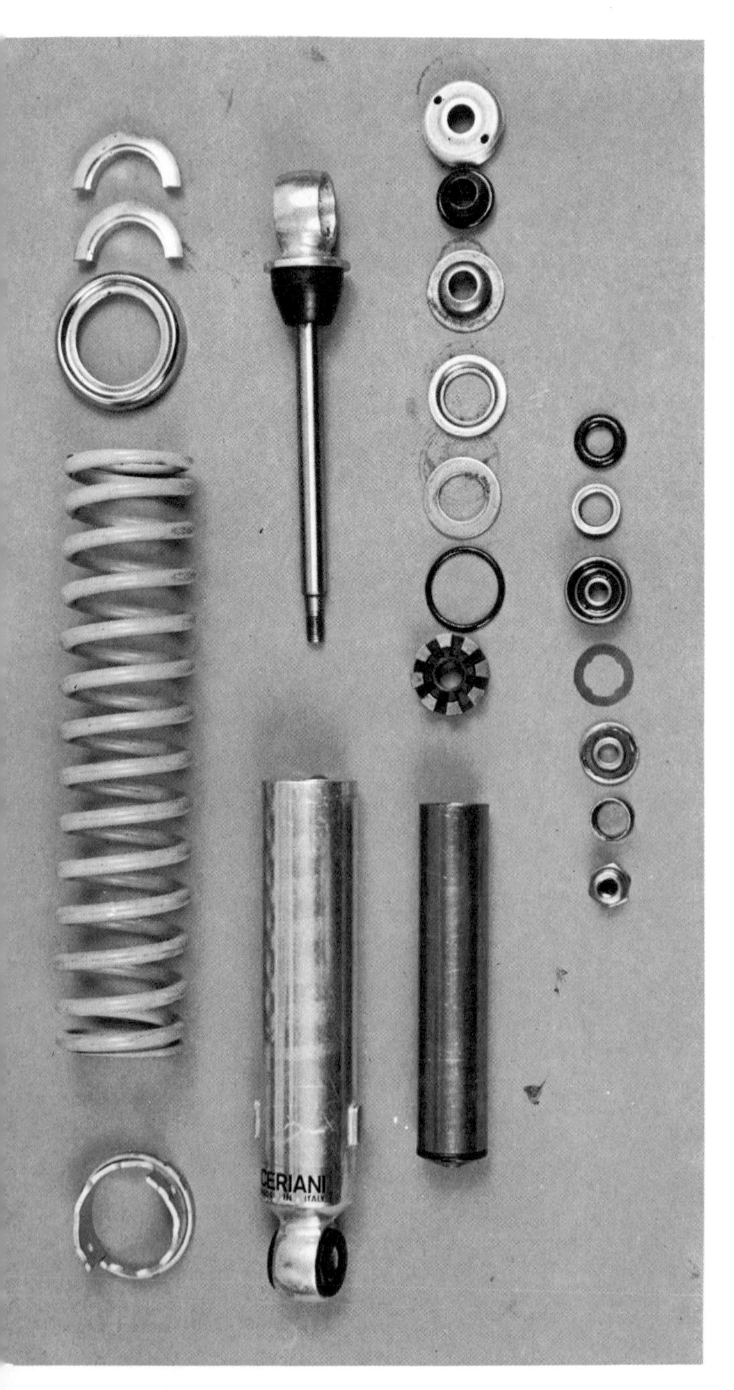

A rear damper spring assembly in exploded form. In practice, however, it is usually impossible to strip a unit to this stage. For diy work, just remove the spring and refit it to a new or service-exchange damper

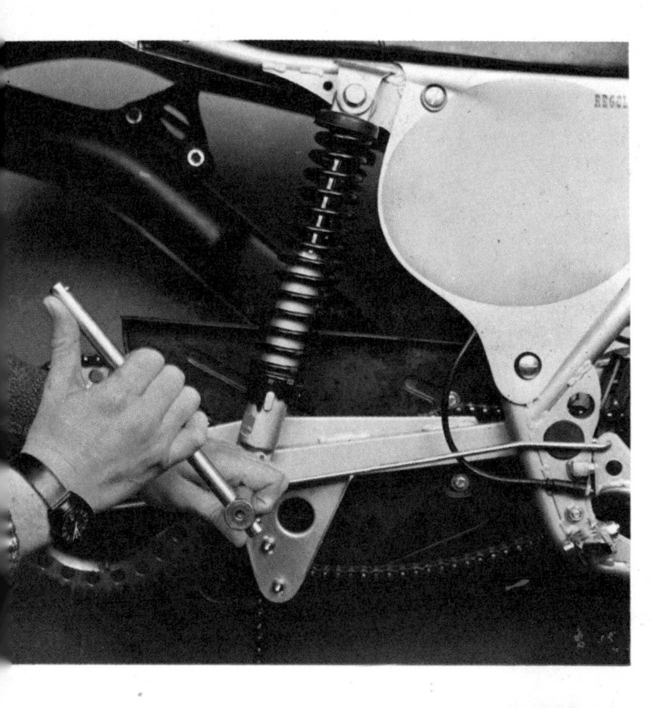

Left: before the rear fork pivot can be checked the rear spring units should be removed
Below: the pivot bush can be tapped out with a shouldered drift

try to steer the bike, which is an unnerving experience.

To rectify the problem, remove the rear wheel, rear spring units and any incumbrance on the fork itself. Undo the spindle nut and tap out the spindle, using a soft drift to get it moving.

Pivot bushes can be driven out with a shouldered drift, or pressed out by using a spacer, long bolt, nut and collar to push the old bush out as the new one is inserted. This is the tidiest way, wherever possible, since it does both jobs simultaneously.

After the new bushes have been fitted, they may need to be reamed – a point on which it is impossible to generalise. The spindle must also be checked for distortion, preferably between centres and using a dial

Right: with the pivot removed the swinging arm will come away
Below: here new bushes are being driven into place – they may then need reaming

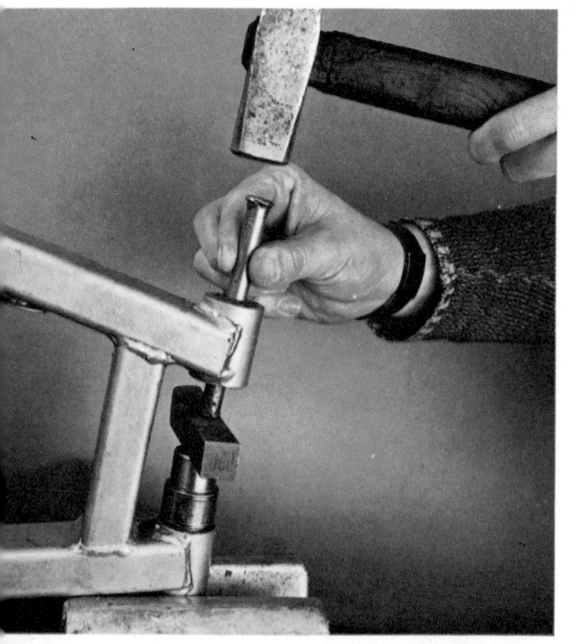

gauge, although a series of measurements with feelers taken with the spindle shank flat on a face-plate is a possible diy alternative. A typical service limit would be any distortion greater than 0.5mm.

Tyre changing

For some reason, tyre changing is an operation which seems to deter amateurs; yet it is basically an easy one. To remove a tyre, take out the wheel and set it flat on the ground. Remove the valve core, so that all air can be expelled, then tread right round one side of the tyre with all your weight to break the bead seal and push the tyre bead right down into the well.

Undo the locknut or ring on the valve, wipe soapy water right round the opposite side of the tyre to ease it later on, and start lifting the already displaced bead with tyre levers. Start immediately alongside the valve, inserting two levers about 300mm apart. Press down on both levers at once and a section of bead will be lifted from the rim. Take out one lever, move it along about 150mm and reinsert it. Press it to raise that length of bead off the rim, then hold it and take out the second lever. That, in turn, should be inserted 150mm further on in the other direction, pressed, lifted out and inserted again an equal distance along. Keep leap-frogging from side to side with the levers until you have lifted half the bead from the rim. The tyre should now pull off by hand if you brace yourself with one hand flat on the spokes, and the other grasping the tyre. This speeds the operation up, although there's no reason why the entire cover shouldn't be freed by use of the levers if you prefer.

Remove the tube by pulling it out until it is held just by the valve, then pressing the end of the valve in until it is clear of its hole.

This is as far as you need go for puncture repairs, but for a tyre change the whole cover needs to be removed, which requires the levers again. Free the second bead by treading it, as before, and then insert your pair of levers across the beads from above, engaging them on the opposite side of the rim. A couple of hearty pushes on the levers should lift about 400mm of bead across the wheel and off the other side. A repeat operation with each lever

Standing on the tyre wall will break the bead seal

Tyre levers should be used approximately 300mm apart

about 100mm further round should free enough of the cover for the rest to be pulled away. Grasp the cover with one hand, at the point where it is clear of the wheel. Grasp the wheel with the other, and pull the wheel towards you and the cover away from you. It should come away like the skin from a banana.

Check the condition of the rim tape – which today is more usually a rubber ring – and remove it so that you can clean up the inside of the rim. Brush away any loose rust, and check for any protruding spoke ends. Grind these down before they can puncture the tube. Wash the rim tape and refit it if it is in good condition, but take no chances with a split one. Renew it if you're in doubt, remembering that when the tube is inflated it takes up the shape of the rim well, and that the tape is the only thing that prevents the spoke ends digging in to it.

To fit the new tyre, first thoroughly lubricate the beads. Soapy water will do the trick, although you can use plain washing-up liquid or a professional tyre bead lubricant. Check which way the cover has to be fitted. It almost certainly has an arrow moulded on it to indicate the direction of rotation, and this can differ depending on whether the cover is to be used on the front wheel or the back. It is usually there to show which way round will give the longest tyre life, since the treads will normally perform as well in either direction.

With the wheel again flat on the ground, offer up the tyre. The section that has to go nearest the valve is usually marked with dots and this should be accurately aligned so that the balance is correct.

Now inflate the tube just enough for it to take up its recognisable shape and feed the valve through the hole. Screw the valve locking ring on by just a few turns, so that the valve cannot withdraw, and feed the tube round the cover, one section in each direction alternately. Make certain that it sits properly, with no twists or bunching.

Now start to fit the cover over the rim. With the wheel still flat, press into place that section of the beading that is at the side directly opposite the valve. Use both hands for the job but not, at this stage, tyre levers. If the cover feels stiff, give it a bit more lubrication.

Working, as before, in sections about 150mm long, continue to ease the beads over the rim. If you work accurately from side to side, you'll end up with a final section, adjacent to the valve, where perhaps 600mm of tyre bead is stretched tight, straight across the wheel.

Some mechanics can twist this last section on by hand, but it's quite permissible to use a pair of tyre levers instead, providing it's done properly. Insert the levers, one at each side, after giving the beading a really thorough lubrication – wipe the liquid on with rag, so that it really covers all the beading. Then press the valve stem right in, as far as the lockring. This lifts the tube completely clear of the rim. Keep the valve in this position and twist one of the levers. Another section of bead should slip easily over the rim. Twist the second lever, and you should be down to about 300mm of bead. Take out the levers, grasp the cover from the opposite side and twist it sharply towards you. It should slide into place. If not, insert one lever and lift it in with the valve still held right down.

The inner tube is removed leaving the valve until last

When refitting the tyre, care should be taken not to nip the inner tube

Now pull out the valve, turn down the lockring, and inflate the tube to around $3^1/_2$ bars (45–50lb per sq in) so that it presses the cover hard into place. Check that the line moulded right round the tyre is concentric on the rim. If it isn't, you have an oval wheel instead of a round one: but it's easily corrected by deflating the tyre, again freeing the locknut right to the end of the valve and pushing the valve as far as it will go into the rim, and relubricating the bead. A second inflation to $3^1/_2$ bars should then seat the cover properly.

With the line concentric on both sides, reduce the pressure to the recommended figure. Tighten down the lockring or locknut, and fit the valve cap. This is more than a dust cover, remember: it is also the emergency seal should the valve core fail.

Tubeless tyres

Tubeless tyres, obviously, require no contortions with the valve since there is no tube to be protected from pinching. They pose their own problems, however, in being an exceptionally tight fit on rims that are themselves highly vulnerable to damage. Proceed as above, but take great care to lubricate the beads thoroughly. The seating areas of the rim must be meticulously cleaned before installation of a new cover, and tyre levers should be used sparingly – preferably, not at all, although that is probably an impossible requirement.

A tubeless tyre also demands a heavy initial inflation to seat it hard enough for pressure to build up, and this usually means blasting the beads into place with a garage airline. The traditional diy method is to wrap rope round the circumference of the cover, twisting it down hard with a peg inserted to form a Spanish windlass. This tourniquet presses the beads into place while, hopefully, sufficient pressure can be generated with a car-type foot pump.

Glossary

Allen key A small cranked wrench, of hexagonal section, for use on socket-headed screws

Alternator An electrical generator producing alternating current, which must be rectified to direct current for battery charging

Armature In a generator or starter motor, the shaft carrying the windings. In a relay, the part that is subject to the influence of the magnetic field

Backlash The play between the teeth of a pair of meshing gears, measured radially

Ball bearing An anti-friction bearing in which a series of caged balls runs between inner and outer tracks

Bar The unit of atmospheric pressure in the Système Internationale, roughly equivalent to 14lb per sq in

Bead wire The wire which stiffens each bead of a tyre, enabling it to seal against the bead seat in the wheel rim

Bearing ball A single ball from a ball bearing. Usually applied to the components of an uncaged bearing, as in some steering heads

Bevel gear Used to transmit motion through a right angle. A conical-shaped pinion, which meshes with one of similar profile, as in the final drive unit of a shaft-drive bike

Bleed nipple A small valve in a hydraulic system which can be opened to enable fluid and air to be pumped out by operation of the control lever or pedal

Bore The internal working surface of a cylinder. Usually refers to an engine cylinder, but can apply, for instance, to the brake master cylinder. Also used to define the radius of the cylinder, usually in millimetres

Bridge On motor cycle forks, the top plate linking the two stanchions and the steering head stem

Bucket tappet Normally found in double ohc engines, this type of tappet is a small cylinder closed at one end. The cam bears on the solid end surface, and the tappet transmits motion to the valve stem through an intermediate shim. The shim thickness can be varied to alter the valve clearance

Bush A plain bearing, usually of soft metal such as phosphor-bronze. If closed at one end, it is called 'blind'

Capacitor Also known as a condenser. An electrical shock absorber which minimises sparking at contact-breaker points. Also used to store an electrical charge in CDI systems

Castellations Slots cut across the flats of a nut which enable a pin or spring circlip to be inserted to prevent subsequent movement once the nut has been tightened

Cc or Cm^3 Abbreviations for cubic centimetre – the standard unit of cylinder capacity outside the USA

CDI Capacitor Discharge Ignition. An electronic ignition system which dispenses with the use of contact breakers, using solid-state devices instead

Circlip A split wire circle, or a spring-steel stamping formed like a round horseshoe, used to lock the gudgeon pin into a piston. Also used in various applications to hold components such as some clutch bodies, or to provide end location for pinions on shafts

Clevis A connector, shaped like a 'U', which can slip over an operating arm. It is then held by a clevis pin, which forms a pivot. The end connection of brake and clutch controls is typical

Clutch body The main drum of the clutch containing the

friction and plain plates and the clutch centre. Usually also carries the drive pinion or sprocket

Clutch plate Either a plain plate or one with friction linings. They also differ in their drive tangs, one being designed to fit the clutch centre and the other the clutch body. When pressed together by springs, they transmit drive. When the pressure is released, the plates still driven by the clutch centre revolve but transmit no movement

Collet Used mainly, though not exclusively, to hold valve caps to the valve stems. A split collar, tapered in profile, which can lock in a similarly shaped hole in the cap and in a recess in the stem

Combination spanner A spanner which carries an open jaw at one end and a ring at the other

Compression ring A split ring, seated in a groove cut round the side of a piston, to provide a gastight seal between the piston and the combustion chamber. In two-strokes, it is located by a peg to prevent the ends moving into such a position that they might catch in the ports

Countershaft An intermediate shaft in a transmission train

Crown The upper face of a piston, which, together with the inner surfaces of the cylinder head, forms the combustion chamber

Crosshead A type of screw fastening in which the head carries a cruciform slot. Can be undone with the appropriate cross-headed screwdriver

C-spanner Designed for use on screwed collars with slots or holes in place of hexagons. So called because of its shape

Cush-drive A shock-absorbing system, using a series of rubber cushions and metal vanes, built into the transmission to minimise snatch under light load. On shaft-drive bikes, often supplemented by a system of face cams and springs

Damper A hydraulic system that enables a spring to move easily on shock, but which then slows down the rebound to prevent the suspension oscillating. Can also refer to the face cam and spring shock-absorbing system (*see* Cush-drive)

Decoke Another word for decarbonising. Periodic removal of carbon from the combustion chamber, piston crown, ports and exhaust

Dog An abutment formed on the face of a pinion or selector which can be moved into engagement with a matching slot on the face of an adjoining unit, to lock it to a shaft

Disc valve On two-strokes, a thin spring-steel disc, rotating with the crankshaft, which opens and closes the inlet port to the crankcase

Dowel A small pin, sometimes tubular, which enters a close-tolerance hole to locate mating parts

Drawbolt The bolt/locknut system used to pull the rear wheel spindle backwards to tension the final drive chain

Electrode In a sparking plug, either the central rod down which HT current passes, or the small projection from the body to which the spark jumps

Electrolyte The solution of distilled water and sulphuric acid in a lead-acid motor cycle battery

End float The end play of an assembly such as a crankshaft or gear shaft when installed in its housing

EP Extreme Pressure. A designation used for a lubricant for heavily loaded surfaces such as the bevel pinion and crown wheel in a shaft final drive unit

Filter For oil, usually a renewable cartridge which absorbs impurities from the lubricant. On some machines, a centrifugal device which spins out impurities into catch chambers. For air, either a dry paper element or a wire mesh wetted with oil to trap dust particles. For fuel, a mesh which prevents large solids from passing, or a gravity trap through which petrol flows leaving the solids behind

First motion shaft In a motor cycle gearbox, the mainshaft, which is driven either direct from the crankshaft or through a countershaft

Gear pump An oil pump in which the lubricant is pressurised by the action of a pair of intermeshing gearwheels in a confined housing

Graphite A solid lubricant which can be simulated by rubbing a pencil lead on to a component. Available in powder form

Grinding paste Carborundum grit in an oily base, used for cutting back surfaces. Available as a coarse paste for heavy work or fine paste for lighter jobs

Grommet A ring of neoprene or similar material used to protect leads or cables where they pass through a panel

Grubscrew A headless screw, threaded throughout its length, and slotted at the top. Normally used as a locking device

Gudgeon pin Otherwise called a piston pin or a wrist pin, this short hollow shaft passes through the piston and small-end bearing to hold the piston to the connecting rod

Hooked Damage to the teeth of a sprocket caused by improper tensioning. The upper part of the tooth is pulled out of line with the lower, giving the appearance of a hook

HT High Tension. The high-voltage (approx. 15–18kV) current produced by the ignition system

Hydrometer An instrument used to measure the specific gravity of a liquid. On bikes, normally used only to check the battery; but on liquid-cooled models a version can also be employed to check the antifreeze solution

Idler A free-running gear or sprocket, such as the roller used to tension some types of cam chain

Impact screwdriver A screwdriver which is activated by striking a plunger on its end with a hammer. This jars the threads and spins the bit in one operation. Essential for removing really tight screws

Journal Sometimes wrongly applied to bearings. In fact, strictly refers to the part of a shaft that is in contact with the bearing

Key A metal tang, often half-moon shaped, which is an interference fit in a slot in a shaft, from which it stands proud to provide a positive location for a mating slotted component, such as a rotor or a pinion

Kg/m A measure of the force applied when tightening a fastening; equivalent to a pull of one kilogram at a metre radius. For practical purposes, can be equated with the daNM (deca Newton Metres) in SI (Système Internationale) measurements

Layshaft The shaft in a gearbox driven from the mainshaft. Usually carries the final drive. Also known as the second motion shaft

Lb/ft A measure of the force applied when tightening a fastening; equivalent to a pull of one pound at a foot radius. One lb/ft is equal to 0.138kg/m

Mainshaft *See* First motion shaft

Mandrel A bar or rod used for centring, especially when offering up before assembly

Needle roller Very narrow, elongated rollers. Normally used caged, in some small-end applications or in gearboxes or clutches

Obstruction spanner A spanner which is specially shaped to enable it to be used on awkwardly placed fastenings such as cylinder base nuts on some multi-cylinder bikes

Oil control ring Sometimes referred to as a 'scraper' ring. Used as the lowest-mounted of the rings on a piston, it is slotted and ported so that it can remove excess oil from the bore and feed it back into the sump

Open-ended spanner A spanner with open, angled jaws

Overlap In valve timing, the period when both inlet and exhaust valves are open

Pawl In a ratchet, the pivotted catch which engages with the teeth in one direction but rides over them in the other. The ratchet is thus uni-directional in action

Peg spanner A spanner without jaws, in which a pair or more of pegs or pins projecting from its face locate in holes in the fastener, enabling it to be turned

Penetrating oil Very thin lubricant which is able to permeate through rust to ease the threads of a fastener

Pinion A gearwheel, either fixed to a shaft or idling

Piston skirt The lower part of a piston. If cut away, it is described as a 'slipper skirt'

Plain bearing A bearing either machined from solid soft metal, or shell-type in which soft metal surfaces are deposited on a steel backing. In a few bikes, an unlined bearing area in which the shaft journal rotates

Port The holes through which petrol/air mixture is induced, transferred or – after burning – exhausted

Ramp A raised working surface on to which a bike can be wheeled for servicing or repair

Ratchet *See* Pawl

Reed valve Thin spring-steel non-return valves, operated by the difference in internal and external pressures, used to control the induction of mixture into a two-stroke engine

Ring spanner A spanner in which a serrated ring is used to grip the corners of a fastener

Run-out With a rotating component, the amount by which it is out of true

Roller bearing An anti-friction bearing in which caged rollers run on inner and outer tracks

Second motion shaft *See* Layshaft

Shell bearing A steel-back shell on whose inner face white metal is deposited to act as a bearing surface. Widely used for big ends or mains on four-strokes, but unsuitable for two-stroke engines due to lubrication problems

Slider The lower moving part of a telescopic fork

Socket-head screw Sometimes called an Allen screw. A screw with a hexagon cut internally in its head

Spindle An axle carrying, for example, the wheel hubs

Sprocket Sometimes called a chain wheel. A toothed wheel in which a chain engages to transmit motion

Stanchion In telescopic forks, the fixed static tube which carries the slider

Steering head The tube and bearings on the frame in which the fork stem pivots

Strobe A stroboscopic timing lamp, used to 'freeze' the timing marks with the engine running, and so ensure accurate settings

Subframe The rear part of the motor cycle frame, usually forming a seat and mudguard support and an upper mounting for the rear spring/damper units

Tailpipe The final emission tube in an exhaust system, often made removable so that it can be freed from carbon deposits

Tdc Top dead centre – the uppermost point of piston travel

T-handle screwdriver A cruciform screwdriver which enables greater torque to be applied to a screw fastening

Thermostat An automatic heat-operated valve in a liquid cooling system, designed to give a quick warm-up and then a constant temperature

Thrust washer An accurately machined washer of bearing material used to reduce friction where a rotating member is subject to an axial load

Torque wrench A form of tommy bar which either carries an indicator to show what torque is being applied, or which has a ratchet on which a torque can be preset

Tread The grooves cut in the contact surfaces of a tyre to channel away water

Vacuum gauge A tuning instrument which measures the depression in an engine induction tract

Valve In a four-stroke, the poppet valves that control induction and exhaust gases. In a tyre, the one-way valve through which air is admitted. In a two-stroke, the disc or reed valves controlling mixture induction

Valve seat The area on which the head of a valve is held to seal the port

Vernier gauge A measuring device which uses a sliding scale to give fractional readings of graduations on a second, adjacent scale

Wire wheel A wheel built up by the use of wire spokes and nipples linking the hub and the rim

Yoke The lower bridge of a front fork which carries the stem and the stanchions